Lecture Notes in Artificial Intelligence   1791

Subseries of Lecture Notes in Computer Science
Edited by J. G. Carbonell and J. Siekmann

Lecture Notes in Computer Science
Edited by G. Goos, J. Hartmanis and J. van Leeuwen

T0223361

Springer
*Berlin
Heidelberg
New York
Barcelona
Hong Kong
London
Milan
Paris
Singapore
Tokyo*

Dieter Fensel

Problem-Solving Methods

Understanding, Description, Development, and Reuse

 Springer

Series Editors

Jaime G. Carbonell,Carnegie Mellon University, Pittsburgh, PA, USA
Jörg Siekmann, University of Saarland, Saarbrücken, Germany

Dieter Fensel
Vrije Universiteit Amsterdam
Division of Mathematics and Computer Science
De Boelelaan 1081a, 1081 HV Amsterdam, The Netherlands
E-mail: dieter@cs.vu.nl

Cataloging-in-Publication Data applied for

Die Deutsche Bibliothek - CIP-Einheitsaufnahme

Fensel, Dieter:
Problem solving methods : understanding, description, development,
and reuse / Dieter Fensel. - Berlin ; Heidelberg ; New York ; Barcelona ;
Hong Kong ; London ; Milan ; Paris ; Singapore ; Tokyo : Springer, 2000
   (Lecture notes in computer science ; 1791 : Lecture notes in
   artificial intelligence)
   ISBN 3-540-67816-6

CR Subject Classification (1998): I.2, D.2

ISBN 3-540-67816-6 Springer-Verlag Berlin Heidelberg New York

Springer-Verlag Berlin Heidelberg New York
a member of BertelsmannSpringer Science+Business Media GmbH
© Springer-Verlag Berlin Heidelberg 2000

Typesetting: Camera-ready by author
Printed on acid-free paper   SPIN 10720050   06/3142   5 4 3 2 1 0

"With these abundant beacons, the banishment of snags, plenty of daylight in a box and ready to be turned on whenever needed, and a chart and compass to fight the fog, piloting, at a good stage of water, is now nearly as safe and simpe as driving stage, and it is hardly more than three times as romantic."

Mark Twain, Life on the Mississippi

Preface

Researchers in Artificial Intelligence have traditionally been classified into two categories: the "neaties" and the "scruffies". According to the scruffies, the neaties concentrate on building elegant formal frameworks, whose properties are beautifully expressed by means of definitions, lemmas, and theorems, but which are of little or no use when tackling real-world problems. The scruffies are described (by the neaties) as those researchers who build superficially impressive systems that may perform extremely well on one particular case study, but whose properties and underlying theories are hidden in their implementation, if they exist at all.

As a life-long, non-card-carrying scruffy, I was naturally a bit suspicious when I first started collaborating with Dieter Fensel, whose work bears all the formal hallmarks of a true neaty. Even more alarming, his primary research goal was to provide sound, formal foundations to the area of knowledge-based systems, a traditional stronghold of the scruffies - one of whom had famously declared it "an art", thus attempting to place it outside the range of the neaties (and to a large extent succeeding in doing so). However, even an unreconstructed scruffy such as myself can recognize a good neaty when he comes across one. What Dieter has managed to produce with his research on problem solving methods is what all neaties hope to do, but few achieve: a rigorous and useful theory, which can be used analytically, to explain a range of phenomena in the (real) world and synthetically, to support the development of robust and well defined artifacts.

Specifically, this book provides a theory, a formal language and a practical methodology to support the specification, use, and reuse of problem solving methods. Thus, knowledge engineering is not characterized as an art any longer, but as an engineering discipline, where artifacts are constructed out of reusable components, according to well-understood, robust development methods. The value of the framework proposed by Dieter is illustrated extensively, by showing its application to complex knowledge engineering tasks - e.g., diagnosis and design - and by applying it to the specification of libraries with both scope and depth (i.e., both usable and reusable). Another important contribution of this book is that it clarifies the similarities and the differences between knowledge-based and 'conventional' systems. The framework proposed by Dieter characterizes knowledge-based systems as a particular type of software architecture, where applications are developed by integrating generic task specifications, problem solving methods, and domain models by means of formally defined *adapters*. The latter can be used to map the terminologies used by the different system components, and also to formally introduce the assumptions on the domain knowledge required by an intelligent problem solver. This notion of assumption is central to Dieter's characterization of knowledge-based systems: these are defined as systems that make assumptions for the sake of efficiency. Thus, Dieter is able to build a continuum of assumption-making systems, ranging from "weak" search methods to "strong", task-specific methods. As a result we can now see clearly the relationship between all these various classes of algorithms, which have traditionally been treated as distinct.

In conclusion, I believe this is the first 'real' theory of knowledge engineering to come out of several decades of research in this area. It describes the class of systems we are talking about, how to model them and how to develop them. I also believe that it is very important that this theory has come out at a time when the explosion of internet-based services is going to provide unprecedented opportunities for deploying and sharing knowledge-based services. I advise anybody who plans to be a player in this area to read this book and learn what robust knowledge engineering is about.

January 2000   Enrico Motta

Acknowledgments

First of all, I would like to thank Rudi Studer for providing me with the possibilities to continue my research after my Ph.D. in 1993. He always stimulated my research and encouraged me to relate my work to the international state of the art. He showed great patience and provided the degree of freedom necessary for a creative atmosphere.

In the last few years I have cooperated intensively with a number of colleagues who I would like to thank at this point. During my guest stay at the University of Amsterdam I profited much from cooperating with Richard Benjamins, Remco Straatman, Frank van Harmelen, Annette ten Teije, and Bob Wielinga in getting a better understanding of what problem-solving methods for knowledge-based systems are about. Putting this understanding into a software engineering flavoured framework and formulas of modal logic would not have been possible without the cooperation with Rix Groenboom and Gerard Renardel de Lavalette[1] from the University of Groningen, a small town in the North of The Netherlands with highly skilled researchers. Back in Karlsruhe I worked on realizing a verification framework for knowledge-based systems that took into account the ideas I collected and developed abroad. I found an excellent tool environment KIV and the helping hand of Arno Schönegge whenever the task exceeded my limited skills in mathematical proof techniques. Discussions with him and Wolfgang Reif (University of Ulm) provided many fruitful ideas on how to provide a development framework for problem-solving methods. Finally it was the cooperation with Enrico Motta from the Open University in England which allowed me to ground my ideas with an existing library of problem-solving methods dealing with real-world problems. In addition to these key players there were also a lot of colleagues from different places who provided me with helpful hints and new insights. So I would like to thank Joost Breuker (University of Amsterdam), Stefan Decker (University of Karlsruhe), Joeri Engelfriet (Vrije Universiteit Amsterdam), Pascal van Eck (Vrije Universiteit Amsterdam), Gertjan van Heijst (CIBIT, The Netherlands), Yde Venema (Vrije Universiteit Amsterdam), Marc Willems (Vrije Universiteit Amsterdam), and Zdenek Zrdahal (Open University in Milton Keyens, England) for helpful discussions and contributions. Shame on me for all the further names I do not mention. However, I should not forget Jeffrey Butler who carried out the Sisyphus-VI project of improving mein English.

Clearly, my thanks are also devoted to Estela who kept life going on watching my back in front of a computer.

---

[1] The mathematical theory and knowledge underlying MCL (see Chapter 4) is contributed by him.

Table of Contents

Section III
How to Develop and Reuse Problem-Solving Methods

Introduction

Knowledge-based systems are computer systems that deal with complex problems by making use of knowledge.[1] This knowledge may be acquired from humans or automatically derived with abductive, deductive, and inductive techniques. This knowledge is mainly represented declaratively rather than encoded using complex algorithms. This declarative representation of knowledge economizes the development and maintenance process of these systems and improves their understandability. Therefore, knowledge-based systems originally used simple and generic inference mechanisms to infer outputs for provided cases. Inference engines, like unification, forward or backward resolution, and inheritance, covered the dynamic part of deriving new information. However, human experts can exploit knowledge about the dynamics of the problem-solving *process* and such knowledge is required to enable problem-solving in practice and not only in principle. [Clancey, 1983] provided several examples where knowledge engineers implicitly encoded control knowledge by ordering production rules and premises of these rules, which together with the generic inference engine, delivered the desired dynamic behavior. Making this knowledge explicit and regarding it as an important part of the entire knowledge contained by a knowledge-based system is the rationale that underlies *problem-solving methods*. Problem-solving methods refine the generic inference engines mentioned above to allow a more direct control of the reasoning process. Problem-solving methods describe this control knowledge independent from the application domain thus enabling reuse of this strategical knowledge for different domains and applications. Finally, problem-solving methods abstract from a specific representation formalism in contrast to the general inference engines that rely on a specific representation of the knowledge.

Problem-solving methods enable the reuse of reasoning knowledge. [Clancey, 1985] reported on the analysis of a set of first generation expert systems developed to solve different tasks. Though they were realized using different representation formalisms (e.g. production rules, frames, LISP) and applied in different domains, he discovered a common problem solving behavior. Clancey was able to abstract this common behavior to a generic inference pattern called *heuristic classification*, which describes the problem-solving behavior of these systems on an abstract level (cf. [Newell, 1982]). When considering the problem-solving method *heuristic classification* in some more detail (see Fig. 1) we can identify the three basic inference actions *abstract*, *heuristic match*, and *refine*. Furthermore, four knowledge roles are defined: *observables*, *abstract observables*, *solution abstractions*, and *solutions*. It is important to see that such a description of a problem-solving method is given in a generic way. Thus the reuse of such a problem-solving method in different domains is made possible.

In the meantime various problem-solving methods have been identified and the concept *problem-solving method* is present in a large number of current knowledge-engineering frameworks (e.g. GENERIC TASKS [Chandrasekaran, 1986]; ROLE-LIMITING

---

1. A good introduction to the field is provided by [Stefik, 1995]. However, the horizont of this book ends at the American borders and we would also very much like to recommend the reader the textbook on CommonKADS [Schreiber, 1999]. A survey on the state of the art can be found in [Studer et al., 1998].

METHODS [Marcus, 1988], [Puppe, 1993]; KADS [Schreiber et al., 1993] and CommonKADS [Schreiber et al., 1994]; the METHOD-TO-TASK approach [Eriksson et al., 1995]; COMPONENTS OF EXPERTISE [Steels, 1990]; GDM [Terpstra et al., 1993]; MIKE [Angele et al., 1998]). Libraries of problem-solving methods are described in [Benjamins, 1995], [Breuker & Van de Velde, 1994], [Chandrasekaran et al., 1992], [Motta & Zdrahal, 1996], and [Puppe, 1993]. In general a problem-solving method describes which reasoning steps and which types of knowledge are needed to perform a task. This description should be domain and implementation independent. Problem solving methods are used in a number of ways in these frameworks (see e.g. [Chandrasekaran et al., 1992]): as a guideline for acquiring problem-solving knowledge from an expert, as a guideline for decomposing complex tasks into subtasks, as a description of the essence of the reasoning process of the expert and knowledge-based system, as a skeletal description of the design model of the knowledge-based system, and as a means to enable flexible reasoning by selecting methods during problem solving.

Given this amount of literature the reader may ask why there should be a need for another volume on this subject. The motivation for this volume stems from an analysis of the problem-solving method *propose & revise* and its application to the configuration of a vertical transportation system (VT-domain, cf. [Marcus et al., 1988], [Schreiber & Birmingham, 1996]). This example was used by several research groups in knowledge engineering as a common case study. The solution in which we participated is reported in [Poeck et al., 1996]. In [Fensel, 1995a], we analysed our solution in more depth having the goal of deriving a precise and reusable specification of *propose & revise*. However, we encountered a number of difficulties. First, *propose & revise* makes a great number of very strong assumptions for solving the given configuration problem. Different variants of *propose & revise* can be identified according to the precise

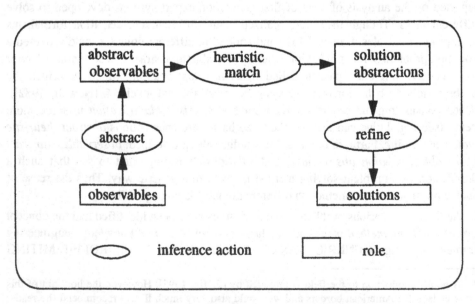

Fig. 1 The problem-solving method *heuristic classification.*

definition of these assumptions. These assumptions influence the definition of elementary inferences as well as the control and competence of the method. In fact, *the competence of the method can only be defined in terms of the underlying assumptions*. Some of the assumptions we encountered are rather strong and as showed by [Zdrahal & Motta, 1995], they are not always fulfilled in the VT-domain [Yost & Rothenfluh, 1996]. In consequence, we identified three aspects that require some deeper mining as a precondition to providing reusable problem-solving methods and seriously considering libraries of them.[2]

(i)   What is the rationale and the role of the numerous assumptions we encountered when taking a closer look at *propose & revise*? Do they imply that *propose & revise* is a strange and poorly designed method or is there some more deeper rationale for introducing them?

(ii) We felt the need to give assumptions a much more prominent role when describing a problem-solving method. They characterize the conditions under which a method can be applied to a domain and a task and are necessary for understanding most of the inferences of a method. Existing work on problem-solving methods only treated them as a side aspect. KADS-like inference and task structures [Schreiber et al., 1994] focus on an operational description of the method. However, for successful reuse of methods it seems much more important to establish a notation that describes a method in terms of assumptions and the competence as a consequence of these assumptions. The operational description is in that sense only an explanation of how the competence can be achieved by making use of the underlying assumptions.

(iii) In [Fensel, 1995a] we identified numerous variations of *propose & revise*. None of them could be determined to be the gold standard of this method. Therefore, hardwiring all assumptions of one variant in a specific operational description with a fixed competence may lead to non-reusable problem-solving methods. Actually, this was the experiences of many shell developers who derived shells from some applications and encountered serious problems when trying to apply it to new and slightly different tasks and domains. Putting all possible variants of *propose & revise* into the library also does not look very promising given the large number of different variants. *Propose & revise* is only one method. Applying this strategy to all problem-solving methods would result in a nearly infinitely large library. In consequence, there seems to be only one reasonable strategy: (1) Identifying generic patterns from which the numerous variants can be derived by adaptation and (2) providing support for this adaptation process.

These three aspects already roughly summarize the content of this volume which—not surprisingly—consist of three sections. In the following, we will briefly sketch each section.

What are problem-solving methods: reasoning strategies that gain efficiency through *assumptions*. Section I deals with the question why problem-solving methods have to introduce *assumptions* and why this is not a bug but a feature. We discuss this perspective in chapter 1 and continue in chapter 2 with an empirical survey of

---

2. Providing a library of problem-solving methods was the initial goal of the research project.

assumptions used in model-based diagnosis to ground our argument.

How can problem-solving methods be described: with a software architecture, MCL and KIV. The structured development of problem-solving methods requires a structured framework to describe them. This is the subject of section II. In chapter 3, we provide a *software architecture* for describing knowledge-based systems focusing on the problem-solving method and its related parts. KADS-like operational specifications are supplemented by describing the competence and assumptions of a method and using adapters to relate them to the task and domain. "A specification can provide a way of making explicit those assumptions which are otherwise hidden consequences of an algorithm." [Jones, 1990] Chapter 4 investigates the requirements of a logical framework for formalizing problem-solving methods and presents the two logics *MLPM* [Fensel & Groenboom, 1996] and *MCL* [Fensel et al., 1998 (c)] which both integrate the specification of dynamics in a declarative framework. Chapter 5 provides a framework for verifying such architectural specifications of knowledge-based systems. It is based on the Karlsruhe Interactive Verifier (KIV) [Reif, 1995] which shifts verification from a task that can be done in principle to a task that can be done in practice. KIV can be used to establish the competence of a problem-solving method given some assumptions or to find the assumptions that are required to achieve such a competence. The latter aspect is discussed in chapter 6.1 as *inverse verification*.

How can problem-solving methods be developed and reused: by *stapling adapters* and hunting for assumptions with *inverse verification*. Section III provides the means for the structured development and reuse of problem-solving methods. Chapter 6 discusses the context dependency of knowledge which arises as a problem when trying to reuse it. We provide two methods that deal with this problem. We discuss a method called *inverse verification* to support the explication of context and *adapters* to support the adaptation to a new context (i.e., domain or task). Chapter 7 uses this principle to describe a library of methods for solving design problems. This methods library was developed at the Knowledge Media Institut (cf. [Motta & Zdrahal, 1996], [Motta, 1999]) and used in several applications[3]. We identify a small number of key patterns and derive all possible variants of problem-solving methods through a navigation process in a three dimensional space. The organizational principles for this library provide a solution for dealing with all the different variants of problem-solving methods: a small number of generic patterns and support in their adaptation.

---

3. Office allocation problem, elevator design, sliding bearing design, problems of simple mechanics, initial vehicle (truck) design, design and selection of casting technologies, and sheet metal forming technology for manufacturing mechanical parts [Motta, 1999].

"Experts can perform faster than novices" [VanLehn, 1989]

Section I:

What Are Problem-Solving Methods

1 Making Assumptions for Efficiency Reasons

Problem-solving methods are present in most of the current knowledge engineering frameworks.[1] They are used to describe the reasoning steps and types of knowledge which are needed to perform a task by a knowledge-based system. However, a question that has not been answered clearly is the connection between problem-solving methods and the *efficiency* of the problem-solving process. Most descriptions of problem-solving method frameworks do point to problem-solving methods as being somehow related to efficiency, however no framework makes this relation explicit, i.e. explains how problem-solving methods achieve their efficiency. Other approaches interpret the knowledge level paradigm of [Newell, 1982] such that the description of problem-solving methods should exclude all efficiency concerns, which are regarded as being dealt with at the symbol level. Finally, some approaches claim not to be concerned with efficiency since their problem-solving methods are only used to capture the expert's problem-solving behavior. But we must be aware that experts also have to solve the task given their real-life limitations. In fact, a large share of expert-knowledge is concerned exactly with efficient reasoning given these limitations [VanLehn, 1989]. The conceptualization of a domain by an expert differs from the conceptualization of a novice because the former reflects the learning process that led to efficiency in problem solving.

We see the main intent of a problem-solving method to be providing the *required* functionality in an *efficient* fashion. In general, problems tackled with knowledge-based systems are inherently complex and intractable, e.g., [Bylander, 1991], [Bylander et al., 1991], and [Nebel, 1996].[2] A problem-solving method has to describe not just any realization of the functionality, but one which takes into account the constraints on the reasoning process and the complexity of the task. The constraints have to do with the fact that we do not want to achieve the functionality *in theory* but rather *in practice*. When this relation between problem-solving methods and efficiency is ignored or kept as an implicit notion, neither the selection nor the design of problem-solving methods can be performed in an informed manner. Besides the efficiency in terms of computational effort of a problem-solving method, there are further dimensions for defining the notion of efficiency (cf. [O'Hara & Shadbolt, 1996]): The efficiency of the entire knowledge-based system, the optimality of the interaction of the system with its environment (e.g., minimizing the number of tests a patient has to undergo in medical diagnosis), and the efficiency of the development process of the knowledge-based system.

After making the claim that problem-solving methods provide functionality in an efficient way, the next question is then: *how* could this be achieved if the problems are intractable in their general form? Usually, efficient data structures and algorithmic

---

[1] [Chandrasekaran, 1986], [Marcus, 1988], [Steels, 1990], [Chandrasekaran et al., 1992], [Puppe, 1993], [Schreiber et al., 1993], [Terpstra et al., 1993], [Breuker & Van de Velde, 1994], [Schreiber et al., 1994], [Benjamins, 1995], [Eriksson et al., 1995], [Motta & Zdrahal, 1996], [Angele et al., 1998].

[2] Exceptions are classification problems which are known to often have polynomial time complexity (see [Goel et al., 1987]).

Dieter Fensel: Problem-Solving Methods, LNAI 1791, pp. 7 - 25, 2000.

optimizations are a means to achieve efficient solutions (see e.g. [Smith, 1990]). However these techniques are of less interest for our purpose. These techniques can be applied during the design and implementation phase to improve the efficiency of the realized systems. They are of less interest during the specification and knowledge level modeling phase. In this context, we look for means stemming from a domain expert and his heuristic knowledge that improve the efficiency. This type of knowledge is necessary because no efficient data structure and algorithmic optimization technique can transform intractable problems into tractable ones (assuming NP≠P). In our view, the way problem-solving methods achieve an efficient realization of functionality is by making *assumptions*. The assumptions put restrictions on the context of the problem-solving method, such as the domain knowledge and the possible inputs of the method or the precise definition of the functionality (i.e., the goal which can be achieved by applying the problem-solving method). These restrictions enable reasoning to be performed in an efficient manner. In summary, assumptions play two roles: they formulate requirements on reasoning support that is assumed by the problem-solving methods and they put restrictions on the reasoning support that is provided by the problem-solving methods (see Fig. 2). In consequence, assumptions link problem-solving methods with the domain knowledge they use and the tasks they are applied to:

- One role of the assumptions of a problem-solving method is to define the domain knowledge that it requires. These assumptions describe the *domain dependency of a problem-solving method in domain-independent terms*. These assumptions are *proof obligations* for the domain knowledge (i.e., one has to prove that the given domain knowledge fulfills the assumptions) or goals for the knowledge acquisition and domain modeling process (i.e., they define what is required as domain knowledge).

- The second role of assumptions of a problem-solving method is to define the task (i.e., the problem) that can be tackled successfully by the problem-solving method.

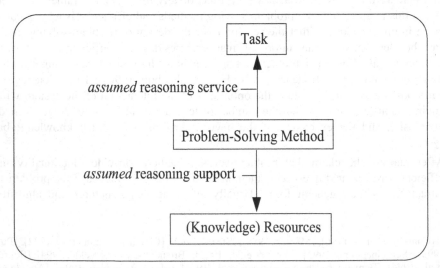

Fig. 2. Relation between a Problem-Solving Method and Its Context

For example, the termination of a problem-solving method may only be provable when assuming that a solution exists and a diagnostic task may only be solvable by a problem-solving method when assuming a single fault [Davis, 1984].

We will provide several assumptions that are made by *propose & revise* [Marcus et al., 1988] when applied to *parametric design* tasks [Fensel et al., 1997]. Later on, further examples in the area of diagnostic problem solving are provided.

The role that assumptions play in the efficient realization of functionality suggests that the process of designing problem-solving methods should be based on these assumptions. [Akkermans et al., 1993] and [Wielinga et al., 1995] introduce a general approach that views the construction process of problem-solving methods for knowledge-based systems as an assumption-driven activity. A formal specification of a task is derived from informal requirements by introducing assumptions about the problem and the problem space. This task specification is refined into a functional specification of the problem-solving method by making assumptions about the problem-solving paradigm and the available domain theory. Further assumptions are introduced in the process of defining an operational specification of the method. We will use this approach as a general framework and make it more concrete. Our focus lies thereby on assumptions which are related to the efficiency of a problem-solving method. We propose to view the process of constructing a problem-solving method for a given functionality as the process of incrementally adding assumptions that enable efficient reasoning.

We use the task *parametric design* and the problem-solving method *propose & revise* to illustrate our main points. Sisyphus-II [Schreiber & Birmingham, 1996] aimed at comparing different approaches to knowledge engineering. The task was to design a vertical transportation system (an elevator). This task was originally described in [Marcus et al., 1988], who developed the problem-solving method *propose & revise* to solve this configuration task. The presentation of the general conclusions in this chapter is based on our own contribution to Sisyphus-II [Poeck et al., 1996] and initial considerations in [Fensel, 1995a].

In the following, we formally define the task[3] *parametric design* ([Motta & Zdrahal, 1996], [Fensel et al., 1997]). Then we define a problem-solving method *generate & test* that can theoretically be used to solve this task. This method can be derived straightforwardly from the task specification. Because this method is very inefficient, we then discuss a more efficient problem-solving method *propose & revise* as introduced by [Marcus, 1988] and [Marcus et al., 1988]. *Propose & revise* weakens the task and makes additional assumptions about available domain knowledge in order to gain efficiency.

We are aware that there are much richer and more complex ways for defining the design task and design problem solving. However, the purpose of our description of parametric design and *propose & revise* is to illustrate our general point of view on problem-

---

[3] A *task* defines the goal that must be achieved by a problem-solving method. In terms of software engineering, a task describes the required functionality of a system. In that sense, *problem definition* would be a better term (see [Breuker, 1997]). However we will follow the established naming convention of the knowledge engineering community.

solving methods and not to provide a rich and detailed picture of design problem solving. For more details see [Mittal & Frayman, 1989], [Chandrasekaran, 1990], [Tank, 1992], [Poeck, 1994], [Faltings & Freuder, 1996], and [Motta & Zdrahal, 1996].

1.1   A Definition of a Task

A parametric design problem can be defined by a *design space, requirements, constraints*, and a *preference* (i.e., an utility). The *design space* describes the space which contains all possible designs. The concrete definition of the design space is domain-specific knowledge. Furthermore, a finite set of *requirements* is assumed to be given by the user. A design that fulfills all requirements is called a *desired design*. In addition to the case-specific user input, a finite set of *constraints* models additional conditions for a valid design. These constraints are domain knowledge describing the regularities in the domain in which the design is constructed. A design that fulfills all constraints is called a *valid design*. A design that is desired and valid is called a *solution*. The *preference* defines a preference function on the design space and can be used to discriminate between different solutions.

In the case of *parametric* design, a design artifact is described by a set of attribute-value pairs. Let $A_1,..., A_n$ be a fixed set of parameters (i.e. attributes) with fixed ranges $R_1,...,R_n$.

Def 1. Design Space
   The *design space* is the cartesian product $R_1 \times ... \times R_n$
Def 2. Requirements and Constraints
   The sets of *requirements* and *constraints* are represented by two relations R and C on the design space which define subsets of this space.
Def 3. Possible Designs, Desired Design, Valid Design, Solution
   A *possible design* is an element of the design space, a *desired design* is an element of R, a *valid design* is an element of C, and a *possible solution* is an element of R and C.

By applying the *preference P*, an *optimal solution* is selected out of all possible solutions.

Def 4. Preference
   The *preference P* is a partial function having all possible designs as its domain and preference values as its range.
Def 5. Optimal Solution
   An *optimal solution* is a solution for which no other solution which has a higher preference value exists.

In general, several optimal solutions could exist. Therefore, one can further distinguish whether the user will receive all of them or a non-deterministic selection. These definitions can be extended by introducing priorities on requirements and constraints or by distinguishing between constraints which must always hold and constraints which should hold etc., but this is beyond the scope of our current interest.

1.2   A Non-efficient Problem Solver

A straightforward operationalization of the declarative task specification can be achieved by applying a variant of `generate & test`. The method defines four different inferences and four different types of knowledge that it requires. The inference structure of this method is given in Fig. 3.[4]

- The inference action `generate` requires knowledge that describes what constitutes a possible design (i.e., the *design space*).
- The inference action `R-test` requires knowledge that describes which possible designs are desired (i.e., the user *requirements*).
- The inference action `C-test` requires knowledge that describes which possible designs are valid (i.e., the domain *constraints*).
- The inference action `select` requires knowledge that evaluates solutions, i.e., knowledge that describes what constitutes a *preferred* design.

To complete the operational method description we must define its control. Again we do this in a straightforward manner (see Fig. 4). The control flow specifies the following

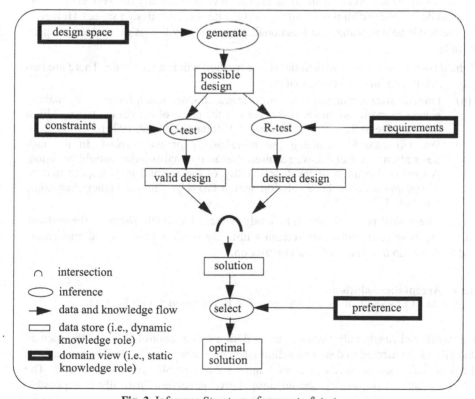

Fig. 3. Inference Structure of *generate & test*

---

[4] See [Schreiber et al., 1994] for an explanation of inference structures and [Fensel et al., 1993] for a comparison with dataflow diagrams.

> *possible design := **generate**_{all};*
> *valid design := **C-test**(possible design);*
> *desired design := **R-test**(possible design);*
> *solution := valid design ∩ desired design;*
> *optimal solution := **select**(solution)*

Fig. 4. Control Flow I of `generate & test`

reasoning process: First, all possible designs are derived. Second, all valid designs are derived. Third, all desired designs are derived. Fourth, valid and desired designs are intersected. Fifth, an optimal solution is selected. The sequence of the second and third steps is arbitrary and could also be specified as parallel activity.

The advantage of this method is that it clearly separates the different types of knowledge that are included in the functional specification of the parametric design task. On the other hand, it is precisely this separation that prevents efficient problem solving. The knowledge about what is a correct (i.e., valid and desired) and good solution is clearly separated from the generation step, and there is no feedback from the results of the test and evaluation steps. This method is clearly not very efficient, as it has to derive and test all possible designs (i.e., the complete design space). However, the method is able to realize the functionality specified by the task if the design space is finite.

If the design space is infinite then the above method will not terminate. There are two ways to deal with infinite search spaces:

(a)   One can always transform each infinite search space into a finite one by making some pragmatic assumptions that restrict the range of the parameters and limit the grainsize of the different values (cf. [Motta & Zdrahal, 1996]).

(b)   We will consider *reducing the functionality of the method*. In the task description (see Def 5.), we required that an optimal solution should be found. A weaker definition of the functionality of the method is to require that an *acceptable solution* be a solution which has a preference higher than some threshold t.

From a theoretical point of view (a) already reduces the functionality of the method. However, these restrictions may remain within the borders of the actual application and therefore do not cause an actual restriction.

Def 6. Acceptable Solution
     Given a threshold t, an *acceptable solution* is a solution x with $P(x) > t$.

The weakened functionality enables us to define a new control flow for the method that allows the method to deal with infinite design spaces (see Fig. 5). The sequence of the four inference actions is repeated until an acceptable solution is found. The inference action `generate` should now derive nondeterministically one possible design per step, which is later processed by the two test steps and the `select` step.[5]

---

[5] For each given probability $0 < \alpha < 1$ we can guarantee that the method finds a solution (if one exists) in finite time with a probability greater than $1 - \alpha$ if each element of the design space has the same chance to be proposed by *generate*.

```
repeat
    possible design := generate_one;
    valid design := C-test(possible design);
    desired design := R-test(possible design);
    solution := valid design ∩ desired design;
    acceptable solution := select(solution)
until ∅ ≠ acceptable solution
```

Fig. 5. Control Flow II of *generate & test*

The weakening of the task to find acceptable solutions also illustrates a problem with using worst-case analysis: In the worst case it takes the same effort to find an optimal solution (i.e., a global optimum) or an acceptable solution as it is now defined. However, in the average case the search need no longer to be complete and can stop when an acceptable solution has been found.

Making the search finite by introducing domain-specific assumptions or reducing the functionality by weakening the solution criteria transform *generate & test* into a method that can solve the problem in theory. However the problem of the tractability of the above method already holds for finite spaces because the size of the space increases exponentially with the number of parameters and their ranges. Dealing with the size of the search space therefore leads immediately to *limited rationality*. Decision procedures with perfect rationality try to find an optimal solution, whereas decision procedures with *limited rationality* also reflect on the costs of finding such an optimal solution. Even for realistic settings with finite search spaces, no computational agent can be implemented that realizes the method in an acceptable way. Arbitrary generated designs are tested as to whether they are desired, valid, and preferred or not. Still, we have an operational description of how to achieve the goal. From the point of view which does not care about efficiency, this could be a valid point to describe the essence of the reasoning process of a system that solves the task. For example, [Rouveirol & Albert, 1994] define a knowledge level model of machine-learning algorithms by applying the *generate & test* scheme and [Davis & Hamscher, 1988], [Bredeweg, 1994], and [ten Teije, 1997] use such a description to define a top-level view on diagnostic tasks and methods.

1.3   An Efficient Problem Solver

The main advantages of *generate & test* as it was described above are:

- It only requires the knowledge that is already part of the functional specification and the four types of knowledge (considering the requirements as knowledge) are clearly separated: each inference uses precisely one knowledge type. The description of the design space is used in the generation step, the requirements and the constraints are used in two test steps, and the preference is used in the select step.
- Its inference structure is cycle-free. That is, its operational specification does not contain feedback loops (i.e., no output of an inference action is directly or indirectly its input) that would make understanding of and formal reasoning about the reasoning process much more difficult.

Generate & test leads to a precise and clear distinction of different conceptual types of knowledge and defines the dynamic behavior of the problem-solving process in a highly understandable manner. On the other hand, these advantages are precisely the reasons for the inefficient problem-solving behavior.

The problem-solving method *propose & revise* as discussed in [Marcus et al., 1988] adds efficiency to the problem-solving process. It introduces static and dynamic feedback into the problem-solving process. This destroys the advantageous properties of *generate & test* as discussed above. An expert has learned which design decisions led to desired, valid, and preferred solutions and which did not. Therefore, *expertise compiles test knowledge into the generation step and provides dynamic feedback from the test step to inform the generation step.* The two principles of *propose & revise* are:

- *Generate & test* requires only the knowledge given by the functional specification. The knowledge about what is a desired, correct, and preferred solution is clearly separated from the generation step. However, "an important issue is the distribution of knowledge between the generator and the tester: Putting as much knowledge as possible into the generator often leads to more efficient search." [Stefik et al., 1983] An expert includes feedback based on experience from solving earlier design problems. A much more clever strategy is therefore to use these knowledge types to guide the generation of possible designs.

- *Propose & revise* "traces errors and inconsistencies back to the inferential step which created them." [Stefik et al., 1983] In *generate & test* there is *no* dynamic feedback from the results of the test and evaluation step of a given design: If a design derived during problem solving is not a solution, a new design is derived in the next step. Dynamic feedback would include the reported shortcomings of the first proposed design as guidance for its modification while deriving the next design.

The use of the test knowledge as guidance for the generation step and the use of the feedback of the test steps as input for the generation step are precisely the main improvements that are incorporated into the *propose & revise* method. This can be pessimistically interpreted as destroying the clear conceptual distinctions of *generate & test*. Optimistically, this can be viewed as introducing new types of knowledge which glue these different aspects together, thereby adding expertise.

The *generate* step is now decomposed into two different activities. The *propose* step derives an initial design based on the requirements and the *revise* step tries to improve an incorrect design based on the feedback of the *C-test* step. To this end, it uses the meta-information that this design is incorrect as well as constraint violations reported by the *C-test*. We obtain the following conceptual structure of the method (see Fig 6.): The *propose* step requires knowledge which enables it to derive desired designs using the requirements as input. The *revise* step requires knowledge which enables it to fix constraint violations of desired designs. In addition, it uses the reported violations to guide the repair process. Revise delivers an acceptable solution as its output.

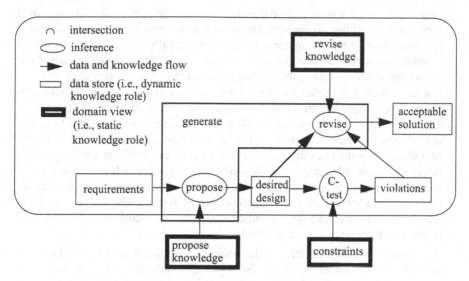

Fig. 6. Inference Structure of *propose & revise*

The third inference action, *C-test*, requires constraints to check desired designs as to whether they are valid. As output it derives the set of constraints violated by a design.

As discussed in [Marcus et al., 1988], it also makes sense to regard repair activities as soon as possible. That is, instead of proposing a complete design which is then repaired, we can also incrementally develop a design and repair it at each step where a constraint violation occurs. This exploits the fact that we specify *propose & revise* for a subclass of design tasks, namely, for parametric designs. A natural decomposition of the entire design is provided by the parameters describing it. In each *propose* step we can assign to one or some parameters a value and we can apply *revise* to these incomplete designs before we propose the next parameter values. This divide & conquer strategy with regard to intermediate repairs requires that the constraints do not interact to a great degree (see [Marcus et al., 1988]). Otherwise, earlier repair activities would always have to be redone when new constraint violations were reported for another parameter. This variant of *propose & revise* poses a new requirement on the domain knowledge: The constraints must be able to check an incomplete design for constraint violations. In general, *propose & revise* requires a number of further assumptions to prove that its input-output behavior is equivalent to the specified task:

- *Propose.* A parameter which should receive a value in the next *propose* step is selected. A set of propose rules is given in the application domain of [Marcus et al., 1988]. Each rule can be used to derive the value of the parameter that forms its conclusion from the values of the parameters of its premises. Each rule could be further accompanied by guards defining applicability criteria for the rule depending on already derived parameter values. The selection step uses these implicit dependencies between the parameters as domain-specific meta-knowledge, and assumes that this network defines an ordering on the set of parameters. At each step, each parameter that only depends on already computed parameters according to the current applicable propose rules is regarded as a possible choice. One parameter is nondeterministically chosen from this set of possible candidates. That is, *select* does not make further assumptions about knowledge that could guide this second selection step. The implicit assumption is that this selection does not change the performance and quality of the problem-solving process and its result. The *propose* step further assumes that at any time there is *either precisely one applicable* propose rule *or one* user input to derive the value of the selected parameter. This requirement is not as trivial as it seems, as it depends on the rules that are applicable during the problem-solving process. Several propose rules may exist for a parameter, but depending on the already derived values only one should be applicable because no selection step or selection knowledge is part of the method (see [Fensel, 1995a] for more details). Also, a parameter should not depend on itself (i.e., no recursive derivation rules requiring a fixpoint operation are allowed).

- *Revise.* The *revise* step is decomposed into a set of more elementary inferences (i.e., *select-violation, derive-fixes, select-fix,* and *apply-fix*). The *select-violation* step nondeterministically selects one constraint violation from the set of all violations that were detected by *C-test*. Again, the implicit assumption is that this selection does not influence the performance and quality of the problem-solving process and its result. This is a very critical assumption because the method does not backtrack over this selection. *Revise* uses fixes to repair constraint violations. *Derive-fixes* computes the set of all possible fix combinations (i.e., the set of all sets of elementary fixes) that could possibly resolve the selected constraint violation. Each fix combination (i.e., each set of elementary fixes) as well as the set of all fix combinations must be finite. This requirement is not trivial because some fixes (e.g., increment the value by one) can be applied several times, and specific constraints are required to restrict the number of legal repetitions of these fixes to guarantee finiteness. From the set of all possible fix combinations one is selected by the *select-fix* step. A cost function is used to guide this selection step. The application of a fix decreases the quality of a design product because it overwrites user requirements or it increases the cost of the product. The cost function defined on the fixes (more precisely on the fix combinations) must be defined in a way that reflects the preferences between possible designs. *Apply-fix* applies a fix combination. It is again realized by a set of elementary inferences, because it requires the propagation of modified values according to the dependency network of parameter. The precise definition of this step and further aspects of the revise step are beyond the scope of our discussions (see [Poeck et al., 1996], [Fensel, 1995a]).

- *Test. Propose & revise* as described in [Marcus et al., 1988] does not require an explicit R-test. That is, designs are not checked on the requirements. Instead, *propose* is assumed to derive desired designs. It is also assumed that the *revise* step delivers designs that are desired (i.e., this would be an assumption about the domain specific repair knowledge) or that requirements violations that it does not fix must be accepted (i.e., this would weaken the functionality of the method). The remaining *C-test* step requires constraints that define a solvable problem and that exclude all non-valid possibilities.

- *Selection*. Finally, *propose* & *revise* does not contain a selection of a solution using the preferences. That is, it is either assumed that the propose step and the revise step deliver acceptable (or optimal) solutions or that the functionality of the task is reduced to finding an arbitrary solution.

When we take a closer look at *revise* by distinguishing several substeps, we see that the *C-test* inference also appears as a sub-step of *revise* (i.e., as a substep of *apply-fix*, cf. [Fensel, 1995a]). After applying some repair rules on an invalid design, *revise* has to check whether the given violations are overcome and no new violations are introduced by applying the repair rules. Again, test knowledge that was originally separated from the generation step now appears as a sub-activity of it. The *revise* step is computationally the most expensive part of the method (and also the most expensive part in precisely specifying the behavior of the method). The actual efficiency of the method therefore relies heavily on the quality of the repair rules that are required by *revise*, but also on the propose knowledge. The propose knowledge is responsible for ensuring preferred desired designs that require little repair activities. The main improvement of the method in gaining efficiency is not so much that it eliminates the R-test and selection step, but that it reduces the search space from the set of all possible designs (i.e., the complete design space) to the set of preferred desired designs which should be nearly valid.

1.4   Summary of the Case Study

> "A ... rationale for making assumptions is based on a view of
> reasoning as a resource-limited process" [Stefik et al., 1983]

The *propose* step and the *revise* step glue together types of knowledge that were treated separately by *generate* & *test*. These new knowledge types define strong assumptions about the domain knowledge required by the method. The only reason for doing this is to try to gain *efficiency*. That is, we assume that the "refined" problem-solving method *propose* & *revise* will be able to find a solution faster than *generate* & *test* (or a better solution in the same amount of time). Therefore, developing problem-solving methods means blurring conceptual distinctions and introducing assumptions about new types of domain knowledge for reasons of efficiency. The pure and very clear separation of four types of knowledge in *generate* & *test* is destroyed by forcing parts of the test and evaluation knowledge into the generation step in order to improve the efficiency of the problem-solving process. We can conclude that *propose* & *revise* provides the same or less functionality as *generate* & *test*. It makes stronger assumptions to achieve this functionality. Finally, *propose* & *revise* is much harder to understand in detail than *generate* & *test*. Especially the *revise* step requires several levels of refinement to be defined precisely (see [Fensel, 1995a]) and "the non-monotonic nature of the *Propose and Revise* method is difficult to capture in intuitively understandable theories." [Wielinga et al., 1995]. Given this we must face the fact that the only reason why we would still prefer *propose* & *revise* is for reasons of efficiency. The reason for this is that a large share of the problem types tackled by problem-solving methods are computational hard problems. This means that there is no hope of finding a method that will solve all cases in polynomial time. [Rich & Knight, 1991] even define AI as "... the study of techniques for solving exponentially hard problems in polynomial time by exploiting knowledge about the problem domain." Most problem-solving methods in knowledge engineering implement a heuristic strategy to tackle problems for which no polynomial algorithms are known. There are basically three general approaches: (1) applying techniques to define, structure, and minimize the search space of a problem; (2) introducing assumptions about the domain knowledge; and (3) weakening the desired functionality of the system:

- *Applying techniques to define, structure, and minimize the search space of a problem can prevent unnecessary effort.* An appropriate definition of the problem space can immediately rule out most of the effort in finding a solution. In terms of the `generate` & `test` paradigm this implies the transfer of test knowledge into the generate step to reduce the problem space `generate` is working on and to define the sequence in which possible solutions are generated. Such techniques as they are used by branch-and-bound and A* cannot change the complexity class of a problem but can drastically change the actual behavior of a system. Pre-analysis of parameters, constraints, requirements, and preferences of a design problem can be used to exclude large parts of the search space and to define an ordering for the remaining search process [Zdrahal & Motta, 1995]. For example, most systems for model-based diagnosis (e.g. DART and GDE) compile all the hypothesis *testing* knowledge in hypothesis *generation* to achieve efficiency by preventing unnecessary search steps [Davis & Hamscher, 1988].[6)]

- *Introducing assumptions over the domain knowledge which can reduce the functionality of the part of the problem that has to be solved by the problem-solving method.* Actually, these are assumptions on available resources for the reasoning process, i.e. the support may not necessarily be delivered by domain knowledge but it may also be the output of another problem-solving method or the result of user-system interaction. In terms of complexity analysis, the external source is used as an oracle that solves complex parts of the problem. In general, the search strategy of `propose` & `revise` is incomplete. That is, a solution may exist even if `propose` & `revise` was not able to find it. Completeness can only be guaranteed by introducing strong assumption over the provided propose and revise knowledge. One has to assume that the propose knowledge always leads to the best (partial) design and that the revise knowledge can always replace a design which violates constraints or requirements with a best design that is valid and desired.

- *Weakening the desired functionality of the system to reduce the worst-case or average-case complexity of the problem by introducing assumptions about the precise problem type.* An example of this type of change is dropping the requirement for an optimal solution, and only searching for an acceptable one. Another example is the problem-solving method GDE [de Kleer & Williams, 1987] which applies the *minimality assumption* to reduce the complexity of model-based diagnosis. In general, model-based diagnosis is exponential in the

---

[6)] The problem in model-based diagnosis is to find diagnoses that explain the faulty behavior of a device based on a model of its behavior (see Chapter 2).

number of components of a device. Each element of the power set of all components is a possible diagnosis [Bylander et al., 1991]. However, if the minimality assumption holds, the complexity grows with the square or cube of the number of components for practical cases. Therefore this assumption does not change the worst-case complexity of the problem, but aims at improving the average-case behavior of the problem-solving methods. An example of an assumption in the field of model-based diagnosis that changes the worst-case complexity of the problem is the *single-fault assumption* [Davis, 1984]. It assumes that the symptoms of a device are caused by only one faulty component. This can be used to improve the efficiency of the methods, but prevents these methods from dealing with situations where the device suffers from several faults.[7] Further examples of weakening diagnostic problem-solving will be discussed in Chapter 2.

The first approach deals with the complexity problem by applying most efficient algorithms with according data structures. The problem-solving method tackle with a different, more restricted, problem in the second and the third cases. In the second approach, parts of the problem are delegated from the problem-solving method to an external source (either domain knowledge or input of an expert), however, the entire problem solving remains constant. The third approach explicitly reduces the functionality. During the rest of this issue we focus on the second and the third strategy on improving efficiency. That is, algorithmic optimization is beyond our discussions.

1.5   The Twofold Role of Assumptions

When establishing the proper relationship between the problem-solving method and the task *correctness* and *completeness* of the problem-solving method relative to the goals of the task are usually required:

- *Correctness* requires that each output that is derived by the problem-solving method also fulfils the goal of the task:

$$\forall i,o \ (PSM(i,o) \rightarrow TASK(i,o))$$

- *Completeness* requires that the problem-solving method provides an output for each input that leads to a fulfilled goal of the task:

$$\forall i \ (\exists o_1 \ TASK(i,o_1) \rightarrow \exists o_2 \ PSM(i,o_2))$$

  It is not necessarily the same output because the task may not be a function (i.e., several outputs are possible).

However, a perfect match is unrealistic in many cases. A problem-solving method has to describe not just a realization of the functionality, but one which takes into account the constraints of the reasoning process and the complexity of the task. The way problem-solving methods achieve efficient realization of functionality is by making *assumptions*. These assumptions put restrictions on the context of the problem-solving method, such as the domain knowledge and the possible inputs of the method or the precise definition of the goal to be achieved when applying the

---

[7] Actually the single-fault assumption can also be viewed as a requirement on domain knowledge to represent each possible fault as a single fault (compare [Davis, 1984] and later discussions).

problem-solving method. These restrictions enable reasoning to be performed in an efficient manner. Note that such assumptions can work in two directions to achieve this result.

- *Weakening*: Reducing the desired functionality of the system and therefore reducing the complexity of the problem by introducing assumptions about the precise task definition. An example of this type of change is to no longer require an optimal solution but only an acceptable one or to make the single-fault assumption in model-based diagnosis.

- *Strengthening:* Introducing assumptions about the domain knowledge (or the user of the system) which reduces the functionality or the complexity of the part of the problem that is solved by the problem-solving method. In terms of complexity analysis, the domain knowledge or the user of the system is used as an oracle that solves complex parts of the problem. These requirements therefore strengthen the functionality of the method.

Both strategies are complementary. Informally:

$$\text{TASK} - \text{Assumption}_{weakening} = \text{PSM} + \text{Assumption}_{strengthening}$$

That is, the sum of both types of assumptions must be constant for achieving the same functionality. Decreasing the strength of one assumptions type can be compensated by increasing the strength of the other type (see Fig.), i.e.

$$\text{TASK} - \text{PSM} = \Delta = \text{Assumption}_{weakening} + \text{Assumption}_{strengthening}$$

This is called the *law of conservation of assumptions* in [Benjamins et al., 1996]. More formally, both types of assumptions appear at different places in the implications that define the relationship between the problem-solving method and the task:

- *Adapted Correctness*
  $\forall i,o$ $(\text{Assumption}_{strengthening}$ $\wedge$ $\text{PSM}(i,o)$ $\rightarrow$ $(\neg \text{Assumption}_{weakening}$ $\vee$ $\text{TASK}(i,o)))$

- *Adapted Completeness*
  $\forall i,o_1$ $(\text{TASK}(i,o_1) \wedge \text{Assumption}_{weakening}$
  $\rightarrow (\neg \text{Assumption}_{strengthening} \vee \exists o_2\ \text{PSM}(i,o_2)))$

This twofold impact can be explained easily by recalling that an implication is true if the premise is false or if the premise and the conclusion are true. A formula α is weaker than a formula β iff every model of β is also a model of α, i.e. $\beta \models \alpha$ and $\models \beta \rightarrow \alpha$. Assumptions weaken the implication by either strengthening the premise or weakening its conclusion.

The first type of assumptions is used to weaken the goal which must be achieved by the problem-solving method and the second type is used to improve the effect which can be achieved by the method by requiring external sources for its reasoning process. Therefore, we will call the first type teleological assumptions (i.e., *Assumptions*$_{teleological}$) and the second type ontological assumptions (i.e., *Assumptions*$_{ontological}$). Both types of assumptions fulfill the same purpose of closing the gap between the problem-solving method and the task goal which should be achieved by it. On the other hand, they achieve this by moving in quite opposite directions (see Fig. 7).

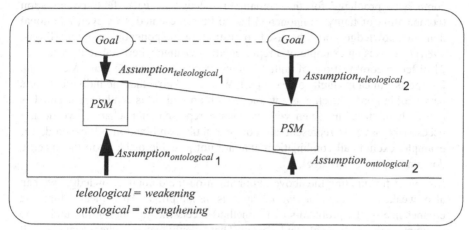

Fig. 7. The Two Effects of Assumptions

The problem-solving method makes less assumptions about available domain knowledge in the second case of Fig. 7. This must be compensated for by stronger teleological assumptions, i.e. by reducing the actual goal which can be achieved by the method. These relationships make it natural to view the sum of the effects of both types of assumptions as constant. The *role* of the two different types of assumptions (i.e., the direction of their influence) remains different. Ontological assumptions are required to define the functionality of a problem-solving method, i.e. they *extend* the effect which can be achieved by the operational specification of a problem-solving method. Teleological assumptions are required to close the gap between this functionality of a problem-solving method and a given goal. They have to *weaken* the goal in cases where the final goal is beyond the scope of the functionality of the problem-solving method.

The joint effort of both types of assumptions leads to the natural question whether they are interchangeable. The composed outcome of their joined effort is constant. We will illustrate this by an example taken from Chapter 2.

Component-based diagnosis with multiple faults is in the worst case exponential in the number of components. Every element of the powerset of the set of components is a possible hypothesis. If we are not interested in problem-solving in principle but in practice, further assumptions have to be introduced that either decrease the worst-case, or at least the average-case behavior. A drastic way to reduce the complexity of the diagnostic task is achieved by the *single-fault* or *N-fault* assumption [Davis, 1984], which reduces the complexity to be polynomial in the number of components. If the single-fault assumption holds, the incorrect behavior of the device is completely explainable by one failing component. Interestingly, the same assumption can be either interpreted as a requirement on domain knowledge or as a restriction of the functionality provided. The single-fault assumption defines either strong requirements on the domain knowledge, or significantly restricts the diagnostic problems that can correctly be handled by the diagnostic system.

- If the single-fault assumption has to be satisfied by the *domain knowledge*, then each possible fault has to be represented as a single entity. In principle this causes complexity problems for the domain knowledge as each fault combination (combination of faulty components) has to be represented. However, additional domain knowledge could be used to restrict the exponential growth. [Davis, 1984] discusses an example of a representation change where a 4-fault case (i.e., 21 different combinations of faults) is transformed into a single fault. A chip with four ports can cause faults on each port. When we know that the individual ports never fail but only the chip as a whole, a fault on four ports can be represented as one fault of the chip. Even without such a representation change, we do not necessarily have to represent all possible fault combinations. We could, for example, exclude all combinations that are not possible or likely in the specific domain (expert knowledge).

- Instead of formulating the above requirement on the domain knowledge, we can also weaken the *task definition* by this assumption. This means that the competence of the problem-solving method meets the task definition under the assumption that only single faults occur. That is, only in cases where a single fault occurs can the method work correctly and completely.

It turns out that the same assumption can either be viewed as a requirement on domain knowledge or as a restriction of the goal of the task. Therefore, it is not an internal property of an assumption that decides its status, instead it is the functional role it plays during system development or problem solving that creates this distinction. Formulating it as a requirement asks for strong effort in acquiring domain knowledge during system development and formulating it as a restriction asks for additional external effort during problem solving if the given case does not fulfill the restrictions and cannot be handled properly by the limited system.

1.6   How Deal Other Approaches with Assumptions and Efficiency

We will briefly relate our discussions to other work on problem-solving methods in the literature. First of all, the work of [Newell, 1982] is important because his *knowledge level hypothesis* is the basis for much of the current work on problem-solving methods. The major difference between our work and that of Newell is that he based his hypothesis on perfect rationality. The knowledge level in its original form is solely concerned with functional specifications that do not reflect the computational limitations of an actual problem-solving process. However, the introduction of efficiency aspects at the knowledge level can already be found as a side issue in [Newell, 1982]. He discusses the case where several actions lead to the same goal or where several goals have to be achieved. In this context he makes a short remark: "If the agent has general goals of minimizing effort, minimizing cost, or doing things in a simple way, these general goals select out a specific action from a set of otherwise equivalent task-specific actions." [Newell, 1982] A refinement of Newell's work that does take efficiency into account is the work on *bounded* or *limited rationality* (e.g. [Russell & Subramanian, 1995]). An important notion there is the utility of a reasoning process, where the benefit of reasoning is charged against its costs. Problem-solving methods can be viewed as operationalized models of limited rationality for specific tasks.

ROLE-LIMITING METHODS ([Marcus, 1988], [Puppe, 1993]) and the METHOD-TO-TASK APPROACH [Musen, 1989] are clearly aimed at providing efficient problem solvers. Unlike our approach, this concern is so strong that no separation is made between efficiency and functionality. In their terminology, a problem-solving method is "an algorithm which determines how domain-specific knowledge is used for solving problems." [Puppe, 1993] From our point of view a problem-solving method defines a class of possible algorithms by describing their functionality, their common assumptions and their expected efficiency, whereas role-limiting methods hardwire one very specific selection of assumptions and provided functionality which reduces their reusability.

Current work on *PROTÉGÉ-II* [Eriksson et al., 1995]), *SFB* [Klinker et al., 1991], and *CONFIGURABLE ROLE-LIMITING METHODS (CRLM)* [Poeck & Gappa, 1993] extend the scope of role-limiting methods by breaking them down into components with a smaller grain size. A complete problem solver for a given task can be configurated using these elementary components. Therefore the problem of selecting the appropriate problem solver becomes much more serious. In addition, the complete problem solver is then the result of a configuration activity. Selecting a component and configuring a complete problem solver involves two questions: The functionality of the methods must fit the given task and their assumptions about the domain and task must be fulfilled to enable effectiveness and efficiency. We assert that significant progress in this direction can only be achieved by the systematic explication of underlying assumptions of these methods and their relation to the expected functionality and efficiency as we proposed.

The work on *GENERIC TASKS* [Chandrasekaran, 1986] and *TASK STRUCTURES* [Chandrasekaran et al., 1992] is very similar to ours. A generic task combines a knowledge structure and an inference strategy which can be used to solve a certain kind of problem. [Chandrasekaran et al., 1992] introduces the concepts task, method, subtasks, and task structure and integrates generic tasks into the problem space paradigm of the *Soar* architecture [Newell, 1991]. The distance between a functional specification of the task and the description of the way the task is achieved by a problem-solving method is bridged by stepwise refinement. When a method is chosen, it defines new subtasks which represent smaller pieces of the entire functionality. A task structure is therefore a tree of tasks, alternative methods which can be used to solve the tasks, and subtasks for each method. This refinement stops when subtasks are achieved that can be directly solved by a method which contains no further subtasks. Therefore a task structure contains four types of knowledge. First, a *domain-independent specification of the task by specifying a task* as a transformation from an initial problem state to a goal state. Second, *knowledge which decomposes a task into subtasks.* Third, knowledge about ordering the subtasks which is called *search-control knowledge.* The initial and goal states defined by a task, together with its subtask as defined by a selected method, define what is called the problem space. The (method-specific) search control knowledge guides the search through the problem space. Fourth, *method selection knowledge* in the case that several methods exist for the same (sub-)task.

Each knowledge type also appears in our framework. The domain-independent characterization of a task corresponds either to our task definition or to the functional specification of a problem-solving method. The operational specification of such a method precisely decomposes a task into subtasks and defines control in achieving these subtasks. The fourth type of knowledge (method selection knowledge) is called an assumption in our framework. A method makes assumptions about the available domain knowledge, the input, and the precise functionality of the task in order to achieve effective and efficient problem solving. Also shared with the generic tasks approach is the belief that the task structure is mainly intended as an *analytic tool* and that it is doubtful whether it can be used as a structure of the design or an implementation. The task structure gives a vocabulary for describing the essence of a system which may be implemented by a neural network, production rules, frames, or procedural programming languages. Besides these shared beliefs, we also have to point out some differences:

- In the generic tasks approach, the development process of problem-solving methods is viewed as a process of the hierarchical refinement of generic tasks. This assumption is only fulfilled if no interactions between the method selection for different subtasks in the hierarchy exist. We argue here that global interactions will take place and that the hierarchical refinement process may prevent the development of efficient problem solvers.

- Generic tasks do not introduce a distinction between the task that should be solved and the competence of the problem-solving method. Therefore, weakening the task via assumptions so as to close the gap between the task and the problem-solving method cannot be expressed in this framework.

- Different from our approach, generic tasks assume a given set of methods and assumptions. These assumptions are only used for the process of selecting predefined method building blocks. As a consequence these assumptions are much more abstract, e.g. whether or not a concept hierarchy exists (see [Goel et al., 1987]). Assumptions here are names for different kinds of knowledge. [Chandrasekaran, 1990] states that for each task many kinds of methods may exist. However, a large number of variants even exists for each kind of method (cf. [Fensel, 1995a]). Similarly, assuming a specific knowledge type may lead to numerous different assumptions when stating it precisely. Therefore, we do not aim at a fixed task structure containing a small number of methods accompanied by abstract assumption-based selection labels for each subtask. Instead, we aim at supporting the process of deriving problem-solving methods by operating on their assumptions. In our case, assumptions are mainly viewed as method construction knowledge rather than just method *selection* knowledge (cf. [Van de Velde, 1994]).

The *Generalized Directive Models (GDM)* provide a hierarchical task-decomposition method ([van Heijst et al., 1992], [O'Hara & Shadbolt, 1996]). A generative grammar is used to support the hierarchical refinement of tasks into subtasks. The final problem solver is a sentence, subtasks are non terminal symbols, the elementary inference actions and the knowledge roles (modeling input and output of subtasks and inference steps) are terminal symbols. An initial model must first be chosen. The further model construction is achieved by stepwise application of a rewrite rule on a non terminal symbol (i.e., a subtask) of the sentence which represents the problem solver. Each of the rewrite rules has associated conditions that have to be true before the rule is applied. These conditions model the method selection knowledge. That is, they define assumptions about available domain knowledge required by a problem-solving method. As with *GENERIC TASKS*, these assumptions are abstract and informal labels. As in most other approaches, developing problem solvers is viewed as hierarchical decomposition and the functionality of the problem-solving method is identified with its operational specification. Efficiency aspects remain rather implicit in this approach. A detailed comparison of our approach with GDM can be found in [O'Hara & Shadbolt, 1996].

The COMPONENTS OF EXPERTISE approach [Steels, 1990] shares our concern with the pragmatics of problem-solving methods and distinguishes a *conceptual* and a *pragmatic viewpoint* on methods. At the conceptual level, the general type of inference of the system is described. The pragmatic level can be used to express limitations on time and space or on observations. Therefore, the pragmatic level introduces the idea of bounded rationality in the components of expertise framework. A problem-solving method is a "knowledge-level characterization" of the problem-solving process of the system. Still, as in role-limiting methods and different from our point of view, a problem-solving method is viewed as an algorithm: "A method is an algorithm." [Steels, 1993].

In KADS [Schreiber et al., 1993] and CommonKADS [Schreiber et al., 1994] the concern with the efficiency of problem-solving is less explicit than in COMPONENTS OF EXPERTISE. A collection of problem-solving methods for different tasks is provided in [Breuker & Van de Velde, 1994] and [Benjamins, 1995]. The connection between problem-solving methods and computational efficiency is proposed as epistemological and computational adequacy [Schreiber et al., 1991]. A problem-solving method specifies role limitations in the use of knowledge. The combinatorial explosion of inferences in unstructured knowledge bases is thus prevented [Wielinga et al., 1993]. The underlying idea is that epistemological role limitations as described by a knowledge-level model are connected to computational access limitations.

We already mentioned the ideas presented in [Akkermans et al., 1993] and [Wielinga et al., 1995] as a starting point of our work. Besides the high degree of correspondence we also notice some differences when trying to make these ideas work. First, we had to introduce efficiency as an explicit requirement in this development process. Most problem-solving methods and choices in their development process can only be understood from this point of view. Second, we make explicit the relation between the assumptions, the functional and the operational specifications of the problem-solving method. Third, instead of refining competence theories and transforming these into operational specifications in separate steps, we view the process as transformations of entire problem-solving methods. This process can strengthen the problem-solving method by introducing new assumptions that either put requirements on the domain or restrictions on the tasks, by modifying the operational structure, or it can directly weaken the task definition.

2 An Empirical Survey of Assumptions

Papers on problem-solving methods generally focus on the description of reasoning strategies and discuss their underlying assumptions as a side aspect. We take a complementary point of view and focus on these underlying assumptions as they play important roles:

- Assumptions are necessary to characterize the precise competence of a problem-solving method in terms of the tasks that it can solve, and in terms of the domain knowledge that it requires.

- Assumptions are necessary to enable tractable problem solving and economic system development of complex problems. First, assumptions reduce the worst-case or average-case complexity of computation. Second, assumptions may reduce the costs of the system development process by simplifying the problem that must be solved by the system.

- Finally, assumptions have to be made to ensure a proper interaction of the problem solver with its environment.

In this chapter, we provide an extensive survey of assumptions used in diagnostic problem solving. This survey provides the empirical base for our argument and delivers numerous illustrations for our point. First, we discuss assumptions that are necessary to relate the task definition of a diagnostic system with its real-world environment (see Section 2.1). That is, assumptions on the available case data, the required domain knowledge, and the problem type. Second, we discuss assumptions introduced to reduce the complexity of the reasoning process necessary to execute the diagnostic task (see Section 2.2). Such assumptions are introduced to either change the worst-case complexity or the average-case behavior of problem solving. Third, we sketch further assumptions that are related to the appropriate *interaction* of the problem solver with its environment (see Section 2.3).

The first diagnostic systems built were heuristic systems in the sense that they contained compiled knowledge which linked symptoms directly to hypotheses (usually through rules). With these systems, only foreseen symptoms can be diagnosed, and heuristic knowledge that links symptoms with possible faults needs to be available. One of the main principles underlying model-based diagnosis [Davis, 1984] is the use of a domain model (called Structure, Behavior, Function (SBF) models in [Chandrasekaran, 1991]). Heuristic knowledge that links symptoms with causes is no longer necessary in these systems. The domain model is used for predicting the desired device behavior, which is then compared with the observed behavior. A discrepancy indicates a symptom. General reasoning techniques such as constraint satisfaction or truth maintenance can be used to derive diagnoses that explain the actual behavior of the device using its model. Because the reasoning part is represented separately from domain knowledge, it can be reused for different domains. This paradigm of model-based diagnosis gave rise to the development of general approaches to diagnosis, such as "constraint suspension" [Davis, 1984], DART [Genesereth, 1984], GDE [de Kleer & Williams, 1987], and several extensions to GDE (GDE+ [Struss & Dressler, 1989], Sherlock [de Kleer & Williams, 1989]).

Dieter Fensel: Problem-Solving Methods, LNAI 1791, pp. 26 - 40, 2000.
© Springer-Verlag Berlin Heidelberg 2000

2.1   Assumptions Necessary to Define the Task

In model-based diagnosis (cf. [de Kleer et al., 1992]), the definition of the task of the knowledge-based system requires a *system description* of the device under consideration and a *set of observations*, where some indicate *normal* and others *abnormal* behavior. The goal of the task is to find a *diagnosis* that, together with the system description, *explains* the observations. In the following, we discuss four different aspects of such a task definition and show the assumptions related to each of them. The four aspects are: identifying abnormalities, identifying causes of these abnormalities, defining hypotheses, and defining diagnoses.

2.1.1   Identifying Abnormalities

Identification of abnormal behavior is necessary before a diagnostic process can be started to find explanations for the abnormalities. This identification task requires three kinds of knowledge, of which two are related to the type of input and one to the interpretation of possible discrepancies (see [Benjamins, 1993]):

- *observations* of the behavior of the device must be provided to the diagnostic reasoner;

- a *behavioral description* of the device must be provided to the diagnostic reasoner;

- knowledge concerning the *(im)preciseness* of the observations and the behavioral description as well as *comparison knowledge* (thresholds, etc.) are necessary to decide whether a discrepancy is significant. Other required knowledge concerns the interpretation of *missing values*, and whether an observation can have several values (i.e., its value type).

Relevant assumptions state that the two types of inputs (i.e., observations and behavioral descriptions) need to be *reliable*. Otherwise, the discrepancy could be explained by a measuring fault or a modeling fault. In other words, these assumptions guarantee that if a prediction yields a different behavior than the observed behavior of the artifact, then the artifact has a defect [Davis & Hamscher, 1988].

These assumptions are also necessary for the meta-level decision whether a diagnosis problem is given at all (i.e., whether there is an abnormality in system behavior). This decision relies on a further assumption: the *no design error assumption* [Davis, 1984] which says that if no fault occurs, then the device must be able to achieve the desired behavior. In other words, the discrepancy must be the result of a faulty situation where some parts of the system are defect. It cannot be the result of a situation where the system works correctly but cannot achieve the desired functionality because it is not designed for this. If this assumption does not hold, then there is a design problem and not a diagnostic problem.

2.1.2   Identifying Causes

Another purpose of the system description is the identification of possible causes of faulty behavior. This cause-identification knowledge must be *reliable* [Davis & Hamscher, 1988], or in other words the knowledge used in model-based diagnosis is assumed to be a correct and complete description of the artifact; correct and complete in the sense, that it enables the derivation of correct and complete diagnoses if discrepancies appear. A typical problem of diagnosis without knowledge about fault models (i.e., incomplete knowledge) is that the reasoner provides, in addition to correct diagnoses also incorrect diagnoses. The result is complete but not correct because the domain knowledge is not complete. Depending on the different types of device models and diagnostic methods, these assumptions appear in different forms. In the following, we restrict our attention to component-oriented device models that describe a device in terms of components, their behaviors (a functional description), and their connections. It is a critical modeling decision to select what is viewed as a component and which types of interactions are represented (cf. [Davis, 1984]). Several points of view are possible for deciding what is to be regarded as being a component. Different levels of physical representations result in different entities; the independent entities that are used in the manufacturing process of the artifact could be used as components or functional unities of the artifact could be seen as components.

Causes of observed behavior are assumed modes of components. Such mode descriptions may either distinguish between "$ok(component_i)$" and "$\neg ok(component_i)$" (i.e., the component works correct or is faulty) or may provide additional modes distinguishing between different fault modes of components. The set of all possible hypotheses are derived from these components and their modes. [Davis, 1984] has pointed out that one should be aware of the underlying assumptions for such a diagnostic approach and listed a number of them which we will discuss now.

First, the *localized failure of function* assumption: the device must be decomposable into well-defined and localized entities (i.e., components) that can be treated as causes of faulty behavior. Second, these *components have a functional description* that provides the (correct) output for their possible inputs. If this functional description is local, that is it does not refer to the functioning of the whole device, then the *no function in structure* assumption [de Kleer & Brown, 1984] is satisfied. Several diagnostic methods also expect the reverse of the functional descriptions, thus rules that *derive the expected input from the provided output* called "inference rules" in [Davis, 1984]. If only correct functional descriptions are available, then fault behavior is defined as any other behavior than the correct one. Fault behavior of components can be constrained by including fault models, that is *functional descriptions of the components in case they are broken* (cf. [de Kleer & Williams, 1989], [Struss & Dressler, 1989]). If one assumes that these functional descriptions are complete (the *complete fault knowledge* assumption), then components can be considered to be correct if none of their fault descriptions is consistent with the observed faulty behavior. A result of using fault models is that all kinds of non-specified—and physically impossible—behaviors of a component are excluded as diagnoses. For example, using fault models, it is then impossible to conclude that a fault "*one of two light bulbs is not working*" is explained by a defect battery that does not provide power and a defect lamp that lights without electricity (cf. [Struss & Dressler, 1989]).

Further assumptions that are related to the functional descriptions of components are the *no fault masking* and the *non intermittency* assumption. The former assumption states that a defect in an individual or composite component or in the entire device must be visible through changed outputs (cf. [Davis & Hamscher, 1988], [Raiman,

1992]). According to the latter assumption, a component that receives identical inputs at different points of time must produce identical outputs. In other words, the output is a function of the input (cf. [Raiman et al., 1991]). [Raiman et al., 1991] argue that intermittency results from incomplete input specifications of components.

Another type of assumption underlying many diagnostic approaches is the *no faults in structure* assumption (cf. [Davis & Hamscher, 1988]) that manifests itself in different variants according to the particular domain. The assumption states that the interactions of the components are correctly modeled and that they are complete. This assumption gives rise to three different classes of more specific assumptions. First, the *no broken interaction* assumption states that connections between the components function correctly (e.g. no wires between components are broken). If this is too strong, then the assumption can be weakened by also representing the connections themselves as components. Second, the *no unexpected directions* assumption (or existence of a causal pathway assumption, [Davis, 1984]) states that the directions of the interactions are correctly modeled and are complete. For example, a light bulb gets power from a battery and there is no interaction in the opposite direction. The *no hidden interactions* assumption (cf. [Böttcher, 1995]) assumes that there are no non-represented interactions (i.e., closed-world assumptions on connections). A bridge fault [Davis, 1984] is an example of a violation of this assumption in the electronic domain. Electronic devices whose components unintendedly interact through heat exchange are another example [Böttcher, 1995]. In the worst case, all potential unintended interaction paths between components have to be represented [Preist & Welhalm, 1990]. The no hidden interactions assumption is critical since most models (like design models of the device) describe correctly working devices and unexpected interactions are therefore precisely not specified. A refinement of this assumption is that there are no *assembly errors* (i.e., every individual component works correctly but they have been wired up incorrectly).

2.1.3   Defining Hypotheses

A hypothesis is a set of annotated components where an annotation states the assumed mode of a component. The set of all possible hypotheses is the powerset of all components annotated with their different modes. Above, we have discussed the knowledge that is required to identify a discrepancy and knowledge that provides these hypotheses used to explain these discrepancies. Further knowledge is required to decide which type of explanation is necessary. [Console & Torasso, 1992] distinguish two types of explanations: weak explanations that are *consistent* with the observations (no contradiction can be derived from the union of the device model, the observations, and the hypothesis), and strong explanations that *imply* the observations (the observations can be derived from the device model and the hypothesis). Both types of explanations can be combined by dividing observations in two classes: observations that need to be explained by deriving them from a hypothesis and observations that need only be consistent with the hypothesis. In this case *knowledge that allows one to divide the set of observations* is required. The decision which type of explanation to use can only be made based on assumptions about the environment in which the knowledge-based system is to be used.

2.1.4   Defining Diagnoses

After introducing observations, hypotheses and an explanatory relation that relates hypotheses with observations, the notion of *diagnosis* must now be established. Each hypothesis that correctly explains all observations is not necessarily a desired diagnosis. We could only accept *parsimonious* hypotheses as *diagnoses* (cf. [Bylander et al., 1991]). A hypothesis or explanation H is parsimonious if H is an explanation and no other hypothesis H' exists that also is an explanation and H' < H. We have to make assumptions about the desired diagnosis (cf. [McIlraith, 1994]) in order to define the partial ordering (<) on hypotheses, for example, whether the diagnostic task is concerned with finding all components that are necessarily faulty to explain the system behavior or whether it is concerned with finding all components that are necessarily correct to explain the system behavior. In the first case, we aim at economy in repair, whereas in safety critical applications (e.g., nuclear power plants) we should obviously choose the second case.

As shown by [McIlraith, 1994], the assumptions about the type of explanation relation (i.e., consistency versus derivability) and about the explanations (i.e., definition of parsimony) also make strong commitments on the domain knowledge (the device model) that is used to describe the system. If we ask for a consistent explanation with minimal sets of faulty components (i.e., $H_1 < H_2$ if H_1 assumes less components as being faulty than H_2), we need knowledge that constrains the normal behavior of components. Otherwise we would simply derive all components as correct. If we ask for a consistent explanation with minimal sets of correct components (i.e., $H_1 < H_2$ if H_1 assumes less components as being correct than H_2), we need knowledge that constrains the abnormal behavior of components. Otherwise we would simply derive all components as faulty.

The definition of parsimonious hypotheses introduces a *preference* relationship of hypotheses. This could be extended by defining further preferences on diagnoses to select one optimal one (e.g., by introducing assumptions related to the probability of faults). Again, knowledge about preferences must be available to define a preference function and a corresponding ordering.

2.1.5   Summary

Fig.8 summarizes the assumptions that are discussed above and groups them according to their purpose. All these assumptions are necessary to relate the definition of the functionality of the diagnostic system with the diagnostic problem (i.e., the task) to be solved and with the domain knowledge that is required to define the task. Table 1 provides an explanation of most of the assumptions along with the role they play (function), the area they refer to (case data, domain knowledge, or task), and some references where they are discussed in more detail.

Table 1. Effect Assumptions in Component-Oriented Diagnosis
(cd = case data, dk = domain knowledge, t = task).

Name	Explanation	about	Function	References
existence of observations	observations must be provided to the diagnostic system	cd	It is necessary for detecting discrepancies.	[Benjamins, 1993]

**Table 1. Effect Assumptions in Component-Oriented Diagnosis
(cd = case data, dk = domain knowledge, t = task).**

Name	Explanation	about	Function	References
reliability of observations	The provided observations must be reliable.	cd	It is necessary for assuming that the discrepancy must be explained by a diagnosis.	[Benjamins, 1993], [Davis & Hamscher, 1988]
existence of a behavioral description	The desired system behavior must be known to the diagnostic reasoner.	dk	It is necessary for detecting discrepancies.	[Benjamins, 1993]
existence of knowledge to identify discrepancies	Knowledge is required to compare the observations with the behavioral description.	dk	It is necessary for interpreting discrepancies.	[Benjamins, 1993]
no design error	The discrepancy between expected and actual behavior does not result from the (incorrect) design of the device.	t	The behavioral discrepancy is a fault and not just an impossibility.	[Davis, 1984]
existence of a set of components	The device can be decomposed into a set of components.	dk	The entire device can be decomposed into smaller units that constitute the device.	[Davis, 1984], [Davis & Hamscher, 1988]
localized failure of function, no function in structure	Faulty components can be identified as causes.	dk	The reasons for faulty behavior do not have to be constructed but can be selected from a finite set.	[Davis, 1984], [de Kleer & Brown, 1984]
existence of a set of annotations (i.e., of component modes)	Components could have several behavioral modes that need to be provided.	dk	The diagnostic reasoner can select from the behavioral modes provided for each component.	[Struss & Dressler, 1989], [de Kleer et al., 1992]
completeness of the set of annotations = complete-fault knowledge	All possible modes of the components are known.	dk	It is used to infer the mode of a component if all other behaviors do not (even not partially) explain the fault.	[Struss & Dressler, 1989], [de Kleer et al., 1992]
existence of input-output descriptions of the components	This knowledge defines the input-output behavior of the components.	dk	The behavioral description of the components is required to detect their faulty behavior and to derive the overall behavior of the complete device.	[de Kleer & Williams, 1987], [Davis & Hamscher, 1988]
existence of output-input descriptions of the components	This knowledge defines the output-input relation of the components.	dk	This knowledge can be used to derive additional discrepancies.	[Davis, 1984], [Raiman, 1989]

Table 1. Effect Assumptions in Component-Oriented Diagnosis (cd = case data, dk = domain knowledge, t = task).

Name	Explanation	about	Function	References
existence of functional descriptions of faulty behavior of components	This knowledge defines the input-output behavior of the components in case they are broken.	dk	The behavioral description of the components is required to identify different possible faults of a component.	[de Kleer & Williams, 1987], [Struss & Dressler, 1989]
complete behavioral descriptions (complete fault models)	All possible behaviors of a component are modeled by its functional description.	dk	It is used to completely constrain the possible behavior of a component.	[de Kleer & Williams, 1987], [Struss & Dressler, 1989]
no fault masking	A fault of a component is visible in its behavior and in the behavior of the entire device.	cd & dk	It is necessary for detecting faulty components.	[Davis, 1984], [Davis & Hamscher, 1988], [Raiman, 1992]
non intermittency	The output of a component is a function of the input (e.g., the behavior does not change over time).	cd	It is necessary for interpreting the discrepancy between an observation and an output of a behavioral description of a component.	[Davis, 1984], [Raiman et al., 1991]
existence of a model of the component interactions	It assumes that the possible interactions between components are known to the reasoner.	dk	This model is required to derive the overall behavior of the system and the local inputs of components from the local outputs of the components.	[Davis, 1984], [Davis & Hamscher, 1988]
no fault in structure assumption	Faulty components are the only causes.	dk	Only components need to be treated as possible causes for the faulty behavior.	[Davis, 1984], [Davis & Hamscher, 1988]
no broken interactions	The interactions work properly, i.e., the connections work properly.	dk	Only components need to be treated as possible causes for the faulty behavior and the interaction model describes the real interactions.	[Davis, 1984], [Davis & Hamscher, 1988]
no unexpected direction	The direction of the interaction is as represented.	dk	Only components need to be treated as possible causes for the faulty behavior and the interaction model describes the real interactions.	[Davis, 1984]

Table 1. Effect Assumptions in Component-Oriented Diagnosis (cd = case data, dk = domain knowledge, t = task).

Name	Explanation	about	Function	References
no hidden interactions (closed world assumption)	There are no interactions that are not represented in the model.	dk	Only components need to be treated as possible causes for the faulty behavior and the interaction model describes the real interactions.	[Davis, 1984], [Böttcher, 1995]
no assembly error	The components are not wired incorrectly.	dk	Only components need to be treated as possible causes for the faulty behavior and the interaction model describes the real interactions.	[Davis & Hamscher, 1988], [Böttcher, 1995]
type of explanation relation (type of hypotheses)	Need an observation be consistent with the hypothesis or must it be derivable from it.	dk & t	The problem solving is either constraints satisfaction or abductive inference.	[Console & Torasso, 1992], [de Kleer et al., 1992], [ten Teije & van Harmelen, 1996]
classification of observations	It introduces a distinction between observations that describe normal and abnormal behavior.	dk	In abductive inference only the abnormal behavior must be explained.	[Console & Torasso, 1992]
type of explanation (type of diagnosis)	Should the set of faulty components contain all components that need to be faulty or that could be faulty.	dk & t	The diagnosis is used for an economic repair process versus it is used for safety-critical monitoring.	[McIlraith, 1994]
preference knowledge on diagnoses	It defines preferences between diagnoses.	dk	Necessary for selecting the diagnoses with high preferences.	[de Kleer & Williams, 1987], [Davis & Hamscher, 1988]

All these assumptions are necessary to relate a model of the device with the actual device under consideration. "There is no such thing as an assumption-free representation. Every model, every representation contains simplifying assumptions" [Davis & Hamscher, 1988]. If the assumptions are too strong, one could consider weakening them. For example, they can be weakened by representing all desired interactions as components (e.g., wires) that could fail by representing additional possibilities of interactions (e.g., electronic devices can interact via heat exchange) [Böttcher, 1995]; by representing all potential unintended interaction paths between components [Preist & Welhalm, 1990]; or by representing additional inputs to get rid of intermittency [Raiman et al., 1991]. Each of these weakenings significantly increases the computational complexity of the problem-solving process. This raises another problem in model-based diagnosis, namely its *high complexity or intractability*. This will be discussed in the following section.

2.2   Assumptions Necessary to Define an Efficient Problem Solver

Component-based diagnosis is in the worst case exponential in the number of annotated components ([Bylander et al., 1991]). Every element of the powerset of the set of annotated components is a possible hypothesis. As we are not interested in problem-solving in principle but in practice, further assumptions have to be introduced that either reduce the worst-case or at least the average-case behavior.

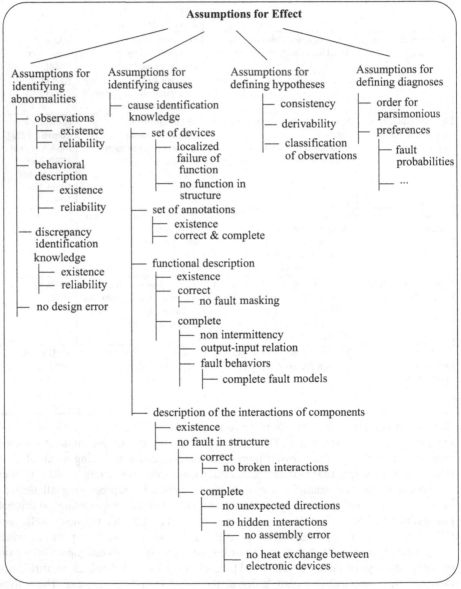

Fig. 8. Assumptions for Effect.

2.2.1   Reducing the Worst-Case Complexity

The *single-fault* or *N-fault* assumptions [Davis, 1984] reduce the complexity of model-based diagnosis to be polynomial in the number of components. If the single-fault assumption holds true, then the incorrect behavior of the device is completely explainable by one failing component. This assumption defines either strong requirements on the provided domain knowledge, or significantly restricts the diagnostic problems that can correctly be handled by the diagnostic system. In the first case, each possible fault has to be represented as a single entity. In the second case, the methods works only in cases where a single fault occurs.

2.2.2   Reducing the Average-Case Behavior

As the single-fault assumption might be too strong an assumption for several applications, either as a requirement on the domain knowledge or as a restriction on the task, [Reiter, 1987] and [de Kleer & Williams, 1987] provide approaches able to deal with multiple faults. However, this reintroduces the complexity problems. To deal with this problem, GDE [de Kleer & Williams, 1987] exploits the *minimality assumption*, which reduces, in practical cases, the exponential worst case behavior to a complexity that grows with the square of the number of components. In GDE, this assumptions helps to reduce the complexity in two ways. First, a conflict is a set of components that cannot work correctly given the provided domain knowledge and the observed behavior. Under the minimality assumption, each super-set of a conflict is also a conflict and all conflicts can be represented by minimal conflicts. Second, a hypothesis contains at least one component of each conflict. Every super-set of such a hypothesis is again a hypothesis. Therefore, diagnoses can be represented by minimal diagnoses. The minimality assumption requires that diagnoses are independent or monotonic (see [Bylander et al., 1991]): a diagnosis that assumes more components as being faulty, explains more observations.

A drastic way to ensure that the minimality assumption holds true, is to neglect any knowledge about the behavior of faulty components. A disadvantage of this is that physical rules may be violated (i.e., existing knowledge about faulty behavior). We already mentioned the example provided in [Struss & Dressler, 1989] where a fault (one of two bulbs does not light) is explained by a broken battery that does not provide power and a broken bulb that lights without power. Knowledge about how components behave when they are faulty (called fault models) could be used to constrain the set of diagnoses derived by the system. On the other hand, it increases the complexity of the task. If for one component m possible fault behaviors are provided, this leads to $m+1$ possible states instead of two (correct and fault). The maximum number of candidates increases from 2^n to $(m+1)^n$.

A similar extension of GDE that includes fault models is the Sherlock system (cf. [de Kleer & Williams, 1989]). With fault models it is no longer guaranteed that every super-set of the faulty components that constitute the diagnosis is also a diagnosis, and therefore the minimality assumption as such cannot be exploited. In Sherlock, a diagnosis does not only contain fault components (and implicitly assumes that all other unmentioned components are correct), but it contains a set of components assumed to work correctly and a set of components assumed to be faulty. A conflict is then a set of some correct and faulty components that is inconsistent with the domain knowledge and the observations. In order to accommodate to this situation, [de Kleer et al., 1992] extend the concept of minimal diagnoses to kernel diagnoses and characterize the conditions under which the minimality assumption still holds. The kernel diagnoses are given by the prime implicants of the minimal conflicts. Moreover, the minimal sets of kernel diagnoses which are sufficient to cover every diagnosis correspond to the irredundant sets of prime implicants (see [McCluskey, 1956]) of all minimal conflicts.[8] These extensions cause significant additional effort, because there can be exponentially more kernel diagnoses than minimal diagnoses and finding irredundant sets of prime implicants is NP-hard. Therefore, [de Kleer et al., 1992] characterize two assumptions under which the kernel diagnoses are identical to the minimal diagnoses. The kernel diagnoses are identical to the minimal diagnoses if all conflicts contain only faulty components. In this case, there is again only one irredundant set of minimal diagnoses (the set containing all minimal diagnoses). The two assumptions that can ensure these properties are the *ignorance of abnormal behavior* assumption and the *limited knowledge of abnormal behavior* assumption.

The ignorance of abnormal behavior assumption excludes knowledge about faulty behavior and thus characterizes the original situation of GDE. The limited knowledge of abnormal behavior assumption states that the knowledge of abnormal behavior does not rule out any diagnosis indicating a set of faulty components if a valid diagnosis indicating a subset of them as faulty components exists and if the additional components assumed faulty are not inconsistent with the observations and the system description.[9] The latter assumption is a refinement of the former, that is, the truth of the ignorance of abnormal behavior assumption implies the truth of the limited knowledge of abnormal behavior assumption.

A similar type of assumption is used by [Bylander et al., 1991] to characterize different complexity classes of component-based diagnosis. In general, finding one or all diagnoses is intractable. The *independent* and *monotonic* assumptions, which have the same effect as the limited knowledge of abnormal behavior assumption, require that each super-set of a diagnosis indicating a set of faulty components is also a diagnosis.[10] In this case, the worst-case complexity of finding one minimal diagnosis grows polynomically with the square of the number of components. However, the task of finding all minimal diagnoses is still NP-hard in regard to the number of components. This corresponds to the fact that the minimality assumption of GDE (i.e., the ignorance of abnormal behavior and limited knowledge of abnormal behavior assumptions), that searches for all diagnoses, does not change the worst-case but only the average-case behavior of the diagnostic reasoner.

---

[8] An implicant is a conjunction of positive and negative literals. Without fault models, minimal hypotheses contain only negative literals ($\neg ok(component_i)$). In the case of fault models we have positive and negative literals ($ok(component_i)$ and $\neg ok(component_i)$) in the hypotheses. Therefore, minimality cannot be simply defined by set inclusion of the literals of a conjunction.

[9] [McIlraith, 1994] generalizes these assumptions for the dual case of diagnosing a minimal set of components proven to be correct and applies these assumptions for characterizing minimal abductive diagnoses.

[10] More precisely, the explanatory power of a hypothesis increases monotonic by adding faulty or correct components.

2.2.3   Search Guidance

The complexity of component-based diagnosis (especially when working with fault models) requires further assumptions that enable efficient reasoning for practical cases (cf. [Struss, 1992], [Böttcher & Dressler, 1994]). Again, these assumptions do not change the worst case complexity but should reduce the necessary effort in practical cases. A well-known means to increase efficiency is a reasoning focus. Defining a focus for the reasoning process can be achieved by exploiting hierarchies or probability information. The *hierarchically-layered device-model* assumption assumes the existence of hierarchically layered models that allow a stepwise refinement of diagnoses to reduce the complexity of the diagnostic process (cf. the complexity analysis of hierarchical structures of [Goel et al., 1987]). The large number of components at the lowest level of refinement is replaced by a small number of components at a higher level. Only the relevant parts of the model are refined during the problem-solving process. The *hierarchically-layered behavioral-model* assumption assumes the existence of more abstract descriptions of the behavior that can improve the efficiency because reasoning can be performed at a more coarse-grained, and thus simpler, level (cf. [Abu-Hanna, 1994]). The *existence of probabilities* assumption assumes knowledge about the probability of faults that can be used to guide the search process for diagnoses by focusing on faults with high probabilities. Usually, these probabilities introduce new assumptions (e.g., the *components fail independently* assumption [de Kleer & Williams, 1989]).

All these knowledge types and their related assumptions rely on further assumptions concerning the utility of this search control knowledge. For example, the hierarchically-layered device model only improves the search process when the faults are not distributed in a way that forces the problem solver to expand each abstract component description to its lowest levels. It significantly improves the search process if the problem solver only needs to refine one abstract component description at each level.

2.2.4   Summary

Fig. 9 summarizes the assumptions and groups them according to their purpose. All these assumptions are introduced so as to reduce the computational effort required to solve the problem. Table 2 provides an explanation of the assumptions along with the role they play (function), the area they pertain to (case data, domain knowledge or task), and some references where they are discussed in more detail.

Table 2. Efficiency Assumptions in Component-Oriented Diagnosis
(cd = case data, dk = domain knowledge, t = task).

Name	Explanation	about	Function	References
single fault (SFA), N-fault	There is one or there are at most N faults.	dk or t	It polynomializes the worst-case complexity for finding one or all diagnoses.	[Davis, 1984]

Table 2. Efficiency Assumptions in Component-Oriented Diagnosis (cd = case data, dk = domain knowledge, t = task).

Name	Explanation	about	Function	References
minimality	Sets of hypotheses can be represented by one minimal hypothesis.	dk	It polynomializes the average-case behavior for finding all diagnoses.	[Reiter, 1987], [de Kleer & Williams, 1987], [Bylander et al., 1991], [de Kleer et al., 1992]
ignorance of abnormal behavior	No knowledge that constrains possible faulty behavior is provided.	dk	It polynomializes the average-case behavior for finding all diagnoses.	[de Kleer & Williams, 1987], [de Kleer et al., 1992]
independency	The explanatory power of a diagnosis is the union of the explanatory power of its elements.	dk	It polynomializes the worst-case complexity for finding one diagnosis.	[Bylander et al., 1991]
monotonicity	The explanatory power of a diagnosis increases monotonic with its size.	dk	It polynomializes the worst-case complexity for finding one diagnosis.	[Bylander et al., 1991]
limited knowledge of abnormal behavior	Valid diagnoses do not become invalid by adding further correct or faulty components to them.	dk	It polynomializes the average-case behavior for finding all diagnoses.	[de Kleer et al., 1992]
existence of search control knowledge	This knowledge is used to guide the search process for diagnoses.	dk	It improves the average-case behavior for finding all diagnoses.	[Struss, 1992], [Böttcher & Dressler, 1994]
existence of a hierarchically-layered device-model	The device model is hierarchically structured.	dk	The hierarchical structure of the device focuses the search process.	[Goel et al., 1987], [Struss, 1992], [Böttcher & Dressler, 1994]
existence of a hierarchically-layered behavioral-model	The behavioral description of the system is hierarchically structured.	dk	Abstract descriptions of the behavior should reduce the search effort.	[Struss, 1992], [Abu-Hanna, 1994], [Böttcher & Dressler, 1994]
existence of probabilities	Faults are annotated by their probability.	dk	Probabilities of faults focus the search process.	[de Kleer & Williams, 1987], [Struss, 1992], [Böttcher & Dressler, 1994]
fault probabilities are independent	Each fault appears independently from other possible faults.	cd & dk	It is used in computing probabilities for hypotheses.	[de Kleer & Williams, 1989]

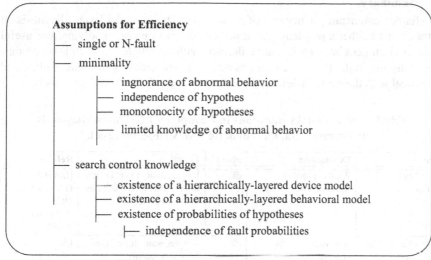

Assumptions for Efficiency

— single or N-fault
— minimality
  — ingnorance of abnormal behavior
  — independence of hypothes
  — monotonocity of hypotheses
  — limited knowledge of abnormal behavior

— search control knowledge
  — existence of a hierarchically-layered device model
  — existence of a hierarchically-layered behavioral model
  — existence of probabilities of hypotheses
    — independence of fault probabilities

Fig. 9. Assumptions for Efficiency.

2.3   Assumptions in System-Environment Interaction

Until now, we have sketched a diagnostic problem solver working in the batch mode. It receives some observations as input and tries to efficiently derive a number of hypotheses that can explain the fault behaviors. This is not a very realistic scenario, however, especially in the case where hypothesis *discrimination* becomes necessary. In general, hypothesis discrimination becomes necessary if the number of hypotheses found exceeds the desired number (cf. [Davis & Hamscher, 1988]). Additional observations must be provided as the initial observations were not strong enough to discriminate between existing hypotheses. Assumptions related to this activity will be discussed now (see Table 3). First, it must be possible to obtain *additional observations*. Examples of more specific versions of this assumption are: can the device be unfastened, are measuring points reachable, can components be replaced easily to test behavior, can new input be provided to the device, etc. Second, assumptions can be made about the *utility of additional observations*. We can assume cost information of additional measurements and knowledge about their discriminatory power (i.e., knowledge about dependencies between hypotheses) to optimize their selection. GDE uses minimal entropy as a measure to minimize the expected number of tests (= additional observations). FAULTY [Abu-Hanna et al., 1991] minimizes the estimated number of tests based on a variety of balanced global factors. Again, NP-hard problems arise if one tries to optimize these decisions. Therefore, assumptions concerning *heuristic knowledge* that guide this process are necessary.

All these assumptions are necessary to optimize the cooperation of the diagnostic system with its environment. In principle, one could assume that all observations that are possible are provided to the system before it starts its diagnostic reasoning. However, collecting observations is often a major cost-determining factor. Therefore, assumptions are introduced concerning the efficiency of gathering information with minimal costs.

2.4   Summary

This chapter enumerates a number of assumptions from model-based diagnosis. It illustrates that neither a problem (i.e., task), nor efficient problem solving, nor useful system-environment interaction can be defined without relying on such assumptions. We will discuss in the following chapters how to make such assumptions explicit and how to deal with their role in developing effective and efficient problem solvers.

Table 3. Interaction Assumptions in Component-Oriented Diagnosis (cd = case data, dk = domain knowledge, t = task).

Name	Explanation	about	Function	References
Possibility of additional observations	What are further possible observations.	dk	It is necessary to get further information for hypotheses discrimination.	[Davis & Hamscher, 1988], [Benjamins, 1993]
Utility of additional observations	How useful are these observations (information gain versus costs).	dk	It is necessary for optimal decisions during hypotheses discrimination.	[de Kleer & Williams, 1987], [Davis & Hamscher, 1988], [Benjamins, 1993]
heuristic search knowledge	This knowledge is used to guide the search process for optimal selection of further observations.	dk	It necessary for efficiently making sub-optimal decisions.	[de Kleer & Williams, 1987], [Davis & Hamscher, 1988], [Benjamins, 1993]

"USER: I need a software system that willhelp me manage my factory.
SOFTWARE ENGINEER: Well, let´s see. I can put together components
that do sorting, searching, stacks, queues, and so forth.
USER: Hmm, that's interesting. But how would those fit into my system?"
[Shaw & Garlan, 1996]

Section II:
How to Describe Problem-Solving Methods

3 A Four Component Architecture for Knowledge-Based Systems

During the last years, several conceptual and formal specification techniques for knowledge-based systems have been developed (see [Studer et al., 1998], [Fensel & van Harmelen, 1994], [Fensel, 1995c] for surveys). The main advantage of these modeling or specification techniques is that they enable the description of a knowledge-based system independent of its implementation. This has two main implications. First, such a specification can be used as a gold standard for the validation and verification of the implementation of the knowledge-based system. It defines the requirements the implementation must fulfil. Second, validation and verification of the functionality, the reasoning behavior, and the domain knowledge of a knowledge-based system is already possible during the early phases of the development process. A model of the knowledge-based system can be investigated independently of aspects that are only related to its implementation. Especially when a knowledge-based system is built out of reusable components is the verification as to whether the assumptions of such reusable building blocks fit to each other and to the specific circumstances of the actual problem and knowledge an essential task.

In this chapter, we discuss a conceptual and formal framework for the specification of knowledge-based systems. The conceptual framework is developed in accordance to the CommonKADS model of expertise [Schreiber et al., 1994] because this model has become widely used by the knowledge engineering community. The formal means applied are based on combining variants of algebraic specification techniques (see [Wirsing, 1990], [Bidoit et al., 1991]) and dynamic logic [Harel, 1984]. We identify several proof obligations that arise in order to guarantee a consistent specification. The overall verification of a knowledge-based system is broken down into different types of proof obligations that ensure that the different elements of a specification together define a consistent system with appropriate functionality.

Our conceptual and formal model can be viewed as a software architecture for a specific class of systems, i.e. knowledge-based systems. Software architectures have found increasing interest by the software engineering community in order to enhance the system development process and the level of software reuse (cf. [Garlan & Perry, 1995], [Shaw & Garlan, 1996]). A software architecture decomposes a system into components and defines their relationships. This recent trend in software engineering works on establishing a more abstract level for describing software artifacts than was previously customary. The main concern of this new area is the description of generic architectures that describe the essence of large and complex software systems. Such architectures specify classes of application problems instead of focusing on the small and generic components from which a system is built up.

This chapter is organized as follows. First, we discuss the different conceptual elements of a specification of a knowledge-based system and which kinds of proof obligations arise in their context. In the following four parts, we introduce our formal means to specify the different elements. In each part, we use an example for illustrating these formalizations. Finally, we add a comparison with related work.

Dieter Fensel: Problem-Solving Methods, LNAI 1791, pp. 43 - 60, 2000.
© Springer-Verlag Berlin Heidelberg 2000

3.1   The Entire Framework

In the following, we will first introduce the different elements of a specification. Then we will discuss how they relate to each other and which proof obligations arise from these relationships.

3.1.1 The Main Elements of a Specification

Our framework for describing a knowledge-based system consists of four elements (see Fig.10): a task that defines the problem that should be solved by the knowledge-based system, a *problem-solving method* that defines the reasoning process of a knowledge-based system, and a *domain model* that describes the domain knowledge of the knowledge-based system. Each of these three elements is described independently to enable the reuse of task descriptions in different domains (see [Breuker & Van de Velde, 1994]), the reuse of problem-solving methods for different tasks and domains ([Puppe, 1993], [Breuker & Van de Velde, 1994], [Benjamins et al., 1996]), and the reuse of domain knowledge for different tasks and problem-solving methods (cf. [Gruber, 1993], [Top & Akkermans, 1994], [van Heijst et al., 1997]). Therefore, a fourth element of a specification of a knowledge-based system is an *adapter* which is necessary to adjust the three other (reusable) parts to each other and to the specific application problem. This *new* element is used to introduce assumptions and to map the different terminologies.

The Task

The description of a *task* specifies goals that should be achieved in order to solve a given problem. A second part of a task specification is the definition of requirements on domain knowledge. For example, a task that defines the derivation of a diagnosis requires causal knowledge explaining observations as domain knowledge. Axioms are used to define the requirements on such knowledge. Natural candidates for the formal task definition are *algebraic specifications*. They have been developed in software engineering to define the functionality of a software artifact (cf. [Bidoit et al., 1991], [Wirsing, 1990]) and have already been applied by [Spee & in 't Veld, 1994] and [Pierret-Golbreich & Talon, 1996] for knowledge-based system. In a nutshell, algebraic specifications provide a signature (consisting of types, constants, functions, and predicates) and a set of axioms that define properties of these syntactical elements.

The Problem-Solving Method

Problem-solving methods describe which reasoning steps and which types of knowledge are needed to perform a task. Besides some differences between the approaches, there is strong consensus that a problem-solving method decomposes the entire reasoning task into more elementary inferences, defines the types of knowledge that are needed by the inference steps to be done, and defines control and knowledge flow between the inferences. In addition, [Van de Velde, 1988] and [Akkermans et al., 1993] define the *competence* of a problem-solving method independently from the specification of its operational reasoning behavior (i.e., a functional black-box specification). Proving that a problem-solving method has some competence has the clear advantage that the selection of a method for a given problem and the verification whether a problem-solving method fulfills its task can be performed independent from details of the internal reasoning behavior of the method.

The description of a problem-solving method consists of three elements in our framework: a *competence description*, an *operational* specification, and *requirements* on domain knowledge.

The definition of the functionality of the problem-solving method introduces the *competence* of a problem-solving method independent from its dynamic realization. As for task definitions, algebraic specifications can be used for this purpose.

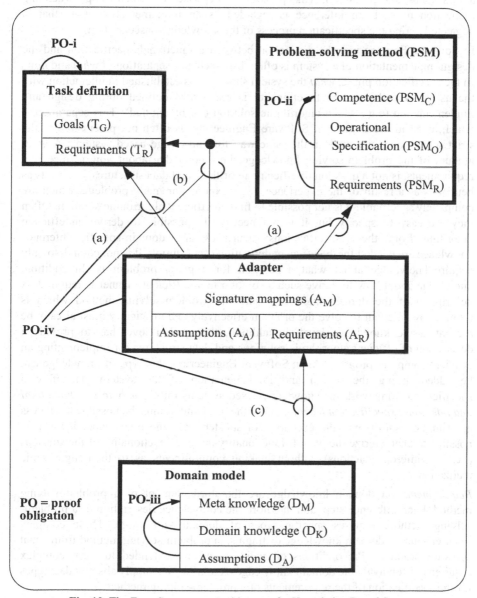

Fig. 10. The Four Component Architecture for Knowledge-Based System

An *operational description* defines the dynamic reasoning of a problem-solving method. Such an operational description explains how the desired competence can be achieved. It defines the main reasoning steps (called *inference actions*) and their dynamic interaction (i.e., the knowledge and control flow) so as to achieve the functionality of the problem-solving method. We use a variant of *dynamic logic* (cf. [Harel, 1984], [Fensel et al., 1998 (c)]) to express procedural control over the execution of inferences. The definition of an inference step could recursively introduce a new (sub-)task definition. This process of stepwise refinement stops when the realization of such an inference is regarded as an implementation issue that is neglected during the specification process of the knowledge-based system.

In Software Engineering, the distinction between a functional specification and the design/implementation of a system is often discussed as a separation of *what* and *how*. In the specification phase, *what* the system should do is established in interaction with the users. *How* the system functionality is realized is defined during design and implementation (e.g., which algorithmic solution can be applied). This separation— which, even in the domain of Software Engineering, is often not practicable in the strict sense—does *not* work in the same way for knowledge-based systems: A great amount of the problem-solving knowledge, i.e. knowledge about *how* to meet the requirements, is not a question of efficient algorithms and data structures, but exists as heuristics as a result of the experience of an expert. For many problems which are completely specifiable it is not possible to find an efficient algorithmic solution. Often they are easy to specify but it is not necessarily possible to derive an efficient algorithm from these specifications; heuristics and domain-specific inference knowledge are needed for the efficient derivation of a solution. It is not enough to only acquire knowledge about what a solution for a given problem is. In addition, knowledge about how to derive such a solution in an efficient manner is required. A description of the domain knowledge and the problem-solving method which is required by an agent to solve the problem effectively and efficiently must already be present at the knowledge level. In addition, the symbol level has to provide a description of efficient algorithmic solutions and data structures for implementing an efficient computer program. As in Software Engineering, this type of knowledge can be added during the design and implementation of the system. Therefore a specification framework for knowledge-based systems must *combine non-functional and functional specification techniques*: on the one hand, it must be possible to express algorithmic control over the execution of substeps. On the other hand, it must be possible to characterize the overall functionality and the functionality of the substeps (i.e., the inference actions) without making commitments as to their algorithmic realization.

Requirements on domain knowledge are the third element of a problem-solving method. Each inference step, and therefore the competence description of a problem-solving method, requires specific types of domain knowledge. These complex requirements on domain knowledge distinguish a problem-solving method from usual software products. Preconditions on valid inputs are extended to form complex requirements on available domain knowledge. Again, we will apply abstract data types for the specification of the requirements of a problem-solving method.

Both the competence description of the problem-solving method and the task definition are declarative specifications. The former specifies the actual functionality of the knowledge-based system (given that the domain knowledge fulfills the requirements of the problem-solving method) and the latter specifies the problem that should be solved by applying the knowledge-based system. We make a distinction between the two for two reasons:

- First, a problem-solving method introduces requirements on domain knowledge in addition to the task definition. This knowledge is not necessary to define the problem but required to describe the solution process of the problem.

- Second, we cannot always assume that the functionality of the knowledge-based system is strong enough to completely solve the problem. Problem-solving methods need to introduce assumptions that reduce the problem to a size they can deal with. The adapters, which we will discuss later, are the specification elements that contain the assumptions that have to be made to bridge the gap between the two specifications.

A simple example may clarify these two points. The task of finding a global optimum is defined in terms of a preference relation. A problem-solving method based on a local search technique requires additional knowledge to solve this task. First, such a method based requires a local neighbor relation to guide the search process. This knowledge is not necessary to define the task but to define the problem-solving process and its competence. Depending on the properties of this neighbor relation, different competences of a method are possible (cf. [Gamma et al., 1995]). Second, the task of finding an optimal solution could easily define an NP-hard problem. The problem-solving method based on local search techniques may provide solutions in polynomial time. However, it derives only a local optimum. Therefore, we must either put strong requirements on domain knowledge (each local optimum must also be a global one) or we must weaken the task to local instead of global optima to establish the correspondence of the problem-solving method and the task.

The Domain Model

The description of the *domain model* introduces domain knowledge as it is required by the problem-solving method and the task definition. Ontologies are proposed in knowledge engineering as a means to represent domain knowledge in a reusable manner (cf. [Gruber, 1993], [Top & Akkermans, 1994], [van Heijst et al., 1997], [Fridman Noy & Hafner, 1997]). Our framework provides three elements for defining a *domain model*: a meta-level characterization of properties, the domain knowledge, and (external) assumptions of the domain model.

The *meta knowledge* characterizes properties of the domain knowledge. It is the counterpart of the requirements on domain knowledge introduced by the other parts of a specification. The *domain knowledge* is necessary to define the task in the given application domain and necessary to carry out the inference steps of the chosen problem-solving method. *External assumptions* relate the domain knowledge to the actual domain. These external assumptions capture the implicit and explicit assumptions made while building a domain model of the real world. Technically they can be viewed as the missing pieces in the proof that the domain knowledge fulfills its meta-level characterizations. Some of these properties may be directly inferred from the domain knowledge whereas others can only be derived by introducing assumptions on the environment of the system and the actually provided input. For example, typical external assumptions in model-based diagnosis are: the fault model is complete (no fault appears that is not captured by the model), the behavioral description of faults is complete (all fault behaviors of the components are modeled), the behavioral discrepancy that is provided as input is not the result of a measurement fault, etc. (cf. Chapter 2).

The Adapter

The *adapter* maps the different terminologies of task definition, problem-solving method, and domain model. Moreover, it gives further requirements and assumptions that are needed to relate the competence of a problem-solving method with the functionality given by the task definition. The task, the problem-solving method, and the domain model can be described independently and selected from libraries because adapters relate the three other parts of a specification to each other and establish their relationship in a way that meets the specific application problem. The consistent combination and adaptation of the three different components to the specific aspects of the given application—since they should be reusable they need to abstract from specific aspects of application problems— must be provided by the adapter.

These adapters correspond to the notion of *adapter patterns* in [Gamma et al., 1995] where adapters are given as a pattern to allow the reuse of object classes and the specification of reusable object classes. This is also the main concern of adapters in our architecture. However, adapters also introduce *assumptions* necessary to close the gap between a problem definition (task) and the competence of a problem-solving method. As we will see later in Section III, adapters will also be used to express the *task-specific refinement* of problem-solving methods. In this case, adapters also specify reusable knowledge. They do not only implement an application-specific glue but specify refinements expressing a problem type. Finally, adapters can be stapled on top of each other to express the stepwise refinement of problem-solving methods.

3.1.2   The Main Proof Obligations

Following the conceptual model of the specification of a knowledge-based system, the overall verification of a knowledge-based system is broken down into four kinds of proof obligations (see Fig. 10).

(PO-i)   The consistency of the task definition ensures that a model exists. Otherwise, we would define an unsolvable problem. The requirements on domain knowledge are necessary to prove that the goal of the task can be achieved. Such a proof is usually done by constructing a model via an (inefficient) *generate & test* type of implementation.

(PO-ii)   We have to show that the operational specification of the problem-solving method describes a terminating process which has the competence as specified. This proof obligation returns recursively for each non-elementary inference action of a problem-solving method. In addition to termination, one may also want to include some thresholds for the efficiency of the method by including it as part of the competence description (cf. [Shaw, 1989]).

(PO-iii)   We have to ensure internal consistency of the domain knowledge and domain model. The domain knowledge does not need to be overall consistent but it must be dividable into consistent parts. In addition, we have to prove that given its assumptions the domain knowledge actually implies its meta-level characterization.

(PO-iv)   We have to establish the relationships between the different elements of the specification:

- (a) We have to prove that the requirements of the adapter imply the knowledge requirements of the problem-solving method and the task.

- (b) In addition to the already existing requirements, an adapter may need to introduce new requirements on domain knowledge and assumptions (properties that do not follow from the domain model) to guarantee, that the competence of the problem-solving method is strong enough to carry out the task.

- (c) We have to prove that the requirements of the adapter are implied by the meta knowledge of the domain model.

Notice that PO-i deals with the task definition internally, PO-ii deals with the problem-solving method internally, and PO-iii deals with the domain model internally, whereas PO-iv deals with the external relationships between task, problem-solving method, domain knowledge, and adapter. Thus a separation of concerns is achieved that contributes to the feasibility of the verification (cf. [van Harmelen & Aben, 1996]). The conceptual model applied to describe knowledge-based systems is used to break the general proof obligations into smaller pieces and make parts of them reusable. As problem-solving methods can be reused, the proofs of PO-ii do not have to be repeated for every application. These proofs have to be done only when a new problem-solving method is introduced to the library. Similar proof economy can be achieved for PO-i and PO-iii by using reusable task definitions and domain models. PO-iv is the application specific proof obligation.

Assumptions concerning the input cannot be verified during the development process of a knowledge-based system. However, their derivation is very important because they define preconditions for the validity of inputs that must be checked for actual inputs to guarantee the correctness of the system.

3.2   Task

The description of a task consists of two parts. The first specifies a goal that should be achieved in order to solve a given problem. The second part of a task specification is the definition of *requirements* on domain knowledge necessary to define the goal in a given application domain. Both parts establish the definition of a problem that should be solved by the knowledge-based system. Contrary to most approaches in software engineering this problem definition is kept domain independent, which enables the

---

task *complete and parsimonious explanation*
    sorts
        datum, data : **set of** *datum,*
        hypothesis, hypotheses : **set of** *hypothesis*
    functions
        explain: hypotheses $\rightarrow$ *data*
        observables: data
        goal : hypotheses
    predicates
        complete: hypotheses
        parsimonious: hypotheses
    variables
        x : datum
        H,H' : hypotheses
    axioms
        goal
            complete(goal) $\wedge$ *parsimonious(goal)*
            $\forall$H *(complete(H)* $\leftrightarrow$ *explain(H) = observables)*
            $\forall$H *(parsimonious(H)* $\leftrightarrow$ $\neg\exists$H' *(H'* $\subset$ *H* $\wedge$ *explain(H)* $\subseteq$ *explain(H')))*
    requirement
        $\exists$x (x $\in$ *observables*)
  endtask

Fig. 11. The Task Definition for *abduction*

reuse of generic problem definitions for different applications. We will use a simple task to illustrate our approach. The task *abductive diagnosis* receives a set of observations as input and delivers a complete and parsimonious explanation (see e.g. [Bylander et al., 1991]). An explanation is a set of hypotheses. A *complete explanation* must explain all input data (i.e., *observations*) and a parsimonious explanation must be minimal (that is, no subset of hypotheses explains all *observations*). Fig.11 provides the task definition for our example. Any explanation that fulfills the *goal* must be *complete* and *parsimonious*. The task introduces requirements on domain knowledge: It must provide sets to interpret the sorts *datum* and *hypothesis* and an explanation function to interpret *explain*. The (axiomatic) input requirement ensures that there are *observations*.

3.3   Problem-Solving Method

Finding a complete and parsimonious explanation is NP-hard in the number of hypotheses [Bylander et al., 1991]. Therefore, we have to apply heuristic search strategies. In the following, we characterize a local search method which we call *set-minimizer*. Questions as to whether other methods would be more suitable or how we have selected this method are discussed in Section III of this volume. At the moment,

competence *set-minimizer*
  import *requirements set-minimizer*
  variables *x : object*
  constants *Output : objects*
  axioms
    correct(Output)
    $\forall x\ (x \in Output \rightarrow \neg correct(Output \setminus \{x\}))$
endcompetence

requirements *set-minimizer*
  sorts *object, objects* **set of** *object*
  predicates *correct : objects*
  constants *Input : objects*
  axioms
    correct(Input)
endrequirements

Fig. 12. The Competence and Requirements of the Problem-Solving Method *set-minimizer*

we focus on how to describe such methods. We first provide the black box specification of the method. That is, we specify the competence provided by the method and the knowledge it requires. Then, we provide a white box specification of the operational reasoning strategy which explains how the competence can be achieved. The former is of interest for the reuse of problem-solving methods whereas the latter is required for developing problem-solving methods.

3.3.1 The Black Box Description: Competence and Requirements

The competence description of the problem-solving method and the task definition are declarative specifications. Thus we apply the same formal means for their specifications: The task specifies the problem that should be solved by applying the knowledge-based system and the problem-solving method specifies the actual functionality of the knowledge-based system (given that the domain knowledge fulfills the requirements of the problem-solving method). A problem-solving method introduces additional requirements on domain knowledge and may weaken the task definition. However, both aspects can be directly covered by algebraic data types.

The competence theory in Fig.12 defines the competence of a problem-solving method that we call set-*minimizer*. *Set-minimizer* is able to find a correct and locally minimal set. Local minimality means that there is no correct subset of the output that only has one less element. The method has one requirement: it must receive a correct initial set (cf. Fig.). The competence and the requirement illustrate the additional aspects that are introduced by the problem-solving method:

- The task of finding a parsimonious set is reduced to local parsimonious sets.
- Constructing an initial correct set is beyond the scope of the method. It is assumed as being provided by the domain knowledge, by a human expert, or by another problem-solving method. The method only minimizes this correct set.

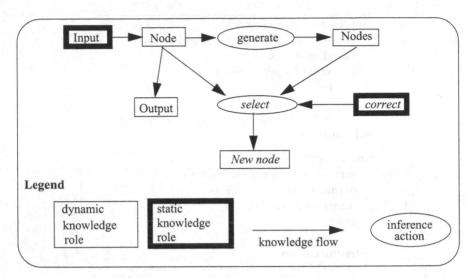

Fig. 13. Knowledge Flow Diagram of *set-minimizer*

3.3.2   The Operational Specification

Our method *set-minimizer* uses depth-first search through a search tree that is derived by set inclusion. The entire method is decomposed into the following two steps: The inference action *generate* generates all successor sets that contain one less element. The inference action *select* selects one correct set from the successors and the predecessor. The inference structure of this method is given in Fig.13 following the conventions of CommonKADS [Schreiber et al., 1994]. It specifies the main inferences of a method (i.e., its substeps), the dataflow between the inferences (i.e., the knowledge flow and the dynamic knowledge roles), and the knowledge types (i.e., the static knowledge roles) that they require. In the following, we will define each of these elements in more detail. In addition, we will have to define the control flow between the inference steps. The latter introduces a strong new requirement on our means for formalization requiring a logic of changes.

Inference Actions and Knowledge Roles

Again we use algebraic specifications to specify the functionality of inference actions and knowledge roles. Dynamic knowledge roles (dkr) are a means to represent the state of the reasoning process and axioms can be used to represent state invariants. They introduce dynamic signatures and correspond roughly to state schemas in Z [Spivey, 1992]. The interpretation of constants, functions and predicates may change during the problem-solving process. Static knowledge roles (skr) are means to include domain knowledge into the reasoning process of a problem-solving method. Our

inf *generate*
  sorts *object, objects* **set of** *object*
  variables *z : object, x,y : objects*
  axioms
    generate $(x,y) \leftrightarrow \exists z \, (z \in y \wedge x = y \setminus \{z\})$
endinf

inf *select*
  sorts *object, objects* **set of** *object*
  variables *x,y′,z : object, y : objects*
  axioms
    $\forall x,y,z \, (\exists y' \, (y' \in y \wedge correct(y')) \rightarrow select(x,y,z) \wedge correct(x) \wedge x \in y)$
    $\forall x,y,z \, (\neg \exists y' \, (y' \in y \wedge correct(y')) \rightarrow select(x,y,z) \wedge x = z)$
endinf

---

dkr *New node*
  sorts *object, objects* **set of** *object*
  constant *New node : objects*
enddkr

dkr *Node*
  sorts *object, objects* **set of** *object*
  constant *Node : objects*
enddkr

dkr *Nodes*
  sorts *object, objects* **set of** *object*
  predicate *Nodes : objects*
enddkr

dkr *Output*
  sorts *object, objects* **set of** *object*
  constant *Output : objects*
endskr

skr *Correct*
  sorts *object, objects* **set of** *object*
  predicates *correct : objects*
endskr

skr *Input*
  sorts *object, objects* **set of** *object*
  constant *Input : objects*
endskr

Fig. 14. The Specification of the Inference Actions and the Knowledge Roles of *set-minimizer*

method *set-minimizer* requires knowledge about correct sets and an initial set. This is modeled by the static knowledge roles. Fig.14 provides the definitions of the inference actions and the knowledge roles. Basically, *generate* derives all subsets that have one less element and *select* selects a successor (one of these reduced sets) if a correct successor exists. Otherwise it selects the original node.

Control Flow

The operational description of a problem-solving method is completed by defining the control flow (see Fig.15) that defines the execution order of the inference actions. The specification in Fig. 15 uses the *Modal Change Logic (MCL)* [Fensel et al., 1998 (c)] which was developed to combine the functional specification of substeps with procedural control over them. MCL is a generalized version of the Modal Logic of

Creation and Modification (MLCM, [Groenboom & Renardel de Lavalette, 1994], [Groenboom, 1997]) and the Modal Logic for Predicate Modification (MLPM, [Fensel & Groenboom, 1996]). Each of these languages are variants of dynamic logic. Dynamic logic [Harel, 1984] was developed to express states, state transitions, and procedural control of these transitions in a logical framework. Dynamic logic uses the *possible-worlds* semantics of [Kripke, 1959] for this purpose. A state is represented by a possible world through the value assignments of the program variables. The variable assignments x:=t are the atomic programs and the usual procedural constructs such as sequence, if-then-else, choice, and while-loop are provided to define complex transition. MCL extends the representation of a state and provides richer elementary state transitions. A state is represented by an *algebra* following the *states-as-algebras* paradigm of Abstract State Machines. A state transition is achieved by changing the truth values of a predicate or the values of a term. A complete introduction to MCL is beyond the current scope (see the next chapter for more details). We will only mention the features that are used in our example: First, dynamic logic uses the value assignment of free variables to characterize a state. In MCL, the representation of a state is enriched. An algebra is used to model states, and state changes are expressed by modifying this algebra. In consequence, constants, functions, and predicates may be used to characterize states. Second, due to the richer state representation, the atomic programs are

- $f:=\lambda x.t$ and $p:=\lambda x.A$
  changing the interpretation of a function or predicate such that $f(x)=t(x)$ and $p(x)=A(x)$ resp.;
- NEW creation of a new object denoted by new; and
- $\cup x.\alpha$ do α for a non-deterministically chosen x for a given program α.

Besides the atomic programs, MCL has the normal imperative statements for sequential composition, choice and repetition. In our example, we apply $p:=\lambda x.A$ to express that *Nodes* is updated by all successor sets of the set contained by *Node* and $\cup$ x.α to express that *New node* is updated (non-deterministically) by one correct successor set if it exists or the predecessor if not.

```
Node := Input;
if Node = ∅
  then Output := ∅
  else
    repeat
      Nodes := λx.generate(x,Node);
      ∪x.((select(x,Node,z) ∧ Nodes(z))?; New node := λy.(x=y))
    until New node = Node
    Output := Node
endif
```

Fig. 15. The Specification of the Dynamics of *set-minimizer*

3.4   Domain Model

A domain model consists of three main parts: the domain knowledge, its meta-level characterization, and its external assumptions. In addition, a signature definition is provided that defines the common vocabulary of the other three elements.

The medical domain model we have chosen for our example is a subset of a large case-study in the formalization of domain knowledge for an anesthesiological support system. The support system should diagnose a (limited) number of hypotheses, based on real-time acquired data. This data is obtained from the medical database system Carola [de Geus & Rotterdam, 1992] which performs on-line logging of measurements. The formal model includes knowledge about how to interpret these raw measurements (quantitative data) and causal relations between qualitative data (see [Renardel de Lavalette et al., 1998] for details).

Some of the simplifications we have made include:

- In this simplified domain we have a "one step" causal relation R. In practice we have the transitive and irreflexive closure R+. Note that we do not have the reflexive transitive closure R* since a symptom cannot be a hypothesis for itself. In a more complex version of this domain model, a symptom can be the hypothesis for another symptom. This kind of reasoning is left out for expository reasons (see [Renardel de Lavalette et al., 1998] for details).

- We restricted the number of possible hypotheses so as to obtain a complete model. Although this seems to be a major restriction, this assumption was already used in [Renardel de Lavalette et al., 1998]. In consultation with the physician we restrict the number of diagnoses (hypotheses) we want the system to detect. Then we design a system to detect these hypotheses leaving the final diagnosis to the physician. This is also the main reason why the system is a *support system*; the goal of the system is not to replace a physician only to support him.

- A last simplification is the abstraction from time. Although the quantitative data is measures a certain time-points, we model causal-knowledge as non-temporal. The notion of time is handled elsewhere in the domain (see [Groenboom, 1997] and [Renardel de Lavalette et al., 1998] for details).

In this domain we deal with abstract notions derived from interpretations of measurements. The exact meaning of *HighPartm* (which stands for a High mean arterial blood-pressure) is defined elsewhere in the formal domain model (see [Groenboom, 1997]). Another technical term is *ToolowCOP*, which refers to a too low Cellular Oxygen Pressure. *Edema* denotes an excessive accumulation of serous fluid in the tissues. Fig. 16 sketches the causal knowledge and Fig. 17 defines the signature and axioms of our domain model. It contains hypotheses and symptoms and a causal relationship between them. The meta-knowledge ensures two properties of the domain knowledge: there is a cause for each symptom and hypotheses do not conflict. That is, different hypotheses do not lead to an inconsistent set of symptoms. In our domain this is guaranteed by the fact that we do not have knowledge about negative evidence (i.e., a symptom may rule out an explanation). Assuming more causes only leads to a larger

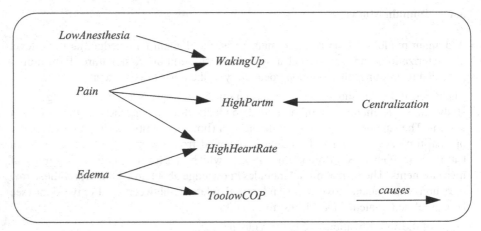

Fig. 16. The Domain Knowledge

set of symptoms that can be explained. The *complete-fault-knowledge assumptions* guarantees that there are no other unknown faults like hidden diseases. Only under this assumption can we deductively infer causes from observed symptoms. However, it is a critical assumption when relating the output of our system to the actual problem and domain. Note that we do not assume complete knowledge of symptoms.

3.5   Adapters

An adapter has to link the different signatures of task, problem-solving method, and domain, and has to add further axioms to guarantee their proper relationships. We use abstract data types for this purpose. First we demonstrate how to link task and problem-solving method by the TP$_{Adapter}$. Then we discuss their relations with the domain model defined by the D$_{Adapter}$.

3.5.1   Connecting Task and Problem-Solving Method

Combining task and problem-solving method requires three activities: establishing syntactical links between different terminologies by mappings, establishing semantic links between different predicates, and the introduction of new assumptions and requirements to establish that the goals of the task are implied by the output of the method.

In our case study, we have to link the sorts *object* and *objects* and the predicate *correct* of the problem-solving method by renaming (see Fig. 18). The appropriate interpretation of predicates has to be ensured by axioms if they cannot be linked directly. The necessity that the output of the method implies the goal of the task is stated as a proof obligation (see Fig.18).

The TP$_{Adapter}$ contains the requirements introduced by task and problem-solving method. This includes (cf. Fig.18) the requirements that any application problem must provide at

domain model *anesthesiology*
   signature
      sorts *hypothesis, hypotheses* **set of** *hypothesis, symptom*
      functions
         HighHeartRate, HighPartm, ToolowCOP, WakingUp : symptom
         Centralization, Pain, Edema, LowAnesthesia : hypothesis
      predicates
         causes: hypothesis x symptom
      variables
         h : hypothesis
         s : symptom
         H,H ': hypotheses
      meta-knowledge
         there is a cause for each symptom
            $\forall s\ \exists h\ causes(h, s)$
         the fault knowledge is monotonic
            $H \subseteq H' \rightarrow \{s \mid h \in H \wedge causes(h,s)\} \subseteq \{s \mid h \in H' \wedge causes(h,s)\}$
      domain knowledge
         causes(LowAnesthesia,WakingUp)
         causes(Centralization,HighPartm)
         causes(Pain,HighPartm)
         causes(Pain,WakingUp)
         causes(Pain,HighHeartRate)
         causes(Edema,HighHeartRate)
         causes(Edema,ToolowCOS)
   assumption
      complete fault knowledge
         $\forall h,s((h \neq Centralization \vee h \neq Pain \vee h \neq Edema \vee$
         $h \neq LowAnesthesia) \vee$
         $(s \neq HighHeartRate \vee s \neq HighPartm \vee s \neq ToolowCOP \vee$
         $s \neq WakingUp) \rightarrow \neg causes(h,s)).$
enddm

Fig. 17. The Domain Model

least one observation and that the set of hypotheses delivered by Input must be a complete explanation of all observations (see Fig.18). These requirements must be fulfilled by the domain knowledge and the input to ensure that the task is well-defined and that the inference steps of the problem-solving method work properly.

Finally, we have to introduce new assumptions and requirements to ensure that the competence of the problem-solving method implies the goal of the task (i.e., to fulfill the proof obligation of the adapter). We already know that *Output* contains a locally-minimal set. Each of its subsets that contains one less element is not a complete explanation. Still this is not strong enough to guarantee that the explanation is parsimonious in the general case. Smaller subsets may exist that are complete

adapter $TP_{Adapter}$
    include *set-minimizer, complete and parsimonious explanation*
    rename *set-minimizer* by *abduction*
        object → *hypothesis, objects* → *hypotheses, correct* → *complete*
    variables *x : datum*
    proof obligations
        complete(Output)
        parsimonious(Output)
    requirements
        ∃x (x ∈ observables)
        complete(Input)
endadapter

Fig. 18. The Initial Version of the $TP_{Adapter}$

adapter $TP_{Adapter}$
    include *set-minimizer, complete and parsimonious explanation*
    rename *set-minimizer* by *abduction*
        object → *hypothesis, objects* → *hypotheses, correct* → *complete*
    variables *x : datum, H,H ': hypotheses*
    axioms
        complete(Output)
        parsimonious(Output)
    requirements
        ∃x (x ∈ observables)
        complete(Input)
    assumptions *∀H,H'(H ⊆ H' → explain(H) ⊆ explain(H'))*
endadapter

Fig. 19. The Intermediate Version of the $TP_{Adapter}$

explanations. In Chapter 6, we will show that the global-minimality of the task definition is implied by the local-minimality if we introduce the *monotonic-problem assumption* (see [Bylander et al., 1991]):

$H ⊆ H' → explain(H) ⊆ explain(H')$

In Chapter 6.1 we will also show how to derive such assumptions. Fig.19 provides the intermediate adapter that contains the fulfilled proof obligation and the newly introduced assumption. Whether the monotonically property must be stated as an assumption or whether it can be formulated as a requirement on domain knowledge in the final version of the adapter can only be decided after specifying the second aspect of the adapter, its connection with the domain knowledge.

adapter $D_{Adapter}$
   include *anesthesiology, TP$_{Adapter}$*
   rename *anesthesiology by TP$_{Adapter}$*
     symptom → datum,
   variables *h : hypothesis, x : datum, H,H ': hypotheses*
   axioms
     $\forall x, H\ (x \in explain(H) \leftrightarrow \exists h\ (h \in H \wedge causes(h,x)))$
   proof obligation
     $\exists x\ (x \in observables)$
     complete(Input)
     $\forall H, H'(H \subseteq H' \rightarrow explain(H) \subseteq explain(H'))$
endadapter

Fig. 20. The Initial $D_{Adapter}$

3.5.2 Connecting with the Domain Model

Finally, we have to link the domain model to the other components using the $D_{Adapter}$ (see Fig.20). We have to map the different terminologies, define the logical relationships between domain knowledge and the other parts of the specification by axioms, and prove the requirements on domain knowledge. For our example, most of these requirements follow straightforwardly from the meta-knowledge of the domain model. Therefore, the monotonically of hypotheses can be stated as a requirement because it follows from the specification of the domain knowledge. If a requirement cannot be derived from the domain knowledge it must be stated as an assumption. In our example, the requirement

   $\exists x\ (x \in observables)$

cannot be derived from the domain knowledge because it is concerned with the input. However, assuming an input for deriving a diagnosis is not a critical assumption. It remains to ensure that *Input* delivers a complete set of hypotheses. An easy way to achieve this is to deliver the entire set of hypotheses (given the monotony of the problem), i.e. $\forall h \in Input$.

3.6 Related Work

The knowledge level [Newell, 1982] has been encountered recently in Software Engineering (cf. [Shaw & Garlan, 1996]). Work on software architectures establishes a higher level to describe the functionality and the structure of software artifacts. The main concern of this new area is the description of generic architectures that describe the essence of large and complex software systems. Our conceptual model fits nicely into this recent trend. It describes an architecture for a specific class of systems: knowledge-based systems. Usually, architectures are described by their components and connectors that establish the proper relationships between the former. In our case, we have three types of components (tasks, problem-solving methods, and domain models) and adapters that connect them. Each problem-solving method could hierarchically refine the architecture by introducing a set of new subtasks through the functional specification of its elementary inference steps (cf. [Cornelissen et al., 1997]).

Work on formalizing software architectures characterizes the functionality of architectures in terms of assumptions about the functionality of their components [Penix & Alexander, 1997], [Penix et al., 1997]. This shows strong similarities to our work where we define the competence of a problem-solving methods in terms of assumptions about domain knowledge (which can be viewed as one or several components of a knowledge-based system) and the functionality of elementary inference steps. However, [Penix & Alexander, 1997], [Penix et al., 1997] abstract from the operational specification of the architecture and keep its specification and verification separate. In our framework, this is treated as an integrated piece of the specification of the entire architecture. This is the reason why we rely on a combination of abstract data types and dynamic logic for specification and verification whereas [Penix & Alexander, 1997], [Penix et al., 1997] only use abstract data types.

An interesting architecture for the specification of problem-solving methods in the area of model-based diagnosis is presented by [ten Teije, 1997]. The specification of the competence of a problem-solving method has a fixed set of component types as parameters. Changing the functionality of a component by selecting a different instantiation for one of the component types modifies the competence of the entire method. This is a very interesting approach, however, we wonder whether it is in fact about specifying problem-solving methods. In our opinion, two key features of problem-solving methods are missing:

- Problem-solving methods describe how a problem is solved and the operational strategy is not covered by the declarative specification of their competence.
- A task introduces knowledge requirements to define a problem in domain-specific terms. A problem-solving method introduces additional knowledge requirements that are necessary to solve the problem. A local search method needs a local structure that is not necessary to define the problem but to define the problem-solving process. This type of knowledge is not present as a parameter in her framework.

In consequence, we think [ten Teije, 1997] presents more an interesting framework for a parameterized specification of model-based diagnosis *tasks* than for problem-solving methods.

4 Logics for Knowledge-Based Systems: MLPM and MCL

Several formal or executable specification languages have been developed for describing knowledge-based systems. Most of them are based on the KADS model of expertise or define their conceptual model as a modification of this model. Surveys of these languages can be found in [Treur & Wetter, 1993], [Fensel & van Harmelen, 1994], and [Fensel, 1995c]. Common to all formal specification approaches for knowledge-based systems is that a formal semantics has to cover three aspects: the specification of static aspects of a knowledge-based system, the specification of the dynamics of a knowledge-based system (i.e., its reasoning), and the combination of both, i.e. its overall semantics. For our study we restrict our attention to the second and third parts, because we think that the main improvements are necessary in the dynamic part. This part also introduces the main distinction between these approaches and many specification languages of software engineering which aim only at a purely functional description of a software system. In addition to a precise functional specification (i.e., the definitions of the goals that should be achieved by the knowledge-based system) specifications of knowledge-based systems have to cover the reasoning process and its use of knowledge, which enable reasonable problem-solving for the expected cases. An important part of the knowledge that must be specified is therefore knowledge about the way to achieve a solution and not just declarative knowledge about what a solution should be.

In this chapter, we will discuss a semantic framework for specifying the dynamic reasoning process of a knowledge-based system. We will start with an analysis of the existing approaches to come up with a framework that integrates these approaches. In fact, we take an analysis of the two KADS-languages KARL [Fensel, 1995b], [Fensel et al., 1998(b)] and $(ML)^2$ [van Harmelen & Balder, 1992] as our point of departure. The language $(ML)^2$ describes the reasoning behavior by combining first-order logic, meta-logic and quantified dynamic logic [Harel, 1984]. The language KARL was developed as part of the MIKE project [Angele et al., 1998] and provides a variant of Horn clause logic and a restricted version of dynamic logic for this purpose. We have chosen KARL and $(ML)^2$ for our exercise as both languages rely on dynamic logic to represent the dynamics of the reasoning process. As the technical core of the semantics of $K_{BS}SF$ [Spee & in 't Veld, 1994] is close to that of KARL, most of our results can also be applied to it. The other specification languages for knowledge-based systems use different means for specifying the dynamics of a knowledge-based system: Petri nets (MoMo [Voss & Voss, 1993]), process algebra (TFL [Pierret-Golbreich & Talon, 1996]), or temporal logic with linear time (DESIRE [Treur, 1994]). We will discuss some of them in the comparison section.

We will introduce the two logics *Modal Logic of Predicate Modification (MLPM,* [Fensel & Groenboom, 1996]) and *Modal Change Logic (MCL,* [Fensel et al., 1998 (c)], [Renardel de Lavalette, 1997]) Both logics stem from the *Modal Logic of Creation and Modification (MLCM,* [Groenboom & Renardel de Lavalette, 1994]) which was developed to provide a formal semantics for the wide-spectrum specification language COLD.[1] MLCM uses the *states-as-algebras paradigm* for specifying states and state transitions of a reasoning process which is also used by

Dieter Fensel: Problem-Solving Methods, LNAI 1791, pp. 61- 77, 2000.
© Springer-Verlag Berlin Heidelberg 2000

Abstract State Machines [Gurevich, 1994]. Basically, MLPM and MCL extend MLCM with new elementary state transition types which cover the grainsize of state transitions in knowledge-based reasoning. As a consequence, we get an approach that integrates existing proposals, overcomes several of their shortcomings and ad-hoc solutions, and provides an axiomatization which enables the use of mechanized proof support.

The structure of this chapter is as follows. First, we introduce the knowledge specification languages $(ML)^2$ and KARL focusing on their dynamics. We use the experience with these languages to derive requirements for an appropriate semantic framework for the specification of the dynamics of the reasoning of knowledge-based systems. Then we introduce the logics MLPM and MCL and provide their syntax and semantics. We use MCL to formalize the inference and control constructs of the KADS languages and Abstract State Machines and provide a comparison with work that uses different solutions.

4.1   Specification Languages for Knowledge-Based Systems

In this subsection we introduce the two languages KARL and $(ML)^2$, focusing on their formal means for specifying the reasoning process of knowledge-based systems. Both use variants of the CommonKADS model of expertise as conceptual framework (i.e., system architecture) for specifying a knowledge-based system. CommonKADS [Schreiber et al., 1994] uses task and inference layers for specifying the reasoning process. The task layer introduces the goal that is to be achieved by the system and it decomposes the overall task into subtasks and defines control over them. It combines a functional specification with the specification of the dynamic reasoning process that realizes the functionality. The inference layer defines the elementary inference steps, the relations between them, and the role of the domain knowledge for the reasoning process. A simple example will be used to illustrate the modeling concepts of both languages (see Fig. 21). The task of the knowledge-based system consists of finding the diagnosis with the highest preference for a given set of symptoms. Our example consists of two inference actions:

- *generate*, which creates possible hypotheses based on the given findings and the causal relationships at the domain layer, and
- *select*, which assigns a preference to hypotheses and selects the diagnosis with the highest preference.

The knowledge role finding provides input to the inference action *generate*, the knowledge role hypothesis delivers the results of the reasoning of *generate* to *select*, and the knowledge role diagnosis provides the results of *select* as output. The two knowledge roles *causality* and *preference* provide knowledge necessary for the inference process. It is mapped from the domain layer. A simple control flow at the task layer is defined by first executing *generate* and then applying *select* to its output.

---

[1] COLD, Common Object-oriented Language for Design, was developed at Phillips Research Eindhoven in several ESPRIT-projects (cf. [Feijs & Jonkers, 1992]).

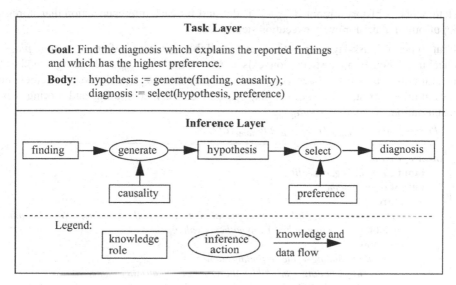

Fig. 21. Inference and Task Layers for a Simplified Diagnostic Task

4.1.1   (ML)²

(ML)² [van Harmelen & Balder, 1992] models each inference action (called primitive inference action in (ML)²) by a predicate and a theory which further specifies this predicate. In our running example, the inference actions generate and select are modeled by two predicates:

pia$_{generate}$(finding(X), causality(finding(X),hypothesis(Y)), hypothesis(Y))
pia$_{select}$(hypothesis(X), preference(Z), diagnosis(Y))

The descriptions of the inference actions generate and select are given in Fig. 22.

It remains to define the different knowledge roles. *Causality* and *preference* provide domain knowledge and *finding* the case data for the inference layer. The inference layer is modeled as a *meta-language* of the domain layer in (ML)². This meta-relation enables the inference-layer to specify properties of relations over domain-layer expressions (predicates and functions). The expressions of object- and meta-language are connected by a naming relation and the truth values of formulas are connected by reflection rules. The input predicates input$_{finding}$, input$_{causality}$, and input$_{preference}$ used in the logical theories of the inference actions pia$_{generate}$ and pia$_{select}$ are defined by reflection rules that connect truth in object- and meta-logic. As we abstract from this aspect of (ML)² we will not go into any detail on this topic (cf. [van Harmelen & Balder, 1992]). The knowledge role *hypothesis*, however, does not provide domain knowledge for the inference actions. It collects the output of the inference action *generate* and provides it as an input to the inference action *select*. This dynamic character of *hypothesis* makes it necessary to define the input predicate input$_{hypothesis}$ at the task layer. The knowledge role *diagnosis* is used as an output role only and therefore requires no input predicate definition at all.

Dynamic logic is used to specify dynamic control at the task layer. The *pia*-predicates, together with the test operator (of the form *pia$_{name}$* ?), are the elementary program statements. A history variable $V_{pia_{name}}$ is defined for each inference action that stores the input-output pairs for every execution step.

Four types of task-layer operations are available for each inference action pia_{name}: checking whether an instantiation exists, *has-solution-pia$_{name}$*, checking whether an instantiation has already been computed, *old-solution-pia$_{name}$*, checking whether more instantiations exist, *more-solution-pia$_{name}$*, and actually computing and storing a new instantiation, *give-solution-pia$_{name}$*:

$$has\text{-}solution\text{-}pia_{name} \ (I,O) =_{def} pia_{name}(I,O)$$

theory *generate*
    input roles *finding, causality;*
    output roles *hypothesis;*
    signature
        sorts *finding-value, finding-name, causality-name, hypothesis-value, hypothesis-name;*
        variables *X : finding-value, Y : hypothesis-value;*
        functions
            finding : finding-value → finding-name,
            *causality : finding-name * hypothesis-name → causality-name,*
            hypothesis : hypothesis-value → hypothesis-name;
        predicates $pia_{generate}$: *finding-name * causality-name * hypothesis-name;*
    axioms
        $pia_{generate}$(*finding(X), causality(finding(X),hypothesis(Y)),hypothesis(Y)*) ←
                $input_{finding}$(*finding(X)*) ∧ $input_{causality}$(*causality(finding(X),hypothesis(Y))*)
endtheory

theory *select*
    input roles *hypothesis, preference;*
    output roles *diagnosis;*
    signature
        sorts
            hypothesis-value, hypothesis-name,
            diagnosis-value, diagnosis-name,
            preference-pairs, preference-pair-set-value, preference-pair-set-name;
        variables *X : hypothesis-value, Y : diagnosis-value, Z : preference-pairs;*
        functions
            hypothesis : hypothesis-value → hypothesis-name,
            preference : preference-pair-set-value → preference-pair-set-name,
            diagnosis : diagnosis-value → diagnosis-name,
            *pref : hypothesis-name * hypothesis-name → preference-pairs;*
        predicates
            pia_{select} : *hypothesis-name * preference-pair-set-name * diagnosis-name;*
    axioms
        pia_{select}(*hypothesis(X), preference(Z),diagnosis(X)*) ←
            $input_{hypothesis}$(*hypothesis(X)*) ∧
            $input_{preference}$(*preference(Z)*) ∧
            ¬(∃Y : $input_{hypothesis}$(*hypothesis(Y)*) ∧ *pref(hypothesis(Y),hypothesis(X))* ∈ Z)
endtheory

Fig. 22. Inference Actions Generate and Select in (ML)^2

$old\text{-}solution\text{-}pia_{name} \ (I,O) =_{def} ((I,O) \in V_{pia_{name}})$

$more\text{-}solution\text{-}pia_{name}(I,O) =_{def}$
$\qquad (has\text{-}solution\text{-}pia_{name}(I,O) \land \neg old\text{-}solution\text{-}pia_{name}(I,O))$

The most important program is give-solution-pia$_{name}$ which gives one possible solution:

$give\text{-}solution\text{-}pia_{name} \ (I,O) =_{def}$
$\qquad (more\text{-}solution\text{-}pia_{name}(I,O)?; V_{pia_{name}} := <(I,O) \mid V_{pia_{name}}>$

The key idea is to non-deterministically choose a value binding of a logical variable using the test operator and store this value in a state variable. Note that *old-solution-pia$_{name}$* and hence $V_{pia_{name}}$ administers the non-deterministic execution of *give-solution-pia$_{name}$* which is necessary to ensure the derivation of new instantiations of the predicate.

These primitive programs and predicates can be combined using sequential composition, non-deterministic iteration and non-deterministic choice.

For our example, we have to define the input predicate input$_{hypothesis}$ and the control flow between the inference actions. The knowledge role *hypothesis* collects the output of the inference action *generate* and provides it as input to the inference action *select*. The following definition of the input predicate is the way in which (ML)^2 can be used to define data flow between inferences.

$\qquad input_{hypothesis}(X) =_{def} \exists I_1, I_2 \text{ with } (I_1, I_2, X) \in V_{pia_{generate}}$

The task layer of our example is given in Fig. .

Dynamic Logic [Harel, 1984] uses *Kripke structures* to define a semantics for programs. A structure has the form S = (D,F,P) consisting of a *domain D*, an interpretation F of the function symbols and an interpretation P of the predicate symbols. A *state over S* is a *function s* interpreting variables as elements of D. The interpretation of functions and predicates is fixed for all states. Let W denote the set of all states. Programs p are interpreted by binary relations between states. Formulas φ are interpreted by the collection of states for which they are true. For example,

$I(p;q) = I(p) \circ I(q) = \{(s_0,s_2) \mid s_0, s_2 \in W \land \exists s_1 \in W \text{ with } (s_0,s_1) \in I(p) \land (s_1,s_2) \in I(q)\}$

$I(\varphi?) = \{(s,s) \mid s \in W \land \varphi \text{ is true in } s\}$

$I(Y := X) = \{(s_0,s_1) \mid s_0, s_1 \in W \land s_1(Y) = s_0(X) \land \forall Z \ (Z \neq Y \rightarrow s_0(Z) = s_1(Z))\}$

The most important program in (ML)^2 is *give-solution-pia$_i$* which gives one possible solution. The essence of this elementary state transition in (ML)^2 is to apply the test operator ? to the predicate *pia$_{name}$* which defines an inference action. *pia$_{name}$(I,O)?* has as successor state a state that interprets (i.e., substitutes) the variables I,O in a way that fulfils *pia$_{name}$(I,O)*. In the successor state, this variable substitution is stored in the

---

while
more-solution-pia$_{generate}$(finding(X),causality(finding(X),hypothesis(Y)),hypothesis(Y))
do   *give-solution-pia$_{generate}$(finding(X),causality(finding(X),hypothesis(Y)),hypothesis(Y))*
enddo
give-solution-pia$_{select}$(hypothesis(X),preference(Z),diagnosis(X))

Fig. 23. A Task Layer in (ML)^2

history variable of the inference action. Slightly simplified, we have the following pattern:

$I(P(X)?;Y := X)$
$$= \{(s_0,s_1) \mid s_0 \in I(P(X)) \wedge (s_0,s_1) \in I(Y := X)\}$$
$$= \{(s_0,s_1) \mid P(X) \text{ is true in } s_0 \wedge s_1(Y) = s_0(X) \wedge \forall Z (Z \neq Y \rightarrow s_0(Z) = s_1(Z))\}$$

4.1.2   KARL

The language KARL (cf. [Fensel, 1995b], [Fensel et al., 1998(b)]) provides a formal and executable specification language for the KADS model of expertise by combining two types of logic: Logical-KARL (L-KARL) and Procedural-KARL (P-KARL). L-KARL, a variant of Frame Logic [Kifer et al., 1995], is provided to specify domain and inference layers. It combines first-order logic with semantic data modeling primitives (see [Brodie, 1984] for an introduction to semantic data models). A restricted version of dynamic logic is provided by P-KARL to specify a task layer. Executability is achieved by restricting Frame logic to Horn logic with stratified negation [Przymusinski, 1988] and by restricting dynamic logic to regular and deterministic programs. Again, we will discuss the inference and task layers.

L-KARL is used for specifying inference actions and knowledge roles at the inference layer. It provides predicates, classes, class taxonomies, single- and set-valued attributes with domain and range restrictions, as well as multiple attribute inheritance for modeling terminological knowledge. KARL distinguishes three types of knowledge roles. *Views* define an upward translation from the domain layer to the inference layer (giving read-access). These roles are only accessible as input roles by inference actions. *Terminators* define a downward translation from the inference layer to the domain layer (giving write-access). These roles are only accessible as output roles by inference actions. *Stores* provide the input or output of inference actions. Therefore, they can be used as input and output roles by inference actions. Whereas views and terminators are used to link a domain layer with a generic inference layer, stores are used to model the data flow dependencies between inference actions. The logical language L-KARL has a minimal Herbrand model semantics [Lloyd, 1987]. Because we allow stratified negation in rules bodies we use a specific minimal model, i.e., the perfect Herbrand model, as the semantics of a set of clauses, cf.[Przymusinski, 1988]. Therefore, L-KARL does not use classical negation but a variant of the closed-world assumption that is common in approaches to logic programming and deductive databases.

P-KARL provides procedural control constructs for the task-layer. The primitive programs correspond to *calling an inference action*. Atomic formulas indicate whether knowledge roles contain elements of a given class. Such primitive programs and atomic formulas can be arranged into sequences, loops, and alternatives. Programs may be combined to form subtasks like procedures in programming languages. The task layer of our example looks like this:

> *hypothesis := generate(finding);*
> *diagnosis := select(hypothesis)*

Each inference action defines a function symbol used in assignments. Each store and terminator is modeled by a (program) variable. Views do not have a counterpart at the task layer because they do not have a dynamic interpretation (i.e., their interpretation is the same in each state). The value assignments of the variables that model stores and terminators are used to represent the current state of the reasoning process. The inference actions pia_{name} appear as a function symbols and each store $store_{name}$ appears as a predicate symbol $\emptyset(store_{name})$ in the signature of P-KARL.

P-KARL is a variant of dynamic logic using again *Kripke structures* as its semantics. The integration of the modal semantics of the task layer and the Herbrand models of L-KARL is as follows: the models of L-KARL are used to define an interpretation for a P-KARL language, i.e. the perfect Herbrand model of the set of clauses which define an inference action pia_{name} is used to interpret a function symbol pia_{name} occurring in assignments in P-KARL. Each store and each terminator is modeled by a (program) variable. The current state is represented by an assignment s of these variables. Notice, that a set of ground facts is assigned to each program variable. Slightly simplified, a transition is defined as:

$I(output\text{-}role(X) :- pia_{name}(input\text{-}role)) =$

$\quad \{(s_0, s_1) \mid s_1(output\text{-}role) = \text{perfect-Herbrand-model}(PIA_{name} \cup s_0(input\text{-}$
$role))\}$

where PIA_{name} is the set of Horn clauses describing pia_{name}.

Finally $\emptyset(store_{name})$ is determined to be true for all states s with $s(store_{name}) = \emptyset$. The domain D is defined by the Herbrand base of the L-KARL language.

4.1.3   Design Rationales for a Logic of Dynamics

In the following, we discuss our design rationales and their relations to the existing approaches. We discuss the following aspects for characterizing a reasoning process: (1) the *state* of a reasoning process, (2) the *history* of a reasoning process, (3) the *elementary state transitions*, (4) the *connection of states* and *state transitions*, and (5) *composed* state *transitions*.

The State of the Reasoning Process

Three choices arise in regard to the representation of a state of a reasoning process. First, whether its characterization is necessary at all, second whether its characterization is syntactic or semantic, and third whether its characterization should be local or global.

Is there a Notion of States. Abstract data types were developed in software engineering for the functional specification of software artifacts [Wirsing, 1990]. They should not make any commitments to the algorithmic process that realizes the functionality. They define the functionality as a relation between input and output but have neither syntactically nor semantically the notion of a state. However, other approaches in software engineering, like VDM [Jones, 1990], Z [Spivey, 1992], and Abstract State Machines ([Gurevich, 1994], [Börger, 1995]), use the notion of states for specifications. In Artificial Intelligence, problem solving is viewed as a search process through a state space. The problems tackled either do not have a complete functional specification or the functional specification defines a computationally hard problem that additionally requires the specification of a heuristic procedure that partly solves it. Therefore, approaches like ATMS [de Kleer, 1986] and situation calculus [McCarthy & Hayes, 1969] use states to specify the dynamics of a reasoning process.

Is this Notion Syntactic or Semantic. Situation calculus reifies the notion of state in first-order logic through the use of a special class of terms. Simplified, a predicate $p(x)$ is enriched by an argument that denotes states, i.e. $p(x,state)$, and the truth values of $p(x,state)$ can therefore be distinguished from the truth values of $p(x,succ(state))$. States are *syntactical* elements of the language in situation calculus. Conversely, dynamic logic provides a *semantic* notion of states. A state is characterized by a value assignment of all free variables. There is no syntactical notion that refers to a state. Therefore its semantics has to extend first-order models to a set of worlds that are used to interpret states.

Syntactical reification of states in situation calculus is achieved by assigning names (i.e., terms that denote states) to them. This brings about the effect that two states that are identical except for having different names are regarded as different. In semantic-based approaches like dynamic logic, two states that have the same variable assignments to all variables cannot be distinguished, i.e. they are treated as equal. Syntactical versions like situation calculus require complex equality axioms to achieve the same purpose.

Is the Characterization of States Local or Global. The *global* representation of states is quite natural for a monolithic sequential problem solver with a procedural control. Procedural control assumes one unique state at each moment of the entire reasoning process. Local representation of states is used for distributed problem-solving agents that cooperate during problem solving without a central control. Here, each component has an internal state. These internal states need not be uniquely related to internal local states of other components. Such approaches can be found in the areas of complex information systems, distributed AI, and multi-agent systems (see [Jungclaus, 1993], [Weiß, 1995], [Brazier et al., 1995]).

Resume: $(ML)^2$ and KARL make the following choices according to our criteria: Both approaches are state-based, both approaches use the semantical notion of states in accordance with dynamic logic, and both approaches have one global state of the reasoning process. MLPM and MCL make precisely the same design decisions. However, the languages differ in the way a state is represented. As mentioned above, a state is represented in dynamic logic by value assignments of all open variables. MLPM and MCL use a richer structure to represent a state in accordance to the *states-as-algebras* setting. In this setting, an algebra (i.e., a rich data structure) instead of a flat list of variables is used to present a state. A state is characterized by an interpretation of all predicates and functions.

The History of the Reasoning Process

Two states are equal in a state-based approach if they do not differ in any property. In a history-based approach they are different if they were achieved through different *paths* of the reasoning process, i.e. the history of the reasoning process is part of the state description. The history of the reasoning process is necessary for software that models real-world processes, like in robotics and work-flow management systems or strategic reasoning about different choices. When modeling the movement of a robot it is not only necessary to end up in a proper terminal state. There are also important constraints on intermediate states and their proper sequence. The situation is similar in work-flow management systems, where decentralized processes need to be synchronized properly. Finally, in strategic reasoning we reason about different paths of the reasoning process. For example, when a system runs into a dead end in its reasoning process it needs information about the path that led to this dead end in order to choose more appropriate reasoning possibilities. Examples for history-based approaches are situation calculus, which reifies history information syntactically using term structures, Transaction Logic [Bonner & Kifer, 1993], which provides a path semantics to express history, and DESIRE [Treur, 1994], which uses temporal models as the semantics of reasoning paths.

The *KADS model of expertise* represents the control of the reasoning process of a knowledge-based system at the task layer. A simple procedural control language is provided for this purpose (cf. [Schreiber et al., 1994]). Restricting ourselves to this type of control also implies that we will not aim at specifying the history of the reasoning process. Like KARL, neither MLPM nor MCL have a notion of history. This restricts our ability to elegantly represent *strategic* reasoning, including the reasoning about earlier states of the problem-solving process, but this goal is beyond the scope of our approach. This type of knowledge was allocated at a different layer (the *strategic layer*) in earlier versions of the KADS model of expertise.

Elementary State Transitions

Inference actions are modeled as relations in $(ML)^2$ and as functions in KARL. In $(ML)^2$, each inference action defines a relation that is used to interpret a predicate symbol used in a test operation in dynamic logic. In KARL, each inference action defines a function which is used to interpret a function symbol used in an assignment in dynamic logic. $(ML)^2$ changes states by selecting precisely one new instantiation of a predicate (i.e. for the given state the predicate is true for one ground variable assignment and false for all others). KARL changes states by declaring all instantiations of a predicate that follow from the logical theory of an inference actions and its input to be true. Both types of inferences appear in formalized KADS models. We see this in our running example. The inference action *generate* should generate all possible hypotheses and the inference action select should select one of them as a diagnosis. It is possible to express one inference type using the other type but it results in an artificial modeling. A loop of updates at the task layer in $(ML)^2$ is required to simulate an update in KARL. KARL needs a random-selection predicate in the definition of an inference action to simulate an update in $(ML)^2$ that non-deterministically selects one instantiation of a predicate. As a consequence, MLPM and MCL provide both types of state transitions (MLPM directly and MCL via a combination of two operators).

We call both update types *bulk* updates as they change the complete extension of a predicate in one step. Each ground literal of a predicate symbol is re-evaluated by such a state transition. MLCM provided only *point-wise* modification of constants, functions, and predicates. The extension in MLPM and MCL is precisely concerned with introducing elementary state transitions of a higher grainsize that can directly express such bulk-updates.

Connecting State Transitions with States

$(ML)^2$ uses the history variables in the definition of the input predicates and the test operator ? of dynamic logic which transform a formula into a state transition to combine the value assignments of the logical and program variables. V_{pia} collects the results of an inference action and can provide them to another inference action via the definition of a corresponding input predicate. This solution relies on the identification of logical and dynamic (state-dependent) variables in dynamic logic. Take as an example the following formula from dynamic logic: the evaluation of the existential quantification more or less "undoes" the states modification of the program in the modal operator.

$$[x := 3] (\exists x (x = 2))$$

A further problem is that $(ML)^2$ requires modeling constructs that are not mentioned in the conceptual modeling context of the KADS model of expertise like *has-solution-pia, old-solution-pia, more-solution-pia$_n$, give-solution-pia*, as well as history variables V_{pia} and complex input predicate definitions for each inference action to connect the specification of statics with dynamic state change.

KARL uses a somewhat nonstandard approach to achieve the combination of the functional specification of state transitions and states. The minimal model semantics of the set of clauses that define a state transitions is used as an interpretation of the corresponding function symbol in dynamic logic.

An important motivation of our exercise is to find a better solution for this integration. We want to separate logical variables used in the definition of elementary transitions and program variables, which express the dynamic state of the reasoning process, without externalizing the definition of a state transition as an interpretation of function symbols. In part we will follow the intuition of KARL, which distinguishes logical variables used to characterize inference actions and program variables used to memorize a state. Part of a state characterization are the literals that hold true. However, this is not achieved by assigning a set of true literals to a program variable but by directly using an algebra to express a state. State changes are expressed by changing this algebra. As a consequence, we do not even need program variables in our framework.

Composed State Transitions

The task layer of a KADS model of expertise defines *sequence, alternative*, and *loops* of inference actions. A specification language has to provide these means to form composed transitions.

Resume

A language for specifying the reasoning process of knowledge-based systems, based on the KADS model of expertise must provide the following:

- It must be possible to express the global state of the reasoning process.
- It is not required to represent the history of the reasoning process.
- It must be possible to only characterize complex substeps functionally without making commitments to their algorithmic realization.
- The description of state transitions must be easily and intuitively related to state changes.
- Finally, it must be possible to express algorithmic control over the execution of substeps.

In the following we present our solutions for these goals.

4.2   Logics for the Dynamics of Knowledge-Based Systems

In the following, we introduce the two logics MLPM and MCL. Both are extensions of MLCM. However, MLPM only extends the point-wise *predicate* update operator of MLCM to bulk-updates and skips other features of MLCM. MCL integrates MLCM and the extensions of MLPM into a new logic. MCL is the more general approach, however, the possibility to introduce new terms and the update-operator for terms make the definition of syntax and semantics much more complex for full MCL compared to MLPM. In a nutshell the difference between MLPM and MCL is that MLPM is a minimalistic approach that unifies the two state transition types of KARL and $(ML)^2$ whereas MCL has a broader scope. Therefore, MLPM can be modeled by a subfragment of MCL and MCL covers approaches from other fields like Abstract State Machines and database update languages like PDDL [Spruit et al., 1995] and DDL [Spruit et al., 1992] (see [Fensel et al., 1998 (c)]). However, this also implies that syntax and semantics of MCL are much more complex than syntax and semantics of MLPM. In the following, we will only mention the aspects of MCL that appear to be relevant in our context and refer the reader to [Fensel et al., 1998 (c)] and [Renardel de Lavalette, 1997].

4.2.1   Modal Logic of Predicate Modification (MLPM)

The *Modal Logic of Predicate Modification (MLPM)* [Fensel & Groenboom, 1996] was introduced for formalizing KADS languages like KARL and $(ML)^2$. MLCM was taken as a departure point for this exercise. For reasons of simplicity, only the predicate modification operator of MLCM was taken. This predicate operator had to be generalized to two types of bulk-updates because KADS inference action may modify a complete extension of a predicate whereas MLCM only offered a point-wise update.

Dynamic logic is often presented with the variable assignments x:=t as its atomic programs. In MLPM however, the atomic programs are p:=εx.A and p:=λx.A (both change the interpretation of a predicate). This program type generalizes the program statement p(s) :↔ A for *point-wise* predicate modification, which were introduced in MLCM. The λ-operator evaluates a predicate p to true for all instantiations where A is true and it evaluates p to false for all instantiations where A is false (i.e., it expresses the KARL-type of state transition). The ε-operator evaluates a predicate p for *exactly* one instantiation where A is true (if it exists) to true and to false for all other instantiations (i.e., it expresses the $(ML)^2$-type of state transition).

For the composition of programs, most dynamic logics (including MLPM) contain the constructs of sequential composition (;), non-deterministic choice (∪), iteration (*) and test (A?, where A is some formula). Some usual program statements can be defined using these constructs:

> **if A then** α **else** β =   (A?;α) ∪ (¬A?;β)
> **while A do** α   = (A?;α)*;¬A?

In the following we introduce the syntax and semantics of MLPM.

Syntax of MLPM

Signatures Σ are collections of (function or predicate) symbols σ, with arity #σ ∈ N. Predicate symbols are denoted by p,q,r,..., function symbols by f,g,h,..., and nullary function symbols (usually called constants) by a,b,c,.... VAR is a countably infinite set of variable symbols, denoted by x,y,z,.... The syntax of MLPM, consisting of the syntactical categories TERM (terms), PROG (programs) and FORM (formulas), is defined by:

TERM $\qquad$ t ::= $\quad$ x | f(t_1,..., t_{\#f})

PROG $\qquad$ α ::= $\quad$ p := λx.A | p := εx.A | A? | α;α | α ∪ α | α*

FORM $\qquad$ A ::= $\quad$ (t = t) | p(t_1,..., t_{\#p}) | A ∧ A | ¬A | ∀xA | [α]A

For the sake of simplicity, we assume here and later that functions f and predicates p are unary. $\top$, $\bot$, ∨, →, ↔, ∃x, and ⟨α⟩ are defined as usual. Substitution of a term for all free occurrences of a variable in a term, formula, or program (denoted (t/x)A etc.; so, e.g., ((f(y)/x)p(g(x,y)) = p(g(f(y),y)))) is defined as usual (renaming bound variables in order to prevent variable clashes).

Semantics of MLPM

MLPM is interpreted in models M = ⟨U,W⟩, where U is the *universe* and W is a collection of *worlds*. Every w ∈ W is an interpretation of the signature elements in the universe. We shall write $σ_w$ for w(σ). Thus every world is a model of the first-order fragment of MLPM. Updates of a world w are defined as follows (P ⊆ U):

w[p ↦ P] is the updated world w′, satisfying w′(p) = P, w′(σ) = w(σ) if σ ≠ p.

ASS = VAR → U is the collection of assignments. Point-wise modification a[x ↦ u] (where x ∈ VAR, u ∈ U) of a ∈ ASS is defined as usual. $⟦t⟧_{w,a}$, the interpretation of term t in world w with assignment a, is defined by:

$⟦x⟧_{w,a}$ $\qquad$ = $\qquad$ $a_w(x)$

$⟦ft⟧_{w,a}$ $\qquad$ = $\qquad$ $f_w(⟦t⟧_{w,a})$

w,a ⊨ A (the interpretation of formula A in world w with assignment a) and $R_{α,a}$ (the accessibility relation of program α w.r.t. assignment a) are defined simultaneously:

w,a ⊨ (s = t) $\qquad$ $=_{def}$ $⟦s⟧_{w,a} = ⟦t⟧_{w,a}$

w,a ⊨ pt $\qquad$ $=_{def}$ $p_w(⟦t⟧_{w,a}) =$ **true**

w,a ⊨ ¬A $\qquad$ $=_{def}$ **not** (w,a ⊨ A)

w,a ⊨ A ∧ B $\qquad$ $=_{def}$ w,a ⊨ A **and** w,a ⊨ B

w,a ⊨ ∀xA $\qquad$ $=_{def}$ **forall** u ∈ U (w,a[x ↦ u] ⊨ A)

w,a ⊨ [α]A $\qquad$ $=_{def}$ **forall** w′ ∈ W (wR_{α,a}w′ ⟹ w′,a ⊨ A)

Modification of the truth values of a predicate applying the λ-operator:

$R_{p:=λx.A,a}$ $\qquad$ $=_{def}$ $\{(w,w[p ↦ \{u ∈ U | w,a[x ↦ u] ⊨ A\}]) | w ∈ W\}$

Modification of the truth values of a predicate applying the ε-operator:

$R_{p:=εx.A,a}$ $\qquad$ $=_{def}$ $\{(w,w[p ↦ \{u\}]) | w ∈ W, u ∈ U, w,a[x ↦ u] ⊨ A\}$

A program using the λ-operator also succeeds in the case where no ground instantiation of the predicate p is evaluated to true (i.e., ¬A holds). A program using the ε-operator fails in the case when no instantiation u exists with w,a[x ↦ u] ⊨ A. Note also that the ε-operator is non-deterministic.

The following four transition relations are standard relations of dynamic logic

$R_{A?,a}$ $\qquad$ $=_{def}$ $\{(w,w) | w,a ⊨ A\}$

$R_{α;β,a}$ $\qquad$ $=_{def}$ $R_{α,a} ∘ R_{β,a}$

$R_{α∪β,a}$ $\qquad$ $=_{def}$ $R_{α,a} ∪ R_{β,a}$

$R_{α*,a}$ $\qquad$ $=_{def}$ $R^*_{α,a}$ (i.e., the transitive closure of $R_{α,a}$)

4.2.2   Modal Change Logic (MCL)

The *Modal Change Logic (MCL)* (cf. [Fensel et al., 1998 (c)], [Renardel de Lavalette, 1997]) integrates the new state transitions of MLPM in the framework of MLCM. The local (i.e. *point-wise*) modification of functions and predicates are generalized to global modification and a choice quantifier is added. In MCL, the atomic programs are f:=λx.t, p:=λx.A (changing the interpretation of a function and a predicate, respectively) and NEW (which creates a new object). Moreover, MCL contains the choice quantifier ∪x. When applied to some program α, the meaning of the resulting program is: do α for some non-deterministically chosen value of x.

In the following we only discuss some of the syntactical and semantical elements of MCL. We skip the introduction of new signature elements and the axiomatic semantics. Complete introductions to MCL can be found in [Fensel et al., 1998 (c)] and [Renardel de Lavalette, 1997] where the mathematical aspects are treated in more detail.

Syntax of MCL

The syntax of MCL, consisting of the syntactical categories TERM (terms), PROG (programs) and FORM (formulas), is defined by:

TERM $\quad$ t ::= $\quad$ x | $f(t_1,..., t_{\#f})$

PROG $\quad$ α ::= $\quad$ f := $\lambda x_1,..., x_{\#f}.t$ | p := $\lambda x_1,..., x_{\#p}.A$ | A? | α;α | α ∪ α |
$\qquad\qquad\qquad$ α* | ∪ x.α

FORM $\quad$ A ::= $\quad$ $(t = t)$ | $p(t_1,..., t_{\#p})$ | A ∧ A | ¬A | ∀xA | [α]A

We have to be carefully for substitutions because it may be possible to substitute a term at an occurrence in the scope of a program that changes one or more signature elements of that term (e.g. (c/x)([c:=f(c)](g(x)=x)). A substitution where this does not occur is called safe.

Semantics of MCL

Modification of the truth values of a predicate:

$R_{p:=\lambda x.A,a}$ $\qquad$ =$_{def}$ $\quad$ {(w,w[p ↦ {u ∈ U | w,a[x ↦ u] ⊨ A}]) | w ∈ W}

Modification of the values of a function:

$R_{f:=\lambda x.t,a}$ $\qquad$ =$_{def}$ $\quad$ {(w,w[f ↦ λu ∈ U.$[\![t]\!]_{w,a[x ↦ u]}$]) | w ∈ W}

A program is executed for one value:

$R_{∪x.α,a}$ $\qquad$ =$_{def}$ $\quad$ {(w,w') | exists u ∈ U, wR$_{α,a[x ↦ u]}$w'}

4.2.3   Modeling MLPM with MCL

MLPM introduces two new operators in MLCM:

- p:= λ.xA, which corresponds to the λ-operator of MCL restricted to unary predicates,

- p:= ε.xA, defining (non-deterministically) p true for exactly one x satisfying A.

The ε operator of MLPM can be expressed by the choice quantifier of MCL (y fresh):

$\quad$ p:= ε.xA $\qquad$ ≡ $\qquad$ ∪x.(A?; p := λy.(x = y))

The generalization of MLCM and MLPM which we achieved with MCL provides the advantage that it reintegrates the generalizations of MLPM into the general setting of

MLCM. Therefore global function updates can also be expressed. In consequence, we get a unified approach that covers many existing approaches from knowledge engineering and other research areas.

4.3   Formalizing Other Approaches

In the following, we discuss first how MCL can be used to formalize the reasoning behavior of knowledge-based systems in a KADS-oriented manner. We do this by showing for a number of KADS-oriented languages how their state transitions can be expressed with the operators of MCL. Second, we illustrate the generality and power of our approach by relating it with other areas of research. We discuss how MCL can be used to formalize Abstract State Machines and we compare MCL with approaches that rely on different specification paradigms.

4.3.1   Formalizing KADS Languages

In this subsection we will discuss the formalization of $(ML)^2$ and KARL with MCL.

$(ML)^2$

The choice quantifier $(\cup x.\alpha)$ of MCL with

$$\alpha \quad \equiv \quad ((x/y)pia_{name}(x,...)\,?;\; output\text{-}role_{name} := \lambda y.(x = z))$$

captures the core of the state transitions in $(ML)^2$. The singleton predicate modeling the output role is true for one ground instantiation (modulo equality) and false for all others. This can be used to model non-deterministic selection. We have decided not to hardwire the mechanism *give-solution-pia* of $(ML)^2$ directly in MCL because there are some problems related to this construct as it can behave in a non-intuitive manner. For example, a deterministic inference action like *multiplication* fails if it receives the same input values a second time.

KARL

The λ-operator of MCL applied to a predicate can be used to model the bulk-update of KARL. The call of an inference action in KARL, for example, the inference action generate

> *hypothesis := generate(finding)*
> with
>> $\forall x,y(finding(x) \wedge causality(x,y) \rightarrow hypothesis(y))$
>> as logical theory defining the inference.

can be expressed in MCL as

> *hypothesis* $:\leftrightarrow \lambda y.(\exists x(finding(x) \wedge causality(x,y)))$.

In the above statement the value of the output role is erased. If we would like to extend the extension of a role, we can formulate this as:

> *role* $:\leftrightarrow \lambda y.(p(y) \vee role(y))$

KARL requires the artificially introduction of two inference actions (one select and one copy step) and an additional placeholder when facts of an input role should be deleted. The KARL statement

> *placeholder := select(input); input := copy(placeholder)*

is formulated in MCL as:

> *input* $:\leftrightarrow \lambda x.(input(x) \wedge select(x))$

However, a significant difference remains between MCL on the one hand and KARL on the other hand. KARL uses minimal and perfect Herbrand model semantics [Lloyd, 1987], [Przymusinski, 1988] to evaluate a set of clauses. Based on this reasoning with the closed-world assumption, negative literals and (in the case of stratification) positive literals of higher strata can be derived from a set of clauses in KARL which are not a logical consequence in the standard model-theoretical framework of first-order logic upon which MCL is based.

Minimal-model semantics of a logical program can be expressed in MCL along the lines of the operational semantics of fixpoint computation. When a fixpoint is reached after a finite number of iterations (which is assumed in KARL [Angele, 1993]), this can be expressed in MCL as a finite number of applications of a program operator. For the unary case this goes as follows: Let H be a logical program, the formula A the disjunction of all clauses in H, p a unary predicate symbol of H, and $\lambda p.\lambda x.A$ a new predicate operator associated with H. Then p equals the fixpoint after termination of the following program α^H with:

$$(p := \lambda x.\bot); (p := \lambda x.A)^*$$

i.e. we have

$$fix(H)x \leftrightarrow <\alpha^H>px$$

In order to deal with non-unary predicate operators, MCL has to be extended by a kind of *parallel* construct. We illustrate this with a binary predicate operator given by $\lambda p.\lambda x.A, \lambda q.\lambda y.B$. The required program α^H then becomes

$$(p := \lambda x.\bot, q := \lambda y.\bot); (p := \lambda x.A, q := \lambda y.B)^*$$

The parallel construct is denoted by a comma (,). The idea is that it can be applied to two programs which do not modify the same signature element(s) (cf. [Groenboom, 1997]).

4.3.2   Using MCL to Formalize Abstract State Machines

The two basic concepts of *Abstract State Machines* [Gurevich, 1994] are *states* and *state transitions*. As in COLD, a *state* is modeled by one static algebra. Let a signature, i.e. a finite collection of function names with given arity (the 0-ary function names model constants), be given. A static algebra of a signature is a nonempty set S together with interpretations on S of functions names. Such a static algebra defines one possible world (i.e., possible state). *Transitions* between states can be expressed by *function updates* of the form $f(t_1,...,t_r) := t$. These updates can be qualified by guards which express preconditions for their application. The point-wise modification corresponds to the grainsize of the transition in MLCM [Groenboom & Renardel de Lavalette, 1994]. Abstract State Machines also provide means to specify parallel algorithms that can be used to express our type of bulk-updates (i.e. the *choose* and the *range* constructs, cf. [Gurevich, 1994]). The formalization of Abstract State Machines in MCL (see Table) is inspired by the work presented in [Groenboom & Renardel de Lavalette, 1995].

An Abstract State Machine program is a set of rules α_i. The execution of such a program (called a run in [Gurevich, 1994]) is defined as the infinite execution of non-deterministically chosen rules α_i. We can encode this in MCL as:

$$EA \quad = \quad (\cup x.\alpha_i)^*$$

Although the formalization presented captures the core of Abstract State Machines, some expressions in Abstract State Machines are not covered. MCL is an untyped logic, therefore we cannot model the different universes of Abstract State Machine directly. Only a syntactic extension of MCL is required, however, in order to mimic Abstract State Machines more directly. More involved is the modeling of the concurrent assignment of Abstract State Machines. [Groenboom & Renardel de Lavalette, 1995] and [Groenboom, 1997] define the parallel execution operator of Abstract State Machines "," in terms of the simultaneous composition operator ⊕. Currently, this operation is not supported by MCL.

Table 4. The Elementary State Transitions of Abstract State Machines.

Abstract State Machines	Characterization	MCL
f(s):=t	sets f at s to t	f:=λx.(if x=s then t else fx fi)
if A then r	execution of r guarded by A	A?;r
choose x in V do r	execute r for a value x from V	∪x.r
range x in V do f(x):=t	let x range over the objects in V and perform update of f	f:=λx.t

Two main differences exist between Abstract State Machines and MCL. First, Abstract State Machines do not aim at a formal specification with formal syntax, semantics, and automated proof support. Instead, they provide a semiformal mathematical notation for definitions and proofs in a textbook-like style (cf. [Börger, 1995]). Second, our approach provides a procedural vocabulary to express control over the execution of transitions. Abstract State Machines do not provide a vocabulary to specify such composed state transitions. The way control is specified in Abstract State Machines is similar in spirit to production rule systems. To put it simply, Abstract State Machines provide a set of local transitions rules and a rule interpreter built into their semantics that selects the next firing rules to be applied.

4.3.3   Approaches Using Different Paradigms

The specification language TFL [Pierret-Golbreich & Talon, 1996] applies abstract data types to specify the functionality and the reasoning process of a knowledge-based system. Abstract data types are applied to specify domain and inference knowledge using loose semantics. Procedural control is specified by so-called process modules which incorporate the control expressions as operations into the framework of abstract data types. Test, sequence, choice, and iteration are specified as operations and axioms are used to further specify these operators (see Fig. 24) as in *process algebra* [Baeten & Weijland, 1990]. The main difference to our approach is that TFL provides neither a syntactical nor a semantical notion of the *state* of the reasoning process and does not provide a predefined set of elementary state transitions. Therefore, TFL has the frame problem just like situation calculus [McCarthy & Hayes, 1969]. For each elementary action the specifier must specify what it changes and what it keeps unchanged. In state-based approaches like dynamic logic and MCL this is already provided by the semantics and axiomatization of elementary state transitions. That is, the semantics of an elementary transition like p :↔λx.A ensures that the other predicates remain unchanged.

$$\cup : process \times process \rightarrow process$$
$$\delta : process$$
$$; : process \times process \rightarrow process$$
$$* : process \rightarrow process$$

$$(p \cup q) \cup r = p \cup (q \cup r)$$
$$p \cup q = q \cup p$$
$$p \cup p = p$$
$$p \cup \delta = p$$
$$(p \cup q); r = (p;r) \cup (q;r)$$
$$r; (p \cup q) = (r;p) \cup (r;q)$$

Fig. 24. Algebraic Specification of the Choice Operator in TFL

The language DESIRE [van Langevelde et al., 1993] uses the notion of meta-layered compositional architecture to specify a knowledge-based system. A knowledge-based system is decomposed into several interacting components. Each component contains a piece of knowledge at its object-layer and its own control is defined at its internal meta-layer. The interaction between components is represented by transactions and the control flow between these modules is defined by a set of control rules. The reasoning modules of DESIRE can be roughly compared with inference actions in $(ML)^2$ and KARL, but DESIRE provides much more sophisticated means to control the reasoning process of an inference action. An important distinction between DESIRE and the languages $(ML)^2$ and KARL is that DESIRE uses its object/meta-level distinction *to specify and reason about* flexible control of object-level inferences whereas languages such as $(ML)^2$ and KARL define control of inferences by means of a procedural language. From a semantic point of view, one difference between DESIRE (see [Treur, 1994]) and $(ML)^2$, KARL, MLPM, and MCL lies in the fact that the former uses temporal logic with linear time for specifying the reasoning process whereas the latter use dynamic logic. In dynamic logic, the semantics of the overall program is a binary relation between its input and output sets (M_i, M_o). Two different paths for computing the same input-output tuple are not distinguished. In DESIRE, the entire reasoning trace that leads to the derived output is used as the semantics. DESIRE uses a sequence of models $M_i, M_1, ..., M_n, M_o$ to define the semantics of a specification. It therefore allows the expression of strategic reasoning about the history of the derivation process.

5   A Verification Framework for Knowledge-Based Systems

Existing work on verifying knowledge-based systems (cf. [Lydiard, 1992], [Plant & Preece, 1996]) is focused on specific representation formalisms (usually production rules and KL-ONE like formalisms) and prove rather abstract properties of knowledge-based systems (so-called *anomalies*). One the one hand, these approaches make very strong meta-assumptions by assuming a specific representation formalism for describing the knowledge-based system. On the other hand, they do not make any (meta-) assumptions about the architecture (i.e., the general structure of a knowledge-based system) that can be used to describe a reasoning system. As a consequence, most of these approaches are situated at a different level of generality than our approach (cf. [Newell, 1982]).

Up to now, we presented an *architecture* for the specification of knowledge-based systems based on different reusable elements. This architecture is a refinement of the CommonKADS model of expertise which has been widely used by the knowledge engineering community. Applying such a model for the verification of knowledge-based systems was proposed by [van Harmelen & Aben, 1996]. In this Chapter, we discuss the precise specification and verification of the different elements and their relationships. Actually we focus on the problem-solving method and its related parts. We use the KIV system (Karlsruhe Interactive Verifier) [Reif, 1995] for the precise specification and verification at the architectural level. It is an advanced tool for the construction of provably correct software. KIV supports the entire design process starting from formal specifications (algebraic full first-order logic with loose semantics) and ending with verified code (Pascal-like procedures grouped into modules). It has been successfully applied in case-studies up to a size of several thousand lines of code and specification (see e.g. [Fuchß et al., 1995]). Roughly, the interactive theorem proving system of KIV is comparable with systems like PVS [Crow et al., 1995] and Isabelle [Paulson & Nipkow, 1990]. The KIV system is especially well suited to our purpose for several reasons.

- First, KIV supports dynamic logic (cf. [Goldblatt, 1982], [Harel, 1984]) which we used to define a formal semantics for the reasoning process of knowledge-based systems (i.e., of problem-solving methods).

- Second, KIV allows the structuring of specifications and the modularisation of software systems. Therefore, the conceptual model of our specification can be realized by the modular structure of a specification in KIV.

- Finally, the KIV system offers well-developed proof engineering facilities: proof obligations are generated automatically, proof trees are visualized and can be manipulated with the help of a graphical user interface and complicated proofs can be constructed with the interactive theorem prover. A high degree of automation can be achieved by a number of implemented heuristics. However, interaction is necessary for two reasons: complex proofs cannot generally be completely automated and proving usually means finding errors either in the specification or in the implementation. The proof process is therefore a kind of search process for errors. Analysis of failed proof attempts and the automatic generation of counter examples support the iterative process of developing

Dieter Fensel: Problem-Solving Methods, LNAI 1791, pp. 78 - 91, 2000.

correct specifications and programs. An elaborated correctness management keeps track of lemma dependencies (and their modifications) and the automatic reuse of proofs allows an incremental verification of corrected versions of programs and lemmas (see [Reif & Stenzel, 1993]). Both aspects are essential to make verification feasible given the fact that system development is a process of continuous modification and revision.

In this chapter we illustrate some of the specification elements and proof processes necessary to establish the correctness of the different elements of a complete specification. In each section, we use different aspects of a running example for illustrating these processes. First, we introduce the structure of our specification in KIV. Then, we illustrate the specification of a task and a problem-solving method. This is used to illustrate the termination and correctness proofs and the proofs that establish the appropriate relationship between the task and the problem-solving method.

5.1   The Architecture in KIV

In KIV, the entire specification of a system can be split into smaller and more tractable pieces. Each *elementary specification* introduces a signature and a set of axioms. The semantics of such a specification is the class of all algebras that satisfy the first-order axioms (i.e., *loose* semantics is applied [Wirsing, 1990]).

KIV provides mechanisms for combining elementary specifications to form more complex ones (e.g. *sum, enrichment, renaming,* and *actualization* of parameterized specifications) which are common to most algebraic specification languages, cf. [Wirsing, 1995].

In addition to (elementary) specifications, KIV provides *modules* to describe implementations in a Pascal-like style. A module consists of an export specification, an import specification, and an implementation that defines a collection of procedures implementing the operations of the export specification.

Fig. 25 provides the structure of the entire specification of our example, i.e. the dependencies between the (sub-)specifications and implementations in KIV. The single specifications (the rectangles in the diagram) and modules (the rhomboid units in the diagram) are discussed in the following sections. The conceptual units we identified above (i.e., task, problem-solving method, domain model, and adapter) must be defined by hand as aggregations of elements of the development graph.

5.2   Formalizing a Task

We use the simple task of Chapter 3 to illustrate the formalization of our approach. The task *abduction* receives a set of observations as its input and delivers a complete and parsimonious explanation that must explain all input and be minimal. Fig. 25 provides the modular structure of the task definition of our example. The internal definitions of some of the specifications are given in Fig. 26. The specification *abduction problem* is an enrichment of *data* and *hypotheses* and introduces a requirement on domain knowledge. *Data* and *hypotheses* specify finite sets of observations and hypotheses, respectively. Their specification is omitted. A function

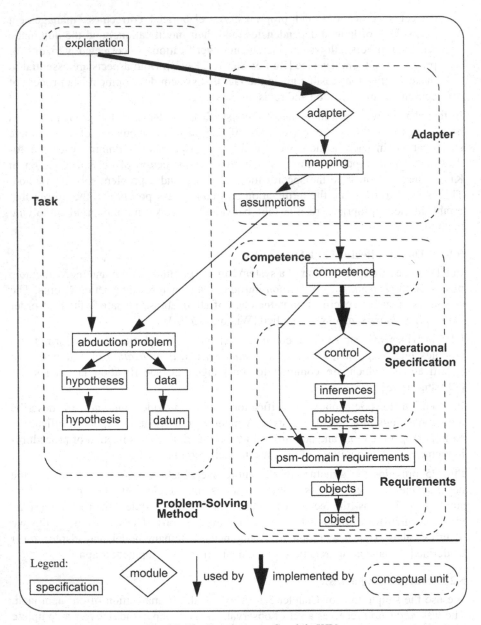

Fig. 25. The Development Graph in KIV

explain relates hypotheses with observations they explain. Further, two predicates *complete* and *parsimonious* are introduced that are required to define a solution of the task. Based on these definitions, we can finally define what an goal must fulfill. It must be complete and parsimonious.

---

explanation = **enrich** *abduction problem* **with**
   constants *goal : hypotheses;*
   axioms
      complete(goal),
      parsimonious(goal)
end enrich

abduction problem = **enrich** *hypotheses, data* **with**
   constants *observables : data;*
   functions *explain : hypotheses* → *data;*
   predicates
      complete : hypotheses,
      parsimonious : hypotheses;
   axioms
      complete(H) ↔ *explain(H) − observables,*
      parsimonious(H) ↔ ¬ ∃ *H′ . H′* ⊂ *H* ∧ *explain(H)* ⊆ *explain(H′),*
      ∃*x . x* ∈ *observables*
end enrich

Fig. 26. The Specification of the Abductive Task in KIV

The main difference from the original specification of the task in Fig. 11 is the separation into two modules *abduction problem* and *explanation*. This is required by the module and proof obligation management concepts of KIV. We will need the axioms to prove whether the competence of the problem-solving method actually fulfills the goal of the task. Therefore, these axioms need to be imported by the adapter which is where the proof obligation is generated by KIV. We will return to this subject later on. Besides this, the internal details of the specification are completely identical to the specification in Chapter 3, Fig. 11.

5.3   Formalizing a Problem-Solving Method

We use the simple problem-solving method *set-minimizer* of Chapter 3 for our example. It receives a set of objects as input and tries to find a minimized version of the set that still fulfills a correctness requirement. The overall structure of the problem-solving method-specification is provided in Fig. 25.

The *competence* in Fig. 27 states that *set-minimizer* is able to find a *local* minimal subset of the given set of objects. The three axioms state that it (1) finds a subset that is correct (2), and minimal (3), i.e. that each set containing one less element is not a correct set. There is one new axiom compared to the original specification in Fig. 12. The first axiom ensures that the output of the method is a subset of its input. Actually we became aware of this axiom during the proof process with KIV. We needed it to establish the correctness of the output as a consequence of the operational search strategy and the correctness of the input. Such axioms are typical examples of things that remain unspecified without verification. For the human modeler, this axiom follows intuitively from the fact that the method should *select* a minimal set. However,

competence = **generic specification**
    parameter *psm-domain requirements* **target**
    constants *output : objects;*
    axioms
        (1) *output $\subseteq$ input,*
        (2) *correct(output),*
        (3) *$x \in output \to \neg correct(output \setminus x)$*
  end generic specification

Fig. 27. The Specification of the Competence of the Problem-Solving Method in KIV

computers still lack intuition. Besides this additional axiom, there are no further differences from the specification in Fig. 12.

The main requirements on available knowledge and input that are introduced by the method are: the existence of a possible set of *objects* (a sort), the existence of a predicate *correct* holding true for some sets, and, finally, the method assumes that the *input* is a correct set. These requirements on knowledge and input data are specified as (formal) parameter of the specification of the method. They are replaced by concrete parameters when the method is applied for a specific task and domain. This parameterization also allows us to obtain different variants of the competence of a method by varying its knowledge requirement. The specification of the requirements in Fig. 28 extends the original specification of Fig. 12 by ensuring explicitly the generatedness of the object-set. In Chapter 3, we skipped this aspect in our informal description style of formal specifications.

psm-domain requirements = **enrich** *objects* **with**
    constants *input : objects;*
    predicates *correct : objects,*
    axioms
        correct(input)
  end enrich

object-sets = **generic specification**
    parameter *psm-domain requirements* **target**
    constants $\emptyset$ *: object-sets;*
    functions *insert : objects x object-sets $\to$ object-sets;*
    predicates *. $\in$. : objects x object-sets;*
    variables o_1, o_2 *: objects, O_1, O_2 :object-sets;*
    axioms
        object-sets **generated by** $\emptyset$*, insert,*
        $\neg o \in \emptyset,$
        $o_1 \in insert(o_2, O_1) \leftrightarrow o_1 = o_2 \vee o_1 \in O_1,$
        $O_1 = O_2 \leftrightarrow (\forall o_1 . o_1 \in O_1 \leftrightarrow o_1 \in O_2)$
  end generic specification

Fig. 28. The Specification of the Requirements of the Problem-Solving Method in KIV

inferences = **enrich** *object-sets* **with**
   functions
      generate : objects → *object-sets,*
      select : objects x object-sets → *objects;*
   axioms
      $O_2 \in generate(O_1) \leftrightarrow \exists o_1 . (o_1 \in O_1 \wedge O_2 = O_1 \setminus o_1),$
      $(\exists O_1 . (O_1 \in OS \wedge correct(O_1)) \rightarrow select(O,OS) \in OS \wedge correct(select(O,OS)),$
      $\neg \exists O_1 . (O_1 \in OS \wedge correct(O_1)) \rightarrow select(O,OS) = O$
end enrich

Fig. 29. The Specification of the Inference Actions in KIV

The problem-solving method works as follows: First, we take the input. Then we recursively generate the successors of the current set and select one of its correct successors. If there is no new correct successor we return to the current set. The functions *generate* and *select* in the specification *inferences* correspond to elementary inference actions and the procedural control is defined by the module *control*. The specification of the functions that model the inferences is provided in Fig. 29 and the procedural control is given in Fig. 30. For the first time we encounter a significant

control = **module**
   export *competence*
   refinement
      representation of operations
         control **implements** *output*
      import *inferences*
      procedures *hill-climbing(objects) : objects*
      variables *output, current, new :objects;*
      implementation

      *control(***var** *output)*
      begin
         hill-climbing(input,output)
      end

      hill-climbing(current, **var** *output)*
      begin
         var *new = select(current,generate(current))*
         if   *new = current*
            then   *output := current*
            else   *hill-climbing(new,output)*
      end

Fig. 30. The Operational Specification of the Problem-Solving Method in KIV

difference between the specification styles of MCL in Chapter 3 (see Fig. 14 and Fig. 15) and the specification in KIV:

- The axiomatic specifications of the inference actions do not differ. However, in Chapter 3, Fig. 14, we used a predicate to model an inference action. Here, we modeled an inference action using a function in Fig. 29. Both are legitimate possibilities. Earlier approaches already used both possibilities. $(ML)^2$ [van Harmelen & Balder, 1992] uses predicates whereas KARL [Fensel et al., 1998(b)] applies functions for this purpose.

- KIV uses variables to model states and state changes are expressed by different value assignments of these variables. In Chapter 3, Fig. 14, we used terms and predicates to model states. This is possible because MCL incorporates the states-as-algebras paradigm. This has not yet been realized in KIV.[2)]

- The specification of control was carried out in an iterative manner in Fig. 15 and Fig. 30 uses a recursive style. Using the recursive style of the specification in KIV for our specification in MCL is not straightforwardly possible. Because we use predicates to model states, we would need to parameterize our procedures with predicates, and local copies of these predicates must be provided for each level of recursion. This is beyond the scope of the current version of MCL.[3)]

5.4   Proving Total Correctness of the Problem-Solving Method

When introducing a problem-solving method into a library we have to prove two aspects of its operational specification. We have to ensure the termination of the procedure and the competence as specified. When reusing the problem-solving method this proof need not to be repeated and can (implicitly) be reused. The according proof obligations are automatically generated by KIV as formulas in dynamic logic. In our example, it derives the following proof obligations (see [Reif, 1995], Section 5.2 for more details on how the correctness of a module is translated into a set of proof obligations formulated in dynamic logic.):

(i)   *<control(output)>* true, i.e. termination.

(ii)   *<control(output)>* output $\subseteq$ input, corresponds to axiom 1 of the competence.

(iii) *<control(output)>* correct(output), corresponds to axiom 2 of the competence.

(iv)   *<control(output)>* o $\in$ output $\rightarrow \neg$ *<control(output)>* correct(output \ o), corresponds to axiom 3 of the competence.

These proof obligations ensure that the problem-solving method terminates and that it terminates in a state that respects the axioms used to characterize the competence of the problem-solving method ("$\diamond$" is the diamond operator of dynamic logic).

The next step is to actually prove these obligations using KIV. For constructing proofs, KIV provides an integration of automated reasoning and interactive proof engineering. The user constructs proofs interactively, but has only to give the key steps of the proof

---

[2)] Integrating this paradigm into a logic is easier than integrating a new paradigm into a verification framework. The former requires semantics and axioms. The latter requires in addition good proof heuristics that support the interactive proof process.

[3)] It would be possible in MCL to use terms and NEW for each recursive level. However, this is more like implementing and not specifying recursive problem solving.

(e.g. induction, case distinction) and all the numerous tedious steps (e.g. simplification) are performed by the machine. Automation is achieved by rewriting and by heuristics which can be chosen, combined, and tailored by the proof engineer. If the chosen set of heuristics gets stuck while applying proof tactics the user has to select tactics on his own or activate a different set of heuristics in order to continue the partial proof constructed up until that point. Most of these user interactions can be performed by selecting alternatives provided by a menu.

For each of the proof obligations we formulate straightforward auxiliary lemmas i-lemma, ii-lemma, iii-lemma, and iv-lemma; one for each of these proof obligations, respectively. These auxiliary lemmas express the corresponding properties of the hill-climbing sub-procedure (cf. Fig. 30):

(i-lemma)$<hill\text{-}climbing(current;output)>$ true
(ii-lemma)$current \subseteq O \rightarrow <hill\text{-}climbing(current;output)>$ output $\subseteq O$
(iii-lemma)$correct(current) \rightarrow <hill\text{-}climbing(current;output)>$ correct(output)
(iv-lemma)$<hill\text{-}climbing(current;output)>$ output $= O \rightarrow \neg\exists o. o \in O \wedge correct(O \setminus o)$

Using these lemmas, each of the proof obligations can now directly be proven using the interactive proof environment of KIV. Activating the standard set of predefined heuristics (by click) and then selecting the auxiliary lemma proper (by click) suffices. KIV automatically unfolds the control procedure, finds the appropriate instantiation of the lemma, and carries out the first-order reasoning (necessary e.g. for (iii)). Thus the proofs of (i), (ii), (iii), (iv) respectively can be carried out with one user interaction.

It remains to prove the four lemmas. All of these proofs work by induction. And to construct them with the help of KIV one has to tell KIV (again by clicking) which kind of induction should be used. KIV is then able to unfold (and symbolically execute) the hill-climbing procedure and find the correct instantiation of the induction hypothesis. While KIV is trying to construct the proofs it comes up with subgoals reflecting certain properties of the inference actions. We then interact by formulating these properties as first-order lemmas in the specification of the inferences and KIV is able to automatically find and use them to close the open subgoals. Thus with a few almost straightforward user interactions (in addition to the formulation of the lemmas) the original proof obligations are reduced to the task of proving some properties of the inferences stated in first-order logic. These in turn can be derived from the axioms. Here again some user interaction is required, mostly selecting the appropriate axioms (and also one quantifier instantiation). Besides this KIV does all the first-order reasoning. We now give a sketch of the proofs:

i-lemma. The termination of the problem-solving method is proven by induction on the first parameter of *hill-climbing*, where the (well-founded) order $\subset$ is used. In the induction step we use the fact that

$select(O,generate(O)) \neq O \rightarrow select(O,generate(O)) \subset O.$

This is equivalent to

$select(O,generate(O)) \subseteq O$

which can be proved as an instantiation of a stronger lemma which is used in the proof of ii-lemma.

ii-lemma. The proof is carried out by induction on the recursive calls of the *hill-climbing* procedure in a terminating run. The proof uses the property that

$$O \subseteq O_0 \rightarrow select(O, generate(O)) \subseteq O_0.$$

This property is proven by using the (three) axioms for the inferences *generate* and *select* and a suitable case-distinction (i.e., four interactions).

iii-lemma. The proof is carried out, as for lemma ii-lemma, by induction on the recursive calls of the *hill-climbing* procedure in a terminating run. For this it is enough to use the property of *select* that it yields a correct object set, whenever it does not yield its first argument as a result. This property follows immediately from the axioms.

iv-lemma. The proof is carried out, as for ii-lemma and iii-lemma, by induction on the recursive calls of the *hill-climbing* procedure in a terminating run. The proof uses the property that

$$\exists o.\ (o \in O \wedge correct(O \setminus o)) \rightarrow select(O, generate(O)) \neq O.$$

This property is proven as follows: First we show that from the condition

$$\exists o.\ (o \in O \wedge correct(O \setminus o))\ \textit{it follows that}$$
$$O_1 := select(O, generate(O)) \in generate(O)$$

From the axiom for *generate* follows that an $o_1 \in O$ must exist such that $O_1 = O \setminus o_1$, i.e. $O_1 \neq O$.

To give an impression of how to work with KIV, Fig. 31 shows a screen dump of the KIV system when proving iv-lemma. The *current proof* window on the right shows the partial proof tree currently under development. Each node represents a sequent (of a sequent calculus for dynamic logic); the root contains the theorem to be proved. In the *messages* window the KIV system reports its ongoing activities. The *KIV-Strategy* window is the main window which shows the sequent of the current goal i.e. an open premise (leaf) of the (partial) proof tree. The user works either by selecting (clicking) one proof tactic (the list on the left) or by selecting a command from the menu bar above. Proof tactics reduce the current goal to subgoals and thereby make the proof tree grow. Commands include the selection of heuristics, backtracking, pruning the proof tree, saving the proof, etc.

5.5   Adapter: Connecting Task and Problem-Solving Method

The description of an *adapter* maps the different terminologies of the task definition, the problem-solving method, and the domain model and introduces further requirements and assumptions. We introduce assumptions using the subspecification *assumptions* (cf. Fig. 32) to ensure that the competence of our method implies the goal of the task. First, we have to require that the input of the method is a complete explanation. Based on the mappings it is now easy to prove that the input requirement of the method is fulfilled (i.e., the input is correct). Second, based on the mappings we can prove that our method *set-minimizer* finds a local-minimal set that is parsimonious in the sense that each subset that contains one element less is not a complete explanation. However, we cannot guarantee that it is parsimonious in general. Smaller subsets of it that are complete explanations may exist. The adapter has to introduce a new requirement on domain knowledge or an assumption (in the case that it does not follow from the domain model) to guarantee that the competence of the problem-

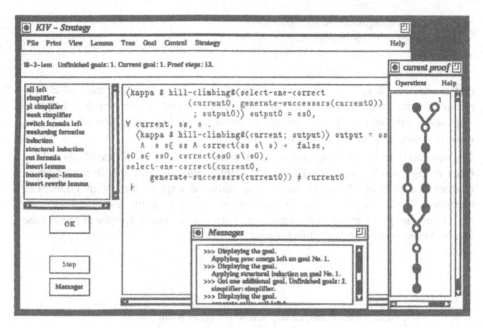

Fig. 31. A Screen Dump of the KIV System

solving method is strong enough to achieve the goal of the task. The *monotony assumption* (cf. Fig. 32) is sufficient (and necessary cf. section III) to prove that the (global) parsimoniousness of the result of the problem-solving method follows from its local parsimoniousness. To ensure the automatic generation and management of this proof obligation by KIV we have to specify the adapter as a module that implements the task goal by importing the mappings and exporting the goal of the task (cf. Fig. 32).

KIV automatically generates three proof obligations for the adapter module, again formulated in dynamic logic.

(i)   <explanation(res)> true
(ii)   <explanation(res)> complete(res)
(iii) <explanation(res)> parsimonious(res)

The proofs of i and ii are trivial and fully automatic. iii is the real proof obligation of this module. The informal proof sketch is as follows: We unfold the definition of parsimonious and it remains to prove that there is no proper subset H of *output* which explains (at least) all the data explained by the *output*, i.e.,

$explain(output) \subseteq explain(H).$

We choose some hypothesis h ∈ *output*, such that

$H \subseteq output \setminus h.$

Due to the monotony assumption we can derive

$explain(H) \subseteq explain(output \setminus h)$

and transitivity of $\subseteq$ yields

$explain(output) \subseteq explain(output \setminus h).$

Since output is complete (see ii) it holds that

explain(output) = all-data

and thus that

explain(output \ h) = all-data

that is, *output \ h* is a complete set of hypotheses. This, however, contradicts the minimality axiom of the (mapped) competence. The proof in KIV requires 14 proof steps and 7 interactions. The seven interactions concern the application of axioms of the different specifications for the proof process.

The monotony assumption defines a natural subclass of abduction (see Chapter 2 for more details). For example [de Kleer et al., 1992] examine their role in model-based diagnosisfor finding all parsimonious and complete explanations with GDE. The question of how to provide such assumptions that close the gap between task definitions and problem-solving methods may arise. In section 6.1, we will present the idea of *inverse verification* for this purpose.

---

assumptions = **enrich** *abduction problem* **with**
    axioms
        complete(all-hypotheses),
        $H \subseteq H' \rightarrow explain(H) \subseteq explain(H')$
end enrich

mapping =
actualize *competence* **with** *assumptions* **by morphism**
    correct $\rightarrow$ *complete, input* $\rightarrow$ *all-hypotheses,*
    objects $\rightarrow$ *hypotheses,*
    all-objects $\rightarrow$ *all-hypotheses,*
    ...
end actualize

adapter = **module**
    export *explanation*
    refinement
        representation of operations
            explanation **implements** *explanation;*
    import *mapping*
    variables *res : hypotheses;*
    implementation
        *explanation(***var** *res)*
        begin
            res := output
        end

Fig. 32. Connecting Problem-Solving Method and Task in KIV

5.6   A Specific Pattern in Specifying Architectures of Knowledge-Based Systems

In the following, we discuss a specificity of the KIV development graph when specifying our architecture for knowledge-based systems in it. Usually the development graph in KIV has the following pattern:

- A specification defines the functionality of operations that are imported by a module, i.e. by an implementation.

- A module imports some operations und uses them to implement new operations that are exported.

- A second specification defines the required functionality of the exported operations. Then a new implementation uses these operations as import.

The left side of Fig. 33 provides the structure of such a typical development graph. The single specifications are the rectangles in the graph and modules are modeled by the rhomboid units in the graph. Such a typical development graph corresponds with the specification and operationalization of a problem-solving method (viewed at the right side of Fig. 33),

- The inference actions are defined in the import specification of the problem-solving method. No algorithmic realization of the inference action is provided. The algorithmic realization of the knowledge requirements is also not part of the problem-solving method because this aspect is assumed to be covered by the domain knowledge or by other agents of the entire problem-solving process. Therefore, its realization is beyond the scope of the specification of the problem-solving method.

- The operationalization of a problem-solving method corresponds to an implementation module. It describes how a specific competence can be achieved by defining control over the execution of imported operations (knowledge and inferences).

- Finally the competence of a problem-solving method corresponds to the specification of the functionality of a module.

A distinction between typical development graphs in KIV and our specifications is introduced by problem definitions and assumptions. Usually in software engineering it is assumed that the problem that should be solved is identical with the functionality of the program. However most problems tackled with knowledge-based systems are inherently complex and intractable (cf. Section I). A problem-solving method can only solve such problems with reasonable computational effort by introducing assumptions that restrict the complexity of the problem or by strengthening the requirements on domain knowledge. Therefore, a specification of the problem independent from the specification of the competence and the specification of assumptions are introduced in our context. A method does not have the direct competence to solve the problem. Only when adding assumptions that limit the problem can this be guaranteed. The entire problem is therefore decomposed into a part that can be solved by the problem-solving method and for which an operationalization is provided and a second part of which the

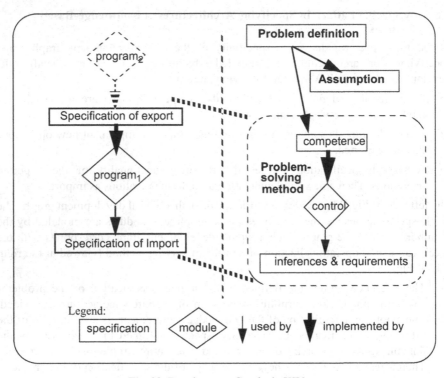

Fig. 33. Development Graphs in KIV

solution is only assumed. This makes quite clear *how assumptions help to reduce the effort of realizing an implementation and computing an actual solution.* They define a part of the entire problem for which no implementation has to be provided. Therefore, the system can be realized more easily and in system runtime this part of the problem does not need to be computed.[4]

In general, there is no distinction between problem specification, assumption specification and the specification of the competence of a method. They are all specification units. Only their roles within the entire specification differ. That is, it is their context that creates their distinction:

- A *problem* defines a specifications that is "realized" by two other specifications. One of these specifies the part that is actually solved (the competence of a problem-solving method) and the other specifies the part that is assumed to be solved (an assumption specification).

- An *assumption* is a specification that has no realization at all. Its realization is only assumed.

- Finally, the *competence* of a problem-solving method is a specification that is directly realized by a module that defines an operationalization. Again this

---

[4] See [O'Hara & Shadbolt, 1996] for a discussion of different dimensions of efficiency.

operationalization relies on a specification defining its knowledge requirements and inferences. Their realization are either external to the specification or introduce a new level of hierarchical refinement by being formulated as new problems.

5.7   Future Work

Two problems were encountered when applying KIV to our architecture and specification language.

The *architecture* used to specify knowledge-based systems can be expressed in the generic module concept of KIV. However, this is connected with a loss of information because the KIV specification does not distinguish the different roles that specifications may have (goals, requirements, adapters etc.). Therefore, not all of the desired proof obligations could be generated automatically or at least not directly. Still, it seems possible to specialize the generic concepts of KIV. This would allow us to provide the automatic generation of according proof obligations and of predefined modules and specification combinations to model the different aspects of knowledge-based systems. Based on this, we plan to develop a methodological framework for the stepwise development of correct specifications of knowledge-based systems.

The *specification languages* MLPM and MCL use the states-as-algebras paradigm to model states and bulk-updates to model state transitions. The current version of KIV relies on the original work of [Harel, 1984], where states are represented by value assignments of free variables. However, current approaches may help to eliminate this difference. [Schönegge, 1995] provides an extension of KIV for a subset of Abstract State Machines that makes a step in eliminating this difference. A state is represented by the actual values of the functions of the signature. The main problem in immediately applying KIV to MCL specifications is that KIV is based on a point-wise modification of functions[5] whereas MCL provides bulk-updates that modify a complete predicate in one step. This problem will disappear when KIV is extended to verify Abstract State Machines of parallel algorithms, as this extension also requires bulk-updates.

Given the fact, that KIV was never designed for knowledge-based systems, the degree of usefulness and applicability was surprising.

---

[5] The extension of [Schönegge, 1995] allows a finite number of pointwise modifications per transition.

"Science does not rest upon solid bedrock. The bold structure of its theories rises, as if were, above a swamp. It is like a building erected on piles. The piles are driven down from above into the swamp, but not down to any natural or 'given' base; and if we stop driving the piles deeper, it is not because we have reached firm ground. We simply stop when we are satisfied that the piles are firm enough to carry the structure, at least for the time being." [Popper, 1959]

Section III:
How to Develop and Reuse
Problem-Solving Methods

6 Methods for Context Explication and Adaptation

Knowledge is *situated* and its usefulness for different situations is limited [Menzies & Clancey, 1999]. Reuse of knowledge has to deal with its situatedness. Knowledge may be powerful in one context and useless or even dangerous in another. It may enable effective and efficient problem-solving if its implicit assumptions are fulfilled. Otherwise, it may produce incorrect results and inefficient search. This *brittleness* of knowledge creates serious problems when trying to reuse knowledge outside the context in which it was developed and used. Problem-solving methods are a specific type of knowledge concerned with the problem-solving process. Therefore, they share this general problem of knowledge reuse. As a consequence, we will first locate our discussion in the general context of sharing and reusing knowledge and will then provide specific solutions which deal with reusing problem-solving methods. Clearly, some of them may also be able to be generalized for reusing different types of knowledge.

Cyc is a prominent and long-term research project aiming for a large knowledge base enabling common-sense reasoning [Guha & Lenat, 1990]. To achieve this goal, large amounts of human common sense knowledge were encoded. However, one encounters a serious problem when formalizing human knowledge. Knowledge can be understood as a model of reality which serves specific (probably implicit) purposes [Agnew et al., 1994]. Trying to represent this situated knowledge recursively creates the same problem. A representation of this knowledge, i.e. a model, reflects a point of view taken by the modeler [Clancey, 1993]. The point of view he takes reflects implicitly or explicitly the intended use of the model. [Guha, 1993] enumerates three aspects of a representation that reflect the situatedness of a knowledge model: the *vocabulary* used to formulate the model, the *granularity and accuracy* of the model, and the assumptions that underlay the model.

[McCarthy, 1993] and [Guha, 1993] present *context logic* as a means to deal with this problem.[1] The notion of context is reified within first-order logic by introducing terms that denote a context, i.e. that provide context names. However, providing a notation for context dependency (i.e., a language that allows to express situatedness) is only half of the work. The second problem is how to become aware of the context dependency of a model. That is, how can we provide methodological support for building a model of the context dependency of our knowledge model. Making the context of a (knowledge) model explicit is a tricky problem that is unsolvable in general, but (heuristically) solvable in practice. It is unsolvable in general because its solution would require us to solve a problem of infinite regress. Making a context explicit needs a perspective that is used as point of reference for this activity. Clearly this creates a new context dependency of the model. "As a consequence, there doesn't seem to be any certain knowledge on which to stop and stand ... that doesn't rely on unproven assumptions" [Agnew et al., 1994]. However, this does not imply that there is no pragmatic solution at all. [Agnew et al., 1994] claim that a concept of purpose

---

[1] See [Akman & Surav, 1996] for a survey of formalizations of contexts and [McCarthy & Buvac, 1997] for a more recent introduction into context logic.

Dieter Fensel: Problem-Solving Methods, LNAI 1791, pp. 95- 115, 2000.
© Springer-Verlag Berlin Heidelberg 2000

realized by a social selection process comparable to the effect of the evolution process in nature, would solve the problem in practice. The assumptions which coincide with the desired purpose and its efficient achievement remain and others are rejected, requiring deeper search for a better (i.e., more suitable) foundation.

The context dependency of knowledge models is more than just a "philosophical" problem. First, when developing a knowledge model for a single application the developer may have a good intuition about which assumptions can be made so as to deal with his problem adequately. In this case, hidden assumptions become apparent in cases where the system fails. The knowledge-based system may not be able to process a given input, or it returns a result that is not the solution as it is required. Using error situations and system breakdowns is the most common (implicit) search method for assumptions. However, this "method" may also cause significant damage. Reliable systems require the explication of their assumptions as an explicit part of their development process. Second, contexts have the problematic feature that they change over time. As a consequence, the knowledge-based system must be maintained [Menzies, 1999]. The notion of context can be used as a guideline of answering the questions as to whether it is necessary to change the system and how this can be done without losing other necessary properties. Third, the problem of context-dependency is immediately present for knowledge models which are intended to be sharable and reusable. In this case they cannot be designed to intuitively fit to a given context because they must be applicable to a broad range of problems not known beforehand.

Making explicit the context of a knowledge model is an infinite process. We cannot expect to reach a solid ground upon which we can built our knowledge model. Therefore, the only thing we can provide are shovels and dredgers that can be used to deepen the fundament and to rebuild the house if required. What can be provided and what is needed is active support in *context explication* and *in changing knowledge or its underlying context assumptions* in the case that we have to adapt it to a new context (i.e., we became aware of the fact that it does not fit well to a context). These are precisely our goals. First, a method that allows to *explicate hidden assumptions of a knowledge model* will be discussed and second, a method that *allows the adaptation of a knowledge model to a changed contexts* by transforming its vocabulary, granularity, and assumptions is presented.

However, we do not investigate knowledge models in general. Instead we focus our attention on a specific knowledge type: *problem-solving methods*. [Fensel, 1995a] attempted to specify the competence of the problem-solving method *propose & revise for parametric design* (cf. [Marcus et al., 1988], [Schreiber & Birmingham, 1996]) enabling its reuse for different tasks. However two significant problems appeared:

- There is not only one *propose & revise* method but there is a large number of slightly different variants and there is no justification for selecting one of them as the gold standard.

- Each of these variants uses slightly different assumptions about what the precise problem is and about the strength of the domain knowledge that can be used for its reasoning process. In general, the competence of a problem-solving method cannot be described independent of these assumptions.

One could ask whether a solution would be to choose the variant of a problem-solving method which makes as few assumptions as possible. However, this fails to grasp the essence of problem-solving methods. Efficient reasoning is only possible by introducing assumptions. These assumptions are necessary for reducing the complexity both of the reasoning task and of the process for developing the reasoning system. Therefore, making *assumptions for efficiency reasons* is an essential feature of problem-solving methods. The more assumptions a problem-solving method makes the more efficient reasoning power it can provide. There are two conclusions that have be drawn for problem-solving methods. There is neither a gold standard for a problem-solving method nor can we expect to ever find a useful assumption-free method. Therefore, what needs to be provided are generic schemes of problem-solving methods and methodological support for adapting such schemes to problem-specific and domain-specific circumstances. Such support has to deal with two aspects (see Fig.):

- A method has to be provided that can be used to make explicit context dependency.

- A method that supports the adaptation of a problem-solving method to a given context has to be found.

Context Explication

We already argued that making strong assumptions on available domain knowledge and problem restrictions is not a bug but a feature of problem-solving methods that should enable efficient reasoning. In Chapter 2, we collected a large number of assumptions and related them to the different subtasks of diagnostic problem solving. This assumption list can be used to check given domain knowledge, to define goals for knowledge acquisition, to restrict the size of the problem that must be solved by the knowledge-based system, or to select a problem-solving method that fits to the given context as characterized by the established assumptions. However, this was a kind of post-analysis. These were the results of a common research project which has been carried out for ca. 20 years. Searching for hidden assumptions was a sort of implicit activity for a research community while developing problem solvers for diagnosis. Chapter 6.1 will present a method called *inverse verification* that allows a pre-analysis for hidden assumptions. It provides support for an active and explicit search process for these assumptions.

Problem-Solving Method Adaptation

The context problem of problem-solving methods was already encountered in the early work on *role-limiting methods* [Marcus, 1988] and *generic tasks* [Chandrasekaran, 1986]. The implemented methods fit well for the application they were developed for. However, the attempt at applying them to similar problems with slightly different

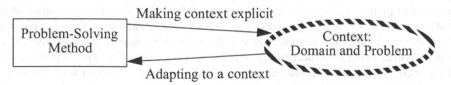

Fig. 34. The Two Directions of the Context Problem

goals and domain knowledge failed because of their brittleness. [Klinker et al., 1991] rephrased this as the usability-reusability trade-off of problem-solving methods. On the one hand, the more assumptions and commitments to a specific problem type that are made the stronger the support of the method in developing a solution for this problem. On the other hand, as more commitments to the specifity of the problem are made less reusability could be expected. Recently [van Heijst & Anjewerden:, 1996] and [Beys et al., 1996] have proposed that problem-solving methods should be described not only in a domain-independent, but also in a completely task-independent manner, so that they can be more broadly reusable. However, this decontextualization of problem-solving methods significantly reduces the usefulness that is usually provided with their task-specific vocabulary, assumptions, and granularity. In their approach, only abstract algorithmic schemas remain, without any relation to the problem. As a consequence, the mapping between such an algorithmic schema and a problem-, domain-, and application-specific problem solver is very complex and little support in knowledge acquisition is provided.

All these discussions deal with the problem of adapting problem-solving methods to a new or modified context. We will provide methodological support for this process. A principled way of developing and adapting problem-solving methods is shown. This is achieved mainly by using *adapters* as a means to express the adaptation of problem-solving methods. Refined versions of problem-solving methods are achieved by combining them with adapters. Therefore problem-solving methods can be used and reused at an arbitrary level of contextualization as shown in Chapter 6.2.

6.1   Inverse Verification of Problem-Solving Methods

Here we discuss how assumptions that are necessary to close gaps between different elements of a specification can be found using *failed* attempts to prove their proper relationship. Again, the *interactive* theorem prover of KIV is used as tool support.

The method consists of two main steps: (1) Establishing the notion of competence of a method in dependence on its assumptions and (2) relating the competence of a method to a problem definition that introduces a general notion of the context in which the problem-solving method can be applied. Both steps are assumption search and construction processes and both rely on the *same principle*. However they both play different *conceptual roles* and require d*ifferent techniques*.

We use failed proofs as a search method for assumptions and analysis of these failures for constructing and refining assumptions. In other words, we attempt to prove that a problem-solving method achieves a goal and the assumptions appear during the proof as missing pieces in proving the correctness of the specification. A mathematical proof written down in a text book explains why a lemma is true under some preconditions (i.e., assumptions and other sublemmas). The proof establishes the lemma by using the preconditions and some deductive reasoning. Taking a look at the proof *process* we get a different picture. Usually, initial proof attempts fail when they run into improvable subgoals. These failed proof attempts point to necessary features that are not present from the beginning. Actually they make aware of further assumptions that have to be made in order to obtain a successful proof. Taking this perspective, a proof process can be viewed as a search and construction process of assumptions. Gaps that can be found in a failed proof provide initial characterizations of missing assumptions. They appear as sublemmas that were necessary to proceed with the proof. An assumption that implies such a sublemma closing the gap in the proof is a possible candidate which we are looking for. That is, formulating this sublemma as an assumption is a first step in finding and/or constructing assumptions that are necessary to ensure that a problem-solving method behaves well in a given context. Using an open goal of a proof directly as an assumption normally leads to very strong assumptions. That is, these assumptions are *sufficient* to guarantee the correctness of the proof, but they are often neither *necessary* for the proof nor *realistic* in the sense that application problems will fulfill them. Therefore, further work is necessary to find improved characterizations for these assumptions. This is achieved by a precise analysis of their role in the completed proof to retrace unnecessary properties.

Such proofs can be done semiformally in a textbook style as proposed by the *Abstract State Machines* community [Börger, 1995]. However, providing specification formalisms with a formal syntax and formal semantics allows (semi-)automated proof support. The great amount of details that arise when proving properties of software (and each problem-solving method finally has to be implemented) indicates the necessity of such mechanization. Therefore, we provide a formal notion for problem-solving methods and semi-automatic proof support by using KIV for our purpose. KIV uses an *interactive* tactical theorem prover that makes it suitable for hunting hidden assumptions. We expect many proofs to fail. Using a theorem prover that returns with such a failed attempt adds nothing. Instead of returning with a failure KIV returns with open goals that could not be solved during its proof process. In addition, KIV provides support for the generation of counter examples. This is precisely the kind of support we are looking for when finding and constructing assumptions. As opposed to verification, here one does not start a proof with the goal to prove correctness. Instead, we start an impossible proof and view the proof process as a search and construction process of assumptions. In the following I will call this method *inverse verification*.

We will illustrate this method by discussing small examples that present our ideas clearly and easy to understand. First, we present the search method *hill-climbing* and relate the competence of this local search method with a problem of finding a global optimum. Second, we discuss our version of abductive diagnosis and the kind of assumptions that can be found when trying to solve this problem with a local search method. The reader may argue that we do not discuss problem-solving methods for knowledge-based system but rather simple search methods. However, we would like to mention four arguments:

- The algorithmic core of problem-solving methods consists of simple search methods. Take *propose & revise* ([Marcus et al., 1988], [Schreiber & Birmingham, 1996]) of Chapter 1 as an example. It is a simple local search method with two different modes: proposing extensions of a state and revising a state if constraint violations occur. Therefore, our results can be immediately applied to this type of methods.
- Problem-solving methods achieve their "intelligence" not through complex algorithmic strategies. Instead, they use strong domain heuristics for the search process, restrict the size of the problem they deal with properly, and make ontological commitments so as to be immediately applicable to a specific problem type.

- We will explain how the search methods that we discuss can be adapted to richer contexts constituting task-specific (or problem-type specific) problem-solving methods in Chapter 6.2 and Chapter 7.

- In the following we will derive rather strong assumptions providing local search techniques with the power to solve global search problems. However, it will be sketched how more realistic assumptions reflecting the heuristic nature of problem-solving methods can be found.

6.1.1   First Example: A Local Search Method

Our methods consists of two main steps: (1) Establishing a notion of the competence of a method in dependence on assumptions and (2) relating a competence of a method with a problem definition. Establishing a competence of an operational algorithm specification requires proof techniques of dynamic logic. We have to relate a procedural specification with a first-order specification of its assumptions and competence. For the second step two declarative specifications must be related. The gap between a competence specification and a problem definition has to be closed via assumptions. The specifications and proofs remain within first-order logic by proving implication between first-order formulas.

Establishing the Competence of a Problem-Solving Method in Dependence on Assumptions

Hill-climbing is a local search algorithm that stops when it has found a local optimum. The control flow is defined in Fig. 35. The method works as follows: First, we select a start object. Then we recursively generate the successors of the current object, and select a successor if we find a better one. Otherwise we terminate and return the current object that does not have better successors. The main requirement on *domain knowledge* that are introduced by *hill-climbing* (and by other local search methods) are the existence of a *preference* relationship and a *successor* relationship between the objects. The former is used for selection and the latter is used to enable the local search process. A third requirement is a selection criterion for the start object of the search process. The performance and competence of the method depends on the properties of these three relations (cf. [Graham & Bailor, 1996]).

We tried to prove that *hill-climbing* always terminates and that it has the competence to find a local optimum (see Fig.). KIV automatically generates all proof obligations in dynamic logic that are necessary to ensure termination and competence of an algorithmic specification. In our case it generates the following proof obligations:

$\vdash$ *<hill-climbing(input)>* true, i.e. termination

$\vdash$ *<hill-climbing(input)> output* $\in$ *input*

$\vdash$ *<hill-climbing(input)>* $\neg\exists x . (successor(output,x) \land x \in input \land output < x)$.

Tool support is provided in unfolding these proof obligations and in applying tactics like inductive proofs. In general the user has to select proof tactics and heuristics from a menu. In our case, user interaction is needed to select axioms of a specification as supporting lemmas for the proof and to select the kind of induction We run into a number of open goals during the proofs:

- We had to ensure that *select-criterion* retrieves an object for each possible input. Otherwise one cannot guarantee that *hill-climbing* will provide any output.
- We have to ensure that the preference we use (<) is a partial order. We have to be sure of irreflexivity and transitivity to ensure that *hill-climbing* cannot be caught up in circles (imagine a < b and b < a and a ∈ *successor(b)* and b ∈ *successor(a)*). Also the finiteness of the input set has to be ensured.

Based on these assumptions that were necessary to complete the proofs we could establish a competence of *hill-climbing* as shown in Fig. 36. This proof ensures that *hill-climbing* finds a local optimum of the input.

Relating the Competence of a Problem-Solving Method with a Task

A *task definition* specifies the goals that should be achieved by the knowledge-based system. It establishes an explicit notion of the context in which the problem-solving

---

operational specification *hill-climbing*

   output := hill-climbing(input)

   hill-climbing(X)
      begin
         current := select-start(X);
         output := recursion(current)
      end

   recursion(X)
      begin
         successors := generate(X);
         new := select-a-best(X,successors)
         if *X = new*
            then   *output := X*
            else   *recursion(new)*
         endif
      end

/* *select-start* must select an element of input and uses a selection criterion. */
   select-start(x) ∈ x ∧ select-start(x) ∈ select-criterion(x)

/* *generates* selects input elements that are in a successor relation with the current object.*/
   x ∈ generate(y) ↔ x ∈ input ∧ successor(y,x)

/* *select-a-best* selects the current object if no better successors exist or a successor if a better successor exists. In the latter case the selected successor must be better than the current object and there must not be another successor that is better than the selected successor. */
   $\neg\exists z . (z \in \{y\} \cup y' \wedge select\text{-}a\text{-}best(y,y') < z)$
   $\neg\exists z . (z \in y' \wedge y < z) \rightarrow select\text{-}a\text{-}best(y,y') = y$
   $\exists z . (z \in y' \wedge y < z) \rightarrow select\text{-}a\text{-}best(y,y') \in y' \wedge y < select\text{-}a\text{-}best(y,y'))$

endoperational spec

Fig. 35. The Operational Specification of *hill-climbing*

competence *hill-climbing*
   axioms
      output $\in$ *input*
      $\exists x . (x \in input \land select\text{-}criterion(input) \land (x < output \lor x = output))$
      $\neg\exists x . (successor(output,x) \land x \in input \land output < x)$
endcompetence

requirements
   axioms
      $\exists x. (x \in input \land x \in select\text{-}criterion(input))$
      $\neg(x < x)$
       $x < y \land y < z \rightarrow x < z$
endrequirements

Fig. 36. Competence and Requirements of *hill-climbing*

method is applied. A general context where *hill-climbing* can be applied is in searching for a (global) optimum. Fig. 37 provides the definition for our running example. The goal describes what an optimum must fulfil. However, the problem-solving method *hill-climbing* has only the competence to find a local optimum in a graph. Again, we start the interactive proof process knowing that it will lead us to further assumptions because in general *hill-climbing* does not have the competence to find a global optimum. Two main problems arise during the proof:

1) We would have to prove that the selected start object is always connected with a global optimum (several global optima may exist because we do not require a total order). Otherwise, the global optimum is not attainable by the recursive search of *hill-climbing*.

2) Even if we could prove (1) we may get stuck at the case distinction
    if X = new
where *hill-climbing* stops due to a local optimum.

A trivial assumption that closes both gaps in the proof is to require that each object is directly connected with each other object.

   totally-connected assumption: successor(x,y)

task *global optimum*
   goal
      global-optimum $\in$ *input*
      $\neg\exists x . (x \in input \land global\text{-}optimum < x)$
   requirements
      $\neg(x < x)$
       $x < y \land y < z \rightarrow x < z$
endtask

Fig. 37. The Task Definition *global optimum*

However this is a very useless assumption. In this case, *hill-climbing* collapses to a complete search in one step because all objects are successors of each possible start object. A less drastic assumption is to require that each object (except a global optimum) have a successor with a higher preference.

better-successor assumption:

$$x \in input \rightarrow (\exists y . (y \in input \land successor(x,y) \land x < y) \lor \neg \exists z . (z \in input \land x < z))$$

This assumption is derived to close the gap in the case distinction of the recursion. If the recursion stops we have found a global optimum. We already know from the termination proof of *hill-climbing* that the problem-solving method always terminates.

The question remains as to whether the assumptions are *minimal*. Here, *minimality* means that the assumptions are not only sufficient but also necessary to guarantee that the competence of the problem-solving method implies the problem definition, formally:

$$(PSM_{competence} \rightarrow Task\ Definition) \rightarrow Assumption.$$

An assumption that is *minimal in the logical sense* (i.e., necessary) has the clear advantage that it maximizes the circumstances under which it holds true. It does not require anything more than what is precisely necessary to close the gap between the competence and the problem. In fact, we have proven with KIV that the *better-successor assumption* is a minimal assumption in the logical sense. Actually this proof process leads to several refinements of the original assumption as we encountered several holes during the proof process. However, besides logical minimality other aspects like cognitive minimality (effort in understanding an assumption) or computational minimality (effort in proving an assumption) may influence the choice of assumptions, too. We will illustrate this in the following subsection. In general, minimizing (i.e., weakening) assumptions can be achieved by analyzing their sufficiency proof with KIV and eliminating aspects that are not necessary for continuing the proof. It was easy to prove with KIV that the *better-successor assumption* is weaker than the *totally-connected assumption*.

The two assumptions that we have introduced are rather trivial. This is a consequence of the simplistic example. In the following section we will define a more complex task and problem-solving method which will lead to more interesting assumptions.

6.1.2   Second Example: Finding an Abductive Explanation

In the following, we use our running abductive example from earlier chapters. It asks for a minimal set of hypotheses that explains a set of observations (see Figure 11 and Figure 26) using *set-minimizer* (see Figure 27 - Figure 30) to compute a solution. It receives a set of objects as input and tries to find a minimized version of the set that still fulfils a correctness requirement. The applied search strategy is one-step look ahead. The *competence* states that *set-minimizer* is able to find a *local* minimal subset of the given set of objects. The three axioms of its competence definition in Figure 27 state that it (1) finds a subset that is correct (2), and (3) that each set containing one element less is not a correct set. We skip all proofs that were necessary to establish this competence. Actually one could reuse the proofs that were done for *hill-climbing* based on our *adaptation method* (see Chapter 6.2) and the proof reuse facilities of KIV. By providing a library of reusable problem-solving methods and support in adaptation, their proofs can be reused, too. Therefore, this type of proof that an operational specification of a problem-solving method has some competence (related to a fixed set of assumptions) only has to be done once when introducing the problem-solving method into the library.

The task and problem-solving method become connected by providing the set of all hypotheses as input and identifying correct sets with complete explanations, i.e. *input* := {x | x is a hypothesis} and *correct(x)* ↔ *complete(x)*, see the adapter in Figure 32.

Again the circumstances that ensure that the problem-solving method achieves the goal as introduced by the problem definition have to be investigated. The same procedure can be used again. We try to prove:

- *complete(output)*
- *parsimonious(output)*

Completeness. The completeness of output follows directly from axioms of the competence of the problem-solving method (see Fig. 27). However, it is based on the input requirement of the method. The problem definition of abduction have to be strengthened. The set of all hypothesis (i.e., the input) must be a complete explanation. This puts a strong restriction on the abductive problem: The function *explain* has to be defined in a way that adding hypotheses to a set of hypotheses does not destroy the explanatory power of the set. In fact, the latter property will be established during the proof of parsimony.

Parsimony. The competence of our method ensures local parsimony. Our method *set-minimizer* finds a local-minimal set that is parsimonious in the sense that each subset that contains one element less is not a complete explanation. However, it cannot be guaranteed that it is parsimonious in general. Smaller subsets of it may exist that are complete explanations. The reader may already have realized the similarity with the problem of *hill-climbing* that only finds local optimal elements. However, with the *better-successor assumption* global optima can be found. A natural way to close our gap is therefore to reformulate the *better-successor assumption* and *global optimum* in terms of the new problem. Instantiating the *better-successor assumption* requires the definition of a preference and of a successor relation:

$$x < y :\leftrightarrow explain(x) \subseteq explain(y)$$
$$successor(x,y) :\leftrightarrow \exists z . (z \in x \wedge y = x \setminus \{z\})$$

The *better-successor assumption* can now be reformulated based on these two definitions and of the definition of the input above:

$$x \subseteq hypotheses \rightarrow$$
$$(\exists y . (y \in x \wedge explain(x) \subseteq explain(x \setminus \{y\})))$$
$$\vee \neg \exists z . (z \subseteq hypotheses \wedge explain(x) \subseteq explain(z))$$

However, this is a minimal but not very intuitive assumption. Again we apply our failed-proof technique. We use it now to *generalize* an assumption. The idea is to prove that the *better-successor assumption* holds based on the problem definition, the input requirements and competence of the *set-minimizer* method, as well as the way the preference was defined. KIV returns with open goals that would be necessary to complete the proof. These open goals are generalizations of the *better-successor assumption* because they imply its truth. This proof attempt with KIV is straightforward and gets stuck in the following subgoal:

$y \subset x \wedge$ *explain(x)* $\subseteq$ *explain(y)* $\rightarrow \exists z \ . \ (explain(x) \subseteq explain(x \setminus \{z\})$

This assumptions requires that if there are smaller subsets of x with greater explanatory power then there must be another subset that differs only in one element from x and also has greater explanatory power. A simple generalization of this implication is to negate its premise. That is, we select the strengthening tactic:

$\neg a \vdash a \rightarrow b$

This tactics leads to

$\neg (y \subset x \wedge$ *explain(x)* $\subseteq$ *explain(y)*)),

i.e.,

$y \subset x \rightarrow \neg$ *explain(x)* $\subseteq$ *explain(y)*

This assumption requires that for any set of hypotheses no subset exists that has a larger explanatory power. Deleting a hypothesis from the set of hypotheses may never lead to a superset of explained observations. Actually, this assumption plays a prominent role in the literature on abductive reasoning and model-based diagnosis.

A strengthened version of this assumption is used by [Bylander et al., 1991] to define polynomial subclasses of abduction. In general, abduction is NP-hard in the number of hypotheses. However, with the following monotonic abduction assumption

$y \subset x \rightarrow$ *explain(y)* $\subseteq$ *explain(x)*

[Bylander et al., 1991] prove that it is possible to find a complete and parsimonious explanation in polynomial time. The assumption they use requires that a superset of hypotheses also explains a superset of observations. The assumption is used to restrict the worst-case effort of a method. [de Kleer et al., 1992] examine their role in model-based diagnosis. The assumption holds for applications, where no knowledge that constrains fault behavior of devices is provided or where this knowledge respects the *limited-knowledge-of-abnormal behavior assumption*. This is used by [de Kleer & Williams, 1987] as the *minimal diagnosis hypothesis* to reduce the *average-case effort* of finding all parsimonious and complete explanations with GDE (compare Chapter 2). A syntactical way to ensure this assumption (i.e., to formulate it as a requirement on the domain knowledge) is the restriction of the domain theory to Horn clauses constraining only the correct behavior of devices, cf. [de Kleer et al., 1992].

It is interesting to see how the very generic *better-successor assumption* transforms into such intuitive and broadly used task-specific assumptions.

6.1.3   Heuristic Assumptions

The assumptions introduced so far ensure that a local method solves a global problem. They ensure that a local search method has the same competence as a global search method. However, that is not what we are usually looking for. Often these assumptions are too strong. In addition, we mentioned that GDE uses the monotonic-abduction problem to reduce the average-case behavior of the problem solver. However, we have not yet provided measurements nor proofs of these aspects. This section discusses how both can be integrated.

Domain-Specific Reformulation and Weakening of Assumptions

We introduced the problem-solving method *propose & revise* ([Marcus et al., 1988], [Schreiber & Birmingham, 1996]) in Chapter 1. It is a local search method consisting of two substeps: *Propose* extends a current state and revise modifies the state if constraint violations occur. Both activities are iterated until a complete and correct state is reached. In general, this cannot be guaranteed because *propose & revise* does not include a backtracking mechanism that would allow us to escape a dead-end of the solution process. Completeness of the search method can only be guaranteed if we introduce strong assumptions about the domain knowledge that is used by the *propose* and the *revise* step (see Fig. 38).

[Zdrahal & Motta, 1995] provide an interesting and in-depth analysis of the problem-solving method *propose & revise* and its application to the vertical transportation (VT) domain ([Marcus et al., 1988], [Schreiber & Birmingham, 1996]). The goal is to design an elevator that meets several requirements and constraints. [Zdrahal & Motta, 1995] identify two key parameters in this domain that influence the difficulty of the problem: the capacity and the required *speed* of the elevator. The larger the values of these two parameters the more difficult it is to find a solution. They investigate how *propose & revise* behaves based on the available domain knowledge for different combinations of these two parameter values. The instantiated method failed for some

---

competence *propose & revise*
    axioms
          /* The output is a complete, correct and optimal state. */
              $Complete(output) \land Correct(output) \land$
              $\neg \exists s \,.\, (s \in State \land Complete(s) \land Correct(s) \land output < s)$
    endcompetence

requirements *propose & revise*
    axioms
          /* The propose knowledge never fails and monotonically extends the state. */
              $\neg\, Complete(s) \rightarrow Partial\ completeness(s) < Partial\ completeness(propose(s))$
          /* The application of a propose leads to an optimal state. */
              $\neg\, Complete(s) \rightarrow$
                    $\neg\exists s' \,(s' \in State \land Correct(s') \land propose(s) < s' \land$
                    $Partial\ completeness(s') = Partial\ completeness(propose(s))$
          /* The revise knowledge never fails. */
              $\neg\, Correct(s) \rightarrow Correct(revise(s))$
          /* The application of revise does not change the completeness of a state. */
              $Partial\ completeness(revise(s)) = Partial\ completeness(s)$
          /* The application of revise leads to an optimal state. */
              $\neg\, Correct(s) \rightarrow$
                $\neg\, \exists s' \,(s' \in State \land Correct(s') \land$
                      $Partial\ completeness(revise(s)) = Partial\ completeness(s') \land$
                      $revise(s) < s')$
    endrequirements

Fig. 38. The Competence of *propose & revise* (see [Fensel et al., 1997])

of the simple cases and, not surprisingly, for many of the difficult ones. Some of the difficult ones could be solved by a complete search method, however it required large amount of storage size and computation time. Failures of *propose & revise* in these cases can be accepted because we are looking for a heuristic problem solver that gains efficiency by restriction to the simple cases. Aiming for a complete and efficient problem solver for the general case would define an unsolvable problem. However, *propose & revise* also fails for some of the simple cases and this must be viewed as due to gaps in the domain knowledge provided. The domain knowledge should be strong enough to enable *propose & revise* to find a solution for these cases.

Based on this domain analysis we could weaken our assumptions of Fig. . Instead of requiring that we always have a *propose* and a *revise* step available that find an optimal successor state we could restrict these requirements to the more simple cases. We could define boundaries for the values of the key parameters in the assumptions. Completeness or optimality may only be guaranteed for domain cases having small values for these key parameters. For difficult cases we either have to use a more complex search method with higher demands on storage and time or we have to ask the human expert to solve them. An according case study for classification methods is described [van Harmelen & ten Teije, 1998].

Specification and Verification Including Thresholds for the Computational Effort

The assumptions of problem-solving methods are motivated by the goal of improving the efficiency of the assumption-based reasoning process compared to a reasoning process using less assumptions. However, we have not yet provided means to specify and verify the efficiency of problem-solving methods. [Shaw, 1989] and [Straatman & Beys, 1995] describe means that can be integrated into our framework. [Shaw, 1989] includes counters and boundaries for the values of these counters into the specification of real-time software. Precisely the same can be done for problem-solving methods. In the case of *hill-climbing* we can add a counter for the number of successors that are derived and compared in one step and a second counter for the number of steps. Then, we can formulate boundaries for their combined value and formulate this in terms of assumptions that either introduce requirements on the domain knowledge or restrict the set of problems that are solved by *hill-climbing* (i.e., *hill-climbing* terminates after it has consumed its computational time). Using this direction, work on anytime algorithms [Zilberstein, 1996] could be integrated into the work on problem-solving methods.

In general, such refinements of specifications by using measurements allow more refined assumptions on the search graph that is used by the search methods. [Stefik, 1995] provides informal examples for such refined assumptions for different variants of different problem-solving methods in what he calls symbol-level analysis of problem-solving methods. For example, he discusses the circumstances under which data-directed search, solution-directed search, and opportunistic search are preferable for classification methods. Each search type requires some knowledge types with specific properties to perform well (i.e., effectively *and* efficiently).

6.1.4   Related Work

> "The problem of performing deduction of new facts from a set of axioms is well-studied and understood. An equally important but far less explored problem is the derivation of hypotheses to explain observed events. In formal terms this involves finding an *assumption* that, together with some axioms, implies a given formula." [Cox & Pietrzykowski, 1986]

[de Kleer, 1986] describes a truth-maintenance system (ATMS) that could in principle be applied to our problem. Actually most of the approaches to model-based diagnosis we discussed in Chapter 2 use adaptations of this technique. However, applying this technique introduces two strong (meta-)assumptions:

- All the assumptions required to solve the gap between the goals of the task and the competence of the PSM must already be known and provided to the system.
- The system needs to know the impacts of the assumptions, i.e. their influence on the truth of the formulas describing the competence of the problem-solving method and the goals of the task.

If this complete knowledge is available, establishing the proper set of assumptions boils down to selecting a minimal set of assumptions, and a bookkeeping mechanism like ATMS can process this task. When such a complete set of assumptions does not exist, finding assumptions is rather a constructive activity.

Constructive approaches to derive such assumptions can be found in program debugging with inductive techniques (cf. [Shapiro, 1982], [Lloyd, 1987]), explanation-based learning (cf. [Minton et al., 1989], [Minton, 1995]) or more generally in inductive logic programming ([Muggleton & Buntine, 1988], [Muggleton & De Raedt, 1994]). However, these approaches achieve automatization by making strong (meta-) assumption about the syntactical structure of the representation formalisms of the components, the representations of the "error", and the way an error can be fixed. Usually, Prolog or Horn logic is the assumed representation formalism and errors or counter-examples are represented by a set of input-output tuples or a finite set of ground literals. Modification is done by changing the internal specification of a component. In this scenario, error detection boils down to backtracking a resolution-based derivation tree for a "wrong" literal. However, we have to aim for new formulas (i.e., an assumption may be represented by a complex first-order formula) and our "counter-examples" are not represented by a set of ground literals but by a complex first-order specification. Again most of the approaches mentioned do not regard architectural descriptions of the entire reasoning system. An exception are the approaches to explanation-based learning that use explicit architecture axioms [Minton, 1995].

We distinguished two roles of assumptions. First, they are necessary to ensure that a problem-solving method has a specific competence. For example, without the assumption that the preference relation is a partial order the termination proof of *hill-climbing* would not be possible. Second, they are necessary to ensure that the competence of a problem-solving method is able to achieve a goal as introduced by a problem definition. For example, with the *better-successor assumption* we can prove that the competence of *hill-climbing* is strong enough to find a global optimum. Both roles differ conceptually and technically.

The first aspect has to be examined when establishing a problem-solving method in a library of reusable elements. Such elements must be reliable in the sense that they guarantee some competence and the conditions necessary to provide this competence. Technically, it is a proof that concerns the algorithmic structure of the method. Therefore, dynamic logic is used to specify the algorithm and the proof obligations are formulas in dynamic logic.

Assumptions → <Operational Specification> true
Assumptions → [Operational Specification] Competence

Finding weakest preconditions for an algorithm has a long tradition in software engineering (cf. the wp calculus [Dijkstra, 1975] and predicate transformers [Chandy & Sanders, 1995]). Since the dynamic logic we use can be regarded as a generalization of Hoare-triples we can employ methods and techniques developed in this area (cf. e.g. the B-Toolkit [Wordsworth, 1996] or Z/EVES [Meisels & Saaltink, 1996]).

However, the second aspect has a different purpose and requires different techniques. Here we are looking for assumptions that ensure that the competence of the method implies the problem definition, i.e.

Assumptions → (Competence → Problem Definition)

That is, we relate two declarative specifications, the functionality of the system and the specification of the required functionality. Assumptions are used to split the required functionality into two parts. One part that is solved by the competence of the problem-solving method (in the case that the assumptions holds) and one part that is only assumed to be solved. That is, this part is either solved by the domain knowledge, by an external possible human agent, or it must be viewed as a restriction of the class of solvable problems. We argued that our problem-solving methods can only provide a limited fragment of the entire functionality because of the intractability of typical problems they are applied to. In software engineering, a different point of view is usually taken. One assumes that the specification of the functionality of the system is also the specification of the required functionality. In this setting, our assumption hunting method makes no sense because the distinction between the two different specifications and their relationship are not present.

6.2   Stepwise Adaptation of Problem-Solving Methods

In the following, a principled way of developing and adapting problem-solving methods to different contexts is shown. This is mainly achieved by using *adapters* as a means to express the refinement of problem-solving methods. *Adapters* were originally introduced in section II to allow the independent specifications of task definitions, problem-solving methods, and domain knowledge. Building knowledge-based systems from reusable elements requires adapters that properly link these elements and adapt them to the application-specific circumstances. Because these elements should be reusable, they must abstract from application-specific circumstances and because they are specified independently from each other there is a need to introduce their mappings. Introduced as glue that brings other elements together *they will now play a central role in refining problem-solving methods.* Actually, a refined version of a problem-solving method is achieved by combining it with an adapter.

The stepwise introduction of adapters can be used to stepwise refine generic problem-solving methods. Three processes are supported by our approach:

- the *terminological structure of states* of a method can be refined by introducing ontological commitments;

- the terminological structure of states can be used to refine *state transitions* of a method; and

- *assumptions* can be introduced to link the competence of a method with problem definitions and domain knowledge.

Again we use examples to illustrate our ideas. A generic algorithmic schema for local search is introduced. First this schema is refined to *hill-climbing* via an adapter. A second adapter is used to refine *hill-climbing* into the *set-minimizer* method. The general search strategy always remains the same, but the ontological commitments of the methods become refined. States and state transitions are described with an enriched vocabulary. A further adapter transforms this method into a method for abductive diagnosis (by adding additional ontological requirements). Besides adding ontological commitments, it is necessary to add assumptions to close the gap between a method and a problem. Adapters will be discussed that ensure that these methods can be applied to problems that define a global optimum and it is shown how this leads to a refinement of problem definitions and assumptions similar to the refinement of problem-solving methods. Finally, a discussion on generalizations and limitations of our approach is provided.

6.2.1   Local Search

The description of the development process of a problem-solving method is started with a very generic search schema. In the following sections this schema will become refined. However, we do not make a commitment to this top-down development process. The process can start at any level of specialization and can take the direction of specialization or generalization because we provide a library containing these generic schemas and their adaptations. *Specialization* is achieved by adding an adapter to an existing problem-solving method adapter combination and *generalization* is achieved by deleting an adapter from an existing problem-solving method adapter combination.

[Smith & Lowry, 1990] present a theory of search algorithms to support the transformation of problem definitions into implementations. Fig. 39 shows their hierarchy of search methods providing local search as an instance of *generate & test* like approaches working on local structures. The general algorithmic structure of a local search graph can be described by an initialization and a recursion that parses the local search structure. Fig. provides the definition of such a generic search strategy. It can be used to describe *breadth-first search, depth-first search, hill-climbing, beam search* etc. This generic specification will be the backbone of all our examples in the following. All other refined versions will be achieved by combining it with adapters.

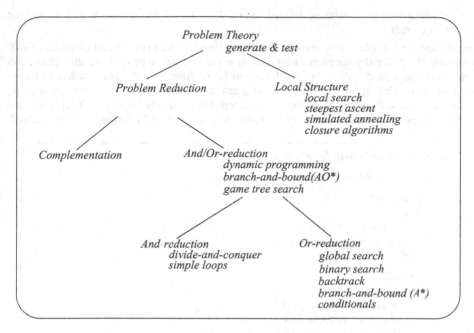

Fig. 39. Refinement Hierarchy of Algorithm Theories [Smith & Lowry, 1990]

6.2.2   Hill-Climbing

Fig. already provided an operational specification of *hill-climbing*. However, we can achieve the same effect by defining an adapter for the generic local search schema of Fig. 40. This adapter has to refine the definitions of the elementary state transitions (i.e., inference actions in terms of CommonKADS) of the method. Axioms have to be added to the definitions of these relations. The adapter that achieves this refinement is provided in Fig. 41.

Hill-climbing refines the generic local search strategy. The output is a local optimal element, however this method is still very generic and can be applied to nearly any type of task. In the next step we will specialize this method to the *set-minimizer* method.

6.2.3   Set-Minimizer

We already presented *set-minimizer* that can be used to find a minimal but still correct subset of a given set (see Fig. 12 and Fig. 27). It returns a correct set that is local minimal in the sense that there is no correct subset that has one element less. This method is obviously a local search method specialized for a specific type of problems. *Set-minimizer* refines *hill-climbing* with the following refinements:

- A generic object of *hill-climbing* is a set in *set-minimizer*. That is, *set-minimizer* adds additional ontological commitments used to characterize states of the search process.

- The successor relationship is hard-wired in *set-minimizer*. A set is a successor of another set if it is a subset with one less element. The ontological commitment which refines state characterizations (i.e, characterizing a state with a set) is used to refine the definition of state transitions.

- A preference of entities is defined implicitly. Smaller sets are preferred if they are still correct.

Set-minimizer describes only one of several possible problem-specific adaptations of *hill-climbing*. Traditionally for each variant the specification has to be re-done, all termination and correctness proofs of the method have to be re-done, and the method has to be re-implemented. Our approach provides adapters as means to add the problem-specific refinement to *hill-climbing*, allowing to keep both aspects separate. Therefore, the complete specifications, proofs, and implementations of *hill-climbing* can be reused.

operational specification *local search*

   output := local search(input)

   local search(X)
      begin
         currents := select$_1$(X);
         output := resursion(currents)
      end

   recursion(X)
      begin
         successors := generate(X);
         new := select$_2$(X,successors)
         if $X = new$
            then   *output := select$_3$(X)*
            else   *recursion(new)*
         endif
      end

/* *select$_1$* must select elements of *input*. */
   select$_1$(x) $\subseteq x$

/* *generates* selects input elements that are in successor relation with the current objects.*/
   $x \in generate(y) \leftrightarrow x \in input \land \exists z . (z \in y \land successor(z,x))$

/* *select$_2$* selects a subset of objects from the union of two sets. The new object set must be constructed in a way that no better objects remain unselected. That is, if we select x and there is a y that is better than x we also have to select y. *select$_2$* selects at least one *object*. */
   $select_2(y,y') \subseteq y \cup y'$
   $\neg \exists x,z . (z \in ((y \cup y') \setminus select_2(y,y')) \land x \in select_2(y,y') \land x < z)$
   $y \cup y' \neq \emptyset \rightarrow \exists x . (x \in select_2(y,y'))$

/* *select$_3$* behaves as *select$_2$*, but specialized local search variants may refine them differently. */
   $select_3(y) \subseteq y$
   $\neg \exists x,z . (z \in (y \setminus select_3(y)) \land x \in select_3(y) \land x < z)$
   $y \neq \emptyset \rightarrow \exists x . (x \in select_3(y))$

endoperational spec

Fig. 40. The Specifications of *local search*

Only the problem-specific aspects have to be specified, proven and implemented by an adapter. Fig. provides the definition of such an adapter. Its main proof obligation is that the way the preference is defined fulfills the requirement on such a relation (i.e., transitivity and irreflexivity).

By keeping the problem-specific refinement separate from the generic core of the method it is easy to overcome the so-called usability/reusability trade-off of problem-solving methods [Klinker et al., 1991]. The original version of *hill-climbing* can be reused for different problems requiring different kinds of refinement. The combination of *hill-climbing* and the *set-minimizer* adapter can be used for problems that can be expressed in terms of minimizing sets. This combined version is less reusable but much more usable for cases it can directly be applied to. For achieving a problem-specific variant of a method it is not necessary to change the method itself. Instead, a problem-specific adapter is added. These adapters can also be stapled to increase the problem specificity of methods. We will show this in the following section where we adapt *set-minimizer* to abductive diagnosis.

6.2.4   Abductive Diagnosis

In Chapter 3, we discussed the task *abductive diagnosis* (see Fig. 11) and described the problem-specific refinement of *set-minimizer*. For reasons of convenience the adapter is repeated in Fig. 41. Assumptions ensure that the output of *set-minimizer* is a complete and parsimonious explanation. First, we have to require that the input of the method is a

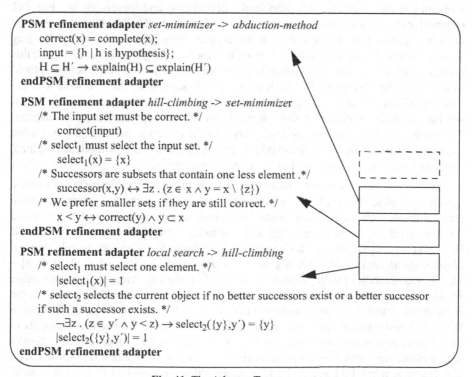

PSM refinement adapter *set-mimimizer -> abduction-method*
   correct(x) = complete(x);
   input = {h | h is hypothesis};
   $H \subseteq H' \rightarrow$ explain(H) $\subseteq$ explain(H')
endPSM refinement adapter

PSM refinement adapter *hill-climbing -> set-mimimizer*
   /* The input set must be correct. */
     correct(input)
   /* select$_1$ must select the input set. */
     select$_1$(x) = {x}
   /* Successors are subsets that contain one less element .*/
     successor(x,y) $\leftrightarrow \exists z . (z \in x \land y = x \setminus \{z\})$
   /* We prefer smaller sets if they are still correct. */
     x < y $\leftrightarrow$ correct(y) $\land$ y $\subset$ x
endPSM refinement adapter

PSM refinement adapter *local search -> hill-climbing*
   /* select$_1$ must select one element. */
     |select$_1$(x)| = 1
   /* select$_2$ selects the current object if no better successors exist or a better successor
   if such a successor exists. */
     $\neg \exists z . (z \in y' \land y < z) \rightarrow$ select$_2$({y},y') = {y}
     |select$_2$({y},y')| = 1
endPSM refinement adapter

Fig. 41. The Adapter Tower

complete explanation. Second, the *monotonicity assumption* (cf. Chapter 6.1) is sufficient to prove that global parsimony follows from its local parsimony.

6.2.5   Generalization and Limitation of Refinement with Adapters

The derivation of a refined problem-solving method for abductive problems from a generic local search frame via adapters was shown in three steps:

- $hill\text{-}climbing := \text{Adapter}_{local\text{-}search \to hill\text{-}climbing}(local\ search)$
- $set\text{-}minimizer := \text{Adapter}_{hill\text{-}climbing \to set\text{-}mimimizer}(hill\text{-}climbing)$
- $abductive\ method := \text{Adapter}_{set\text{-}mimimizer \to abductive\text{-}method}(set\text{-}minimizer)$

The first adapter refines mainly the definition of state transitions of the method. The second adapter refines the notion of states to sets and state transition by defining a successor relationship between sets. The third adapter adds some simple terminological mappings that express the method in terms of abduction and adds assumptions that guarantee that the methods achieves the goal as it is introduced by the problem definition.

In the same way in which we refined problem-solving methods we can also refine task definitions and assumptions necessary to link problem-solving methods and problem definitions. In Chapter 6.1 it was shown that the monotonicity assumption is a problem-specific refinement of an assumption that is necessary and sufficient to prove that *hill-climbing* finds a global optimum. Therefore, it is not only possible to refine problem-solving methods but also task definitions and assumptions. Fig. 42 summarizes the task definitions, assumptions and methods. The black arrows describe the development path we described in the chapter. However, as shown by the gray arrows, we could have refined *hill-climbing* to a method for global optima, refined this method to a method that finds global-minimal but correct sets and this method refined to a method for abduction. For both paths, the dimension of this refinement is the *ontological commitments* made by problem definition, assumptions and problem-solving methods. Notice that these specializations are kept separate via adapters. Therefore, it is always possible to reuse very specific or very generic entities A unified view on problem definitions, assumptions, and problem-solving methods is obtained, where the refinements have a *virtual* existence via adapters.

We view problem-solving methods as task or problem-specific refinements of generic search strategies. However this refinement concerns the characterizations of states, elementary state transitions, and assumptions about specific properties of concepts and relations used to characterize states and transitions. Take the *board-game method* [Eriksson et al., 1995] as an example. It refines the generic search method *chronological backtracking* for one-player board games. In [Fensel et al., 1996b] a formal specification of both methods is analyzed for their differences. It is interesting to note that the *board-game method* does not change the overall control, i.e. the algorithmic structure of *chronological backtracking*. It refines the notion of states in terms of board positions (chronological backtracking does not make commitments to the internal structure of the states it searches through) and uses this refined notion to define elementary state transitions in terms of *moves* that change board positions. As a consequence, it can be more easily (i.e., more efficiently) applied to tasks it is well-

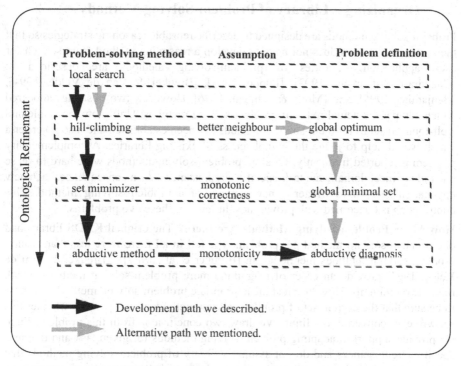

Fig. 42. Refining Problem-Solving Methods, Assumptions and Task Definitions

suited for like the Sisyphus-I assignment problem [Linster, 1994]. Our approach supports precisely these kinds of refinement processes. Developing new generic search procedures or gaining efficiency by algorithmic optimization techniques applied to its overall control structure is beyond its scope. We restrict our attention to assumptions that formulate requirements on domain knowledge or that restrict the problem size and on ontological commitments that improve the efficiency in applying the method to a given application domain and problem. Both are usually beyond the scope of approaches that look for generic optimization because these assumptions and commitments cannot be made in the generic case. Such assumptions reflect specific domain-type or problem-type specific circumstances.

Our approach is complementary to approaches that investigate generic control regimes (see [Bundy, 1990] for a survey of search techniques). Such work can be used by our approach to introduce different starting points for our refinement process like the local search scheme used here. Also, our approach is complementary to the algorithmic optimization methods like the KIDS/SPECWARE approach that refines the control, i.e. the algorithmic structure, to gain efficiency (cf. [Smith, 1996], [Juellig et al., 1996a]). However, they provide valuable support for refining a specification of a problem-solving method into an efficient implementation.

7   Organizing a Library of Problem-Solving Methods

Problem-solving methods are designed to describe reusable reasoning strategies so that the system developers does not have to develop a reasoning method from scratch for each application. Libraries of problem-solving methods are described in [Chandrasekaran et al., 1992], [Puppe, 1993], [Breuker & Van de Velde, 1994], [Benjamins, 1995], and [Motta & Zdrahal, 1996]. However, two obstacles appeared which hamper the actual reuse of problem-solving methods: Until now, no stable and well-founded set of problem-solving methods has been established and also no criteria which would help to judge the completeness of existing libraries. A complementary problem is reported frequently: Existing problem-solving methods were hard to reuse and did not meet domain and task-specific circumstances. As a consequence, each new application seemed to trigger a new version of a problem-solving method. This contribution is concerned with providing solutions for these two problems.

How Many Problem-Solving Methods Are there? The original KADS library had one problem-solving method per problem type (all in all there were less than twenty problem-solving methods mentioned in [Breuker et al., 1987]). [Breuker & Van de Velde, 1994] provide an order of magnitude more problem-solving methods which raises two problems: How to select the appropriate problem-solving methods and how to be sure that the current set of problem-solving methods is complete or whether this set will ever converge to a limit. We draw two conclusions from this problem. First, we provide support in adapting problem-solving methods for given task and domain-specific circumstances and do not assume a library of problem-solving methods that must provide a solution for any application problem and all its specific circumstances. We bypass the completeness problem by enabling easy adaptation. This support in adapting problem-solving methods is also support in developing problem-solving methods for inclusion in a library. Second, we provide more abstract descriptions of problem-solving methods. Therefore we bypass the problem of having too many elements in our library. Our problem-solving methods are frameworks that can be refined later. This leads to our answer to the second question as to why existing problem-solving methods are so hard to reuse.

Why Are Existing Problem-Solving Methods so Hard to Reuse? The literature on problem-solving methods is full of concerns that a problem-solving method developed for one task may also be suitable for other task (however cannot be applied to it because of hardwired problem descriptions) and, conversely, that different problem-solving methods with completely different control regiments may be applicable to the same type of tasks. Current libraries of problem-solving methods interweave these different dimensions (i.e., the control and the problem). We *separate* these issues by identifying different dimensions for developing and describing problem-solving methods to overcome this bottleneck. In consequence, reuse of the different parts of a problem-solving method becomes possible. We distinguish algorithmic schemes, state structures, and inferences. Therefore they can be reused independently from each other as well as in some specific combinations reflecting specific assumptions in regard to the problem type and the domain knowledge available for inferences and control. Therefore, we do not only aim at support for developing and adapting problem-solving methods but also at improving the reusability of existing problem-solving methods.

Dieter Fensel: Problem-Solving Methods, LNAI 1791, pp. 116 - 128, 2000.
© Springer-Verlag Berlin Heidelberg 2000

In the following a case study illustrating our approach will be described. The point of departure is a generic algorithmic scheme describing local search and we will add stepwise refinements until we achieve a set of specialized methods for parametric design. Instead of using the block-world examples of earlier chapters the problem-solving method library for parametric design of [Motta, 1999] is described, which has been applied in a number of technical design problems (office allocation problem, elevator design, sliding bearing design, problems of simple mechanics, initial vehicle (truck) design, design and selection of casting technologies, and sheet metal forming technology for manufacturing mechanical parts [Motta, 1999]). First, a short introduction to the key ideas of our approach is provided. Then, the stepwise development of a set of problem-solving methods for parametric design is shown. We start with a local search scheme and stepwise refine the data structure it is working on. Then, we focus on refining the state transitions of the method, i.e. we refine its inference actions. Assumptions about available knowledge and the problem-specific refinements of the state descriptions will be used to define state transitions more precisely.

7.1   The Three Dimensions in Method Organization

Problem-solving methods for knowledge-based systems are knowledge-level descriptions of effective and efficient procedures that solve the problems the knowledge-based system is designed for by utilitizing the provided knowledge. In consequence a problem-solving method consists of three ingredients.

- a *problem-solving paradigm* that decomposes a task into subtasks and introduces control in their execution in order to proceed with the entire task;

- *ontological commitments* to the *type of problem* that is solved by the problem-solving method;

- *assumptions on knowledge* that is necessary to realize the inference process.

Clearly identifying and separating the problem-solving paradigm, problem commitments, and knowledge requirements enables a principled way to develop a problem-solving method and to structure libraries of problem-solving methods that enable their reuse. Current approaches to problem-solving methods usually glue these different aspects together and encounter problems when characterizing the main rationale of such methods, when trying to define a rational framework for developing such methods, and when trying to reuse them. We present the development and adaptation of problem-solving methods as a navigation process in a three-dimensional space defined by *problem-solving paradigms; problem-specific definition* of the state and the state transitions; and requirements on the availability of *knowledge* introduced by the elementary state transitions. The overall structure of the navigation space is shown in Fig. 43. Each paradigm defines a two-dimensional space for the further refinement according to problem type and the assumed knowledge types.

Problem-Solving Paradigms. Problem-solving paradigms are high-level descriptions which describe a type of problem solving rather than an actual algorithm. They fix some basic data structures, elementary state transitions, and (optionally) a generic control regime. Examples for such algorithmic schemes are: generate & test, local search, problem reduction etc. [Smith & Lowry, 1990]. Such paradigms can be ordered in a hierarchy to define more structure. Such schemes are necessarily vague in the sense that they define only a basic control regime and some very basic data structures required by this regime.

Problem Type (i.e., Task). The ontological commitments introduced by a problem type can be used to refine the competence, the structure of each search state in the search space and the nature of state transitions carried out by a problem-solving method. Thus a generic search method can be transformed into a more specific method for model-based diagnosis or parametric design. A problem-specific refinement of a method is still reusable because it is formulated independently of any domain. That is, the method may be applicable to technical or medical diagnostic problems. However, it is limited to a specific type of problem. The advantage of instantiating search spaces in a task-specific way is that the resulting model provides much stronger support for knowledge acquisition and application development than a task-independent one.

Assumptions on Domain Knowledge. Assumptions are introduced by the state transitions of a method or may be necessary to relate the competence of the method to the given problem (i.e., they are introduced by the state transition that describes the entire method). Assumptions about available domain knowledge are necessary to enable efficient problem solving for complex and intractable problems. They describe parts of the problem solving that remain external to the problem-solving method. It is either

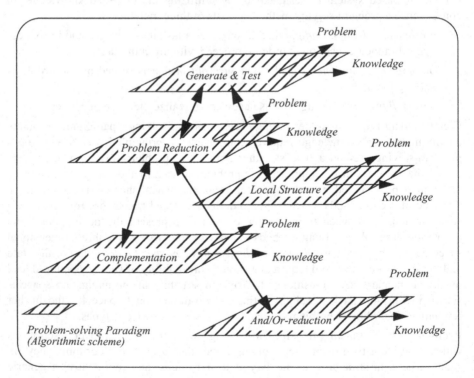

Fig. 43. The Navigation Space for Developing Problem-Solving Methods

assumed that they will be solved by the provided knowledge or that they are irrelevant parts of the problem that need not be solved by the knowledge-based system.

The nature of the navigation process itself differs in respect to the dimension of the development process.

- Moving through the dimension of algorithmic schemes from one problem-solving paradigm to another is *not necessarily structure preserving*. In fact, changing the problem-solving paradigm is a revolutionary act that creates new structures in the problem-solving process. However, we will later see an example for a significant structure-preserving refinement of a search paradigm. An adapter can refine local search either to a *hill-climbing* or a best-first type of search.

- Moving in the direction of refining the problem type or the assumptions on knowledge is a *structure-preserving* activity. Because these movements do not change the structure of the problem-solving methods they can be described by *external* means that refine the atomic data structures and state transitions of a problem-solving method. In fact, these external descriptions transform such an atomic description into a complex one with an internal structure. Adapters can be used to stepwise refine these elements. A problem-solving method can be successively refined for a specific problem by plugging a number of adapters on top of it.

By keeping these refinements *external* in an adapter the problem-solving method can be reused at a more generic or more specific level. The adaptations according to one of the different dimensions problem-solving paradigm, task, and domain knowledge, do not get mixed up. Instead, each aspects is clearly separated and can be treated independently.

7.2   Deriving Task-Specific Problem-Solving Methods

The overall picture of refining the problem specificity of a generic search method is provided in Fig. 44. On the left side we refine the problem definition and on the right side we refine the problem-solving paradigm that guides the problem-solving process. The virtual elements do not require a specification because these specifications follow from a combination of an existing specification and an adapter. However, for convenience, a library may also directly provide these derived specifications.

Defining and Refining the Problem. We start with the general design problem described in terms of requirements, constraints, and cost. Then we add specific terminology for parametric design. We introduce $adapter_1$ that adds parameters and value ranges to the definition of the design problem. The definition of the problem type parametric design is provided by the adapter that imports the problem type design. There are two reasons for separating the definition of the design problem and the parametric design problem:

- The definitions of the generic design problem can be reused for other types of design problems.

- The definitions of the generic design problems can be used to define problem-solving methods for design tasks that do not hardwire specific assumptions of parametric design.

Defining and Refining the Problem-Solving Method. We start with the algorithmic scheme local search that defines the common pattern of all problem-solving methods of [Motta, 1999]. By including the definitions of the problem type design via *adapter$_2$* we obtain an initial refinement of this scheme for design problems and, with *adapter$_3$*, a refinement for parametric design problems.

Three adapters will be used to come up with an initial, still very abstract, method for parametric design. Later the inferences that guide the search process will be further

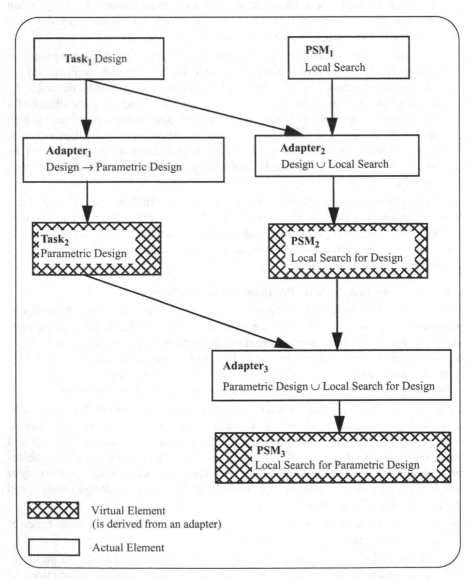

Fig. 44. The Development Graph of a Problem-Solving Method for Parametric Design

refined. However, in the current section we focus on refining the state description based on the problem type.

7.2.1   Problem Type Design

Design can be characterized in generic terms as the process of constructing artifacts. Usually, a constructed artifact should fulfill certain requirements, should not violate certain constraints, and should follow the principle of economy, i.e. should have minimal cost, (cf. [Mittal & Frayman, 1989], [Chandrasekaran, 1990]). A design problem can be characterized according to Fig. 45. The problem solving is not allowed to redefine any of these invariant parts. That is, complex design problems which include meta-level reasoning about weakening constraints, requirements, or cost expectations is beyond its scope.

7.2.2   Local Search

[Motta, 1999] describes a library of different methods for parametric design. Each of these methods shares a common, highly generic, control regime. A generalized version of this control regime independent of the problem type is presented in Fig. 46. Basically, LocalSearch initializes the search process and RecursiveSearch searches until a solution has been found. They define the scheme of local search. The local transition between the states that are searched through is performed by DeriveSuccessorNodes. SelectNode selects a new node for that successors are derived. Finally UpdateNodes decides (in combination with SelectNode) about the kind of local search. We will see below that it defines a best-first search when it updates the Nodes by the union of Nodes and SuccessorNodes and it defines *hill-climbing* when it updates the Nodes only by the SuccessorNodes.

---

task$_1$ Design
   sorts
        DesignModel, Constraint, Requirement, Cost,
        Constraints : set of Constraint, Requirements : **set of** *Requirement;*
   constants
        Goal : DesignModel;
   functions
        violated : DesignModel → Constraints;
        fulfilled : DesignModel → Requirements;
        cost : DesignModel → Cost;
   predicates
        consistent, optimal, suitable, valid , solution : DesignModel;
   axioms
        solution(goal) ∧ optimal(goal)
        solution(x) ↔ valid(x) ↔ consistent(x) ∧ suitable(x)
        consistent(x) ↔ violated(x) = ∅
        suitable(x) ↔ ∀ y (y ∈ fulfilled(x))
        optimal(x) ↔ ¬ ∃ y (cost(y) < cost(x))
   endtask

Fig. 45. Problem Type Design

7.2.3   Local Search as Design Problem Solving

Adapter$_2$ transforms the generic search method into a method for solving design problems (see Fig. 47). Basically, it introduces the term *design model* into the method and defines an OptimalSolution in terms of the task. Still the method is not very operational because we do not know how to select design models, how to derive successor designs, and how to update the set of designs. These aspects will be clarified in Section 7.3. At the moment, further information about parametric design will be given.

PSM$_1$ Local Search

/* There are some simplifications to report: We ignore the case when SelectNode does not deliver an output and when DeriveSuccessorNodes does not deliver an output. In consequence we only terminate when we have found a solution and we do not terminate for intermediate empty inputs. */

control flow

> *LocalSearch()*
> > /* *Initializes and starts the search.* */
> > *Nodes:= Initialize();*
> > *Output := RecursiveSearch(Nodes)*
>
> *RecursiveSearch(Nodes)*
> > /* *Searches.* */
> > *Node := SelectNode(Nodes);*
> > *SuccessorNodes := DeriveSuccessorNodes(Node);*
> > *Nodes := UpdateNodes(Nodes, SuccessorNodes);*
> > IF *OptimalSolution(x) for a x ∈ Nodes*
> > > THEN RETURN *these x's*
> > > ELSE *RecursiveSearch(Nodes)*
> > ENDIF

sorts
> *Object, Objects : **set of** Object;*

functions
> *Node : Object;*
> *Nodes, Output, SuccessorNodes : Objects;*

prediactes
> *OptimalSolution : Object;*

elementary inferences
> *DeriveSuccessorNodes,*
> *Initialize,*
> *SelectNode,*
> *UpdateNodes*

Fig. 46. Problem-Solving Local Search

7.2.4   Problem Type Parametric Design

Configuration design is a restricted class of design problems, which can be defined as design problems where all building blocks are given as input to the design process [Mittal & Frayman, 1989]. A stronger assumption, which further restricts the space of possible designs is that which postulates the existence of a parametrized solution template for the target artifact. In this scenario, design problem solving can be described as the process of assigning values to design parameters in accordance with the given needs, constraints, and desires. Applications for which this assumption holds are called parametric design applications. The VT elevator design problem (cf. [Marcus et al., 1988], [Schreiber & Birmingham, 1996]) provides a well-known example of a parametric design task. Here the problem is to configure an elevator in accordance with the given requirements specification and the applicable constraints. The parametrized solution template consists of 199 design parameters which specify the various structural and functional aspects of an elevator - e.g. number of doors, speed, load, etc.

Adapter$_1$ refines the definition of the design problem to parametric design (see Fig. 48). A parametric design problem introduces parameters and parameter value ranges as a means to describe a design model. Therefore, it extends the definition of a design problem using a set of parameters and a set of value ranges. This extended terminology can be used to define the structure of a design model and to introduce further requirements for a solution of a parametric design problem. A design model can now be defined as a partial function:

$$ParametricDesignModel : Parameter \rightarrow ValueRange_1 \cup ... \cup ValueRange_n$$

where $ParametricDesignModel(p_i) \in ValueRange_i$ for all i=1,..,n;

Also, we get a completeness characterization of design models and solutions. A solution to the parametric design problem is a *valid* and *complete* design model, i.e. it has to assign a value to each parameter.

adapter$_2$ **(Design $\cup$ Local Search $\rightarrow$ Local Search for Design)**
  import
    Problem Type Design,
    Problem Solving Local Seach;
  export
    Problem-Solving Local Seach forDesign;
  terminology mapping
    Object $\rightarrow$ DesignModel;
  axioms
    $\forall x \, (OptimalSolution(x) \leftrightarrow optimal(x) \wedge solution(x)$
  endadapter

Fig. 47. Problem-Solving Local Search for Design

adapter₁ (Design → Parametric Design)
   import
      Problem Type Design;
   export
      Problem Type Parametric Design;
   terminology mapping
      DesignModel → ParametricDesignModel;
   sorts
      Parameter = {$p_1,...,p_n$},
      Parameters : **set of** *Parameter,*
      $ValueRange_1$, ..., $ValueRange_n$;
   functions
      ParametricDesignModel : Parameter → $ValueRange_1$ ∪ ... ∪ $ValueRange_n$
         where DesignModel(p_i) ∈ $ValueRange_i$ for all i=1,..,n;
      assigned : ParametricDesignModel → Parameters;
   predicates
      complete : ParametricDesignModel;
   axioms
      $solution_{Export}(x)$ ↔ $solution_{Import}(x)$ ∧ complete(x);
      complete(x) ↔ ∀ y (y ∈ assigned(x));
endadapter

Fig. 48. Problem Type Parametric Design

7.2.5   Local Search as Parametric Design Problem Solving

Adapting the problem-solving frame to parametric design requires nothing more than importing the problem type *Parametric Design* and the problem solving *Local Search for Design* and exporting the problem solving *Local Search for Parametric Design.*

7.3   Variating the Problem-Solving Paradigm

Up to now, the local search strategy remained rather unspecific. The character of the search process is determined by the four inference steps:

- Initialize which selects the initial design model;
- SelectNode which selects the design model that is to be investigated later when it is used to derive successor models;
- DeriveSuccessorNodes which actually derives the successor models of the design model selected; and
- UpdateNodes which provides the input for the selection step of SelectNode.

Assumptions on the available knowledge used by these inferences can be used to refine the search process. We start the discussion with DeriveSuccessorNodes because its definition in [Motta, 1999] has the strongest commitment to the problem type.

```
adapter (Problem-Solving Parametric Design → Problem-Solving Parametric Design)
    Import
        Problem-Solving Parametric Design;
    export
        Problem-Solving Parametric Design;
    sorts
        Context, Focus, Transformation,
        History : set of (Context x Focus x Transformation);
    Program
        DeriveSuccessorNodes(DesignModel)
            Context := DecideOverContext(DesignModel);
            Focus := DecideOverFocus(DesignModel, Context);
            Transformation:= DecideOverTransformation(DesignModel, Context, Focus);
            Bookmark Context, Focus, and Transformation in History of DesignModel;
            DesignModels := ApplyTransformation(DesignModel, Transformation);
            RETURN DesignModels
endadapter
```

Fig. 49. Refining DeriveSuccessorNodes

7.3.1   Derive Successor Candidates

DeriveSuccessorNodes of [Motta, 1999] uses a rather complex three step procedure instead of directly using a successor relationship between nodes as in the case of an abstract definition of local search in Chapter 6.1. First, a context is derived from the node, second a focus is derived within the context, and third a transformation operator is derived within this focus. The transformation operator then provides the successor relationship between nodes. The procedure that refines DeriveSuccessorNodes is provided in Fig. 49. The use of the three-step selection process is motivated by the structure of the problem type:

- The quality information of a design model distinguishes four different criteria: violation of constraints, fulfillment of requirements, completeness of value assignments, and costs. Four different contexts can be immediately identified according to these four criteria: trying to repair constraint violations, trying to improve fulfillment, trying to improve completeness, and trying to reduce costs.[2]

- Within a context, we can decide about the focus of the design activity by using the structure of the design model (i.e., the object information) in the case of parametric design. A design model is a fixed set of parameters and a transformation can only refer to the value of a parameter. Deciding about the focus is therefore deciding about the parameter or the set of parameters that should be updated next.

---

[2] As the reader may realize, a more pedantic organization would have already introduced three of these context decisions for design problems because they are not specific for parametric design. For reasons of simplicity we skip this intermediate step.

- Finally, we have to select one transformation operator because in the general case, several transformations may be applicable within a context and a focus.

Triples of contexts, foci and transformation operators record history information of the search process that is kept to prevent unnecessary repetition and infinite loops in the search process.

[Graham & Bailor, 1996] provides an analysis of local search. However, the distinctions that we introduced cannot be discussed at the level of local search and optimization problems in general. They require additional ontological distinctions that are not available at the level of generic control regimes. Without the notion of a problem type they need to be introduced during domain adaptation. Therefore, they would not be reusable for related problems in different domains. The refinements we discuss here are basically concerned with the neighborhood relationship that is essential for determining the quality of local search algorithms. Still, general characterizations of this neighborhood relation ([Lowry, 1991], [Graham & Bailor, 1996]) remain valid but we provide a richer vocabulary for formulating them.

7.3.2   Select the Design Model that Is to Be Expanded Next

DeriveSuccessorNodes is mainly concerned with design problem solving and (as we will see below) UpdateNodes is mainly concerned with generic search strategies. The task of SelectNode combines both aspects. It selects a design model according to some filters, an estimation of its feasibility (i.e., whether the design model may lead to a solution), and possibly some further criterion.

A filter may be defined by a context similar to its use in DeriveSuccessorNodes. When we already have a complete and valid design model we may only select successors with lower costs if they are valid. In this context, only valid and complete design models remain as selection candidates. This may differ when we are in a context where we try to repair constraints violations or work on improving the completeness of a design model.

Feasibility may either be a new knowledge requirement (asking for a domain-specific heuristic estimator) for an A* like search or it may be defined in terms of the quality of the design models (assuming that better design models lead with higher probability to solutions).

In addition to just selecting the most feasible design model that passed the context filter a further selection criterion may be introduced to escape local optima in the search space. Methods like simulated annealing do not always select the best local node. Therefore, a third criterion based on random selection is needed to complete the definition of SelectNode covering all search variants.

Finally, [Motta, 1999] uses knowledge about the structure of a design model (a fixed set of parameters) to define the starting point of the search process (i.e., the first selected design model returned by Initialize). The search begins with the empty model that does not assign any value to the parameter.[3]

---

[3] Other initialization strategies are sketched in [Graham & Bailor, 1996].

7.3.3   Update the Set of Future Candidates

UpdateNodes significantly influences the type of search that is performed. In the case that it unifies the SuccessorNodes with the original Nodes, a variant of best-first search is performed where all expanded nodes are available for selecting the next node. In the case that UpdateNodes only regards the SuccessorNodes, the search is restricted to the environment of the selected node. Therefore, a variant of *hill-climbing* is performed where only the neighbors of a selected node are possible candidates for the further search process.

The specified search process is *local* in the sense that it derives the neighbors of a current node. However, it may be *global* in the sense that it also selects the neighbors of earlier nodes. This is decided by the external refinement of the inference UpdateNodes. Therefore, more global search techniques can be covered by the same algorithmic scheme and an adapter can be used to navigate between different search versions based on the same search paradigm.

7.4   Conclusions

We presented a systematic approach enabling the structured development, adaptation, and reuse of problem-solving methods. A large number of different problem-solving method can be described by a structured set of generic problem and problem-solving pattern (one of each) and a couple of adapters that express their refinement. These

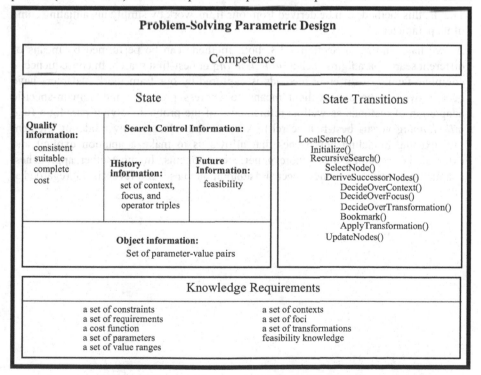

Fig. 50. A Survey of Parametric Design Problem Solving

refinement are kept externally allowing their reuse for new problem types and different problem-solving schemas.

A summary of parametric design problem solving in terms of its states and state transitions is provided in Fig. 50. This is the way the method is presented as a result of choosing an algorithmic scheme and applying several adapters that refine its state descriptions and state transitions. However, this scheme is still more abstract than what is usually called a method in the literature on problem-solving methods. Take the mentioned problem-solving method *propose & revise* for parametric design as an example. *Propose & revise* for parametric design instantiates the framework by distinguishing two contexts when deriving successor design models:

- Propose context: Consistent design models are extended until they are complete or inconsistent.

- Revise context: Inconsistent design models are repaired until they are consistent.

A variant of this method, which first assigns a value to all parameters and then repairs the design models (i.e., complete *propose & revise*, cf. [Motta & Zdrahal, 1996]) is defined by the two contexts:

- Propose context: Incomplete design models are extended until they are complete.

- Revise context: Complete but inconsistent design models are repaired until they are consistent.

That is, this methods can be derived from our framework by simply instantiating some of its parameters.

As we have shown in Section 7.3.3, both methods can be performed by means of different search paradigms such as *hill-climbing* or best-first search. In consequence, a complete family of different methods is captured by our framework. Adapters have been proven to be an excellent means to express problem- and domain-specific adaptation of methods as well as refinements of the problem-solving paradigm (e.g. *hill-climbing* versus best-first search). Adapters introduce a new modeling element into existing modeling approaches that allows us to make adaptation explicit and external, i.e. separated from more generic components. In most other approaches, adaptation is treated as a side-aspect and adaptation via several levels is not regarded at all.

Conclusions and Future Work

This volume is concerned with improving the state of the art of work on problem-solving methods for knowledge-based systems. In a nutshell, we provided the following contributions:

- Problem-solving methods are necessary to enable effective and *efficient* reasoning of knowledge-based systems. This efficiency is not achieved by algorithmic optimization but by introducing *assumptions* that either restrict the size of the problem or that postulate strong requirements on the available domain knowledge. We provided a large number of assumptions to empirically ground our argument and to enable their reuse for developing new methods. We showed how task-specific assumptions like the monotonic abduction problem assumptions can be derived from the generic assumptions used to ensure that a local search finds a global optimum.

- We presented a *software architecture* for knowledge-based systems enabling their conceptual description, formal specification and semi-automatic verification. We used this structured description framework for providing structured support in developing and reusing problem-solving methods. We introduced a new conceptual modeling element, the *adapter*, that enables the reusable specification of the other parts of a model.

- Reusing problem-solving methods has to deal with the context dependency or situatedness of knowledge. When analyzing *propose & revise* in [Fensel, 1995a] we realized that there is neither a gold standard for such methods nor does it appear reasonable to include all the numerous variants of a method in a library. In consequence, we developed the concept of a library that contains only skeletons and we provide strong support in adapting and refining library elements according to domain and task-specific circumstances. By separating generic and specific parts via adapters both become reusable. This helps to overcome the so-called usability-reusability trade-off identified by [Klinker et al., 1991]. We discussed two methods that support reuse of problem-solving methods: we provided the *inverse verification* method to explicate context dependency and the *adapter-stapling* method to adapt methods to context change. Finally, we used our approach to reorganize the library of [Motta, 1999] for parametric problem-solving. A library of problem-solving schemas is organized according to three dimensions: the problem-solving paradigm, the problem type, as well as the inferences and their assumptions on domain knowledge.

We will use the rest of this chapter to discuss some ongoing work that deals with open issues of the framework we presented and we will show a recent line of work that should enable broader reuse of problem-solving methods via ontologies and intelligent brokering services.

Open Issues

We applied the *Karlsruhe Interactive Verifier (KIV)* [Reif, 1995] to verify formal models of knowledge-based systems. It fits excellently to our needs and provides strong support in enabling verification in practice. However, KIV is not yet customized for our purpose. This customization could significantly improve the support in specification and

Dieter Fensel: Problem-Solving Methods, LNAI 1791, pp. 129 - 132, 2000.
© Springer-Verlag Berlin Heidelberg 2000

verification. In fact, we identify three aspects that look worthwhile for specializing KIV (cf. [Fensel et al., 1998 (d)]):

- The *architecture* used to specify knowledge-based systems can be expressed in the generic module concept of KIV. However, this is connected with a loss of information because the KIV specification does not distinguish the different roles that specifications may have (goals, requirements, adapters, etc.).

- The *specification language* MCL uses the states-as-algebras paradigm to model states and bulk-updates to model state transitions. The current version of KIV relies on the original version of dynamic logic, where states are represented by value assignments of variables. Integrating the states-as-algebras concept and bulk-updates in KIV is of general interest because it would also allow to verify specifications with Abstract State Machines.

- We used KIV as a tool for *inverse* verification, for searching and for constructing assumptions that close gaps in proofs. This aspect is not new for KIV because each verification process is usually a process that identifies errors in specifications and implementations. However, the methodological support for this aspect could be improved and we would like to support this process with libraries of reusable assumptions and flexible support in their task-specific adaptation.

When taking a closer look at Chapter 7 of this volume the reader may identify missing details. Some aspects of the formalization are rather sketchy[1] and the competence of the different variants of the methods has not yet been established. A serious shortcoming is that we do not provide any tool support. In consequence, a knowledge engineer has to do all the task- and domain-specific adaptation by hand. As in successful approaches in algorithmic optimization like KIDS/SPECWARE [Smith, 1996] we would need libraries of adapter patterns and tool support for refining specifications by applying a selected adapter operator to a specification. Our proposal, which focuses on the refinement of state definitions via commitments to the problem structure and the refinement of inferences via assumptions on domain knowledge, is complementary to these approaches focusing on algorithmic refinement.

Reasoning Agents in the Cyperspace

Software and knowledge reuse via networks is becoming an increasingly popular topic. Intelligent agents providing reasoning service based on problem-solving methods (cf. [Benjamins et al., 1998]) introduce an interesting application framework and raise very interesting research issues. Providing different libraries of problem-solving methods via the net requires a *broker* that mediates between customers and providers of problem-solving methods (cf. [Benjamins, 1997], [Fensel, 1997a]) by using ontologies. *Ontologies* have been proposed to enhance knowledge sharing and reuse (cf. [Fridman Noy & Hafner, 1997]). An ontology provides a conceptualization, which can be shared by multiple reasoning components communicating during a problem solving process. Using ontological engineering for describing problem-solving methods provides two important benefits with respect to reuse. The resulting method specification (i) is grounded on a common, shared terminology and (ii) its knowledge requirements are conceptualized as ontological commitments [Gruber, 1995].

---

[1] For example, the definition of the sort *parameter* and the *ParametetricDesignModel* as a partial function defined on this sort.

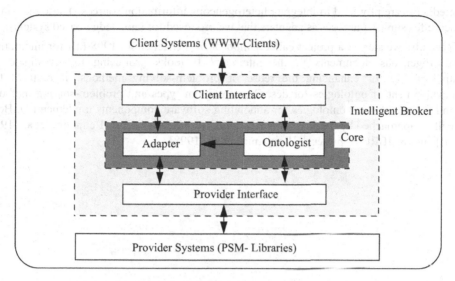

Fig. 51. The Layered Architecture of the Intelligent Broker.

The general layered architecture of such a broker is depicted in Fig. 51. The broker has to communicate with clients via *clients systems*. A client is someone who has a complex problem but can provide domain knowledge that describes it and that supports problem-solving. The providers are developer teams of problem-solving methods. Their *provider systems* are annotated libraries of problem-solving methods. The problem-solving methods are implementations that solve complex tasks by using domain knowledge for defining and solving the problem. Their annotations are necessary to support their selection process and the communication process with the methods. The core of a broker for problem-solving methods consists of two main elements: an *ontologist* and an *adapter*. An ontologist must support the selection and adaptation process of problem-solving methods for a given application. Basically it has to provide support in building or reusing a domain ontology and in relating this ontology to an ontology that describe generic classes of application problems. This problem-type ontology has to be linked with problem-solving method-specific ontologies that allow the selection of a method. The adapter hardwires the results of the ontological engineering that was necessary to establish the appropriate links between domain knowledge and problem-solving method via a problem ontology. It can be automatically derived from these ontological links and it is used to mediate between the domain knowledge and problem-solving method during the problem-solving process.

Mapping the input and output of a problem-solving method via a problem definition on domain-specific data and knowledge can be interpreted as a mapping between different data schemas. Instead of assuming a global data schema, heterogeneous information and knowledge systems have a *mediator* [Wiederhold, 1992] that translates user queries into sub-queries on the different information sources and integrates the sub-answers. E.g. in the projects Infomaster [Genesereth et al., 1997], Information Manifold [Levy et al., 1996], SIMS [Arens et al., 1993], and TSIMMIS [Papakonstantinou et al., 1995] mediators are provided to integrate heterogeneous information sources. These mediators serve for similar purposes as adapters that we proposed for knowledge-based systems.

Recently, we started a project called *Ontobroker* [Fensel et al., 1998 (a)] for integrating heterogeneous documents in the internet.[2] It looks promising to investigate its applicability for enhancing the reuse of problem-solving methods. It requires the development of ontologies for describing problem types and problem-solving methods and the use of these ontologies for annotating software components implementing. Both will be approached by the *Knowledge Annotation Initiative* $(KA)^2$ [Benjamins et al., 1999 (a)] and the IBROW-project[3] [Benjamins et al., 1998].

---

[2] Recent results can be found in [Fensel et al., 1999 (a)] and [Fensel et al., to appear]. Ontobroker has been the nucleus of a project in the Information Society Technologies (IST) Program for Research, Technology Development and Demonstration under the 5th European Framework Program: *On-To-Knowledge: Content-driven Knowledge-Management Tools through Evolving Ontologies.* It has been started in January 2000. Project partner are the Vreije Universiteit Amsterdam (VU); the Institute AIFB, University of Karlsruhe, Germany; AIdministrator, the Netherlands; British Telecom Laboratories, UK; Swiss Life, Switzerland; CognIT, Norway; and Enersearch, Sweden.
http://www.cs.vu.nl/~dieter/ontoknowledge/.

[3] IBROW started with a pre-phase under the 4th European Framework and has become a full-fledged Information Society Technologies (IST) project under the 5th European Framework Program since January 2000. Results of its initial phase are described in [Benjamins et al., 1999 (b)], [Fensel & Benjamins, 1998 (b)], and [Fensel et al., 1999 (b)]. Project partners are the University of Amsterdam; the Open University, Milton Keynes, England; the Spanish Council of Scientific Research (IIIA) in Barcelona, Spain; the Institute AIFB, University of Karlsruhe, Germany: Stanford University, US: Intelligent Software Components S. A., Spain; and the Vrije Universiteit Amsterdam.
http://www.swi.psy.uva.nl/projects/IBROW3/home.html.

References

[Aben, 1993]
M. Aben: Formally Specifying Re-usable Knowledge Model Components, *Knowledge Acquisition*, 5:119—141, 1993.

[Abu-Hanna, 1994]
A. Abu-Hanna: Multiple Domain Models in Diagnostic Reasoning, Ph.D. thesis, University of Amsterdam, 1994.

[Abu-Hanna et al., 1991]
A. Abu-Hanna, V.R. Benjamins and W.N.H. Jansweijer: Device Understanding and Modeling for Diagnosis, *IEEE-Expert*, 6(2):26—32, 1991.

[Agnew et al., 1994]
N.M. Agnew, K. M. Ford, and P. J. Hayes: Expertise in Context: Personally Constructed, Socially Selected, and Reality-Relevant?, *International Journal of Expert Systems*, 7(1), 1994.

[Akkermans et al., 1993]
J.M. Akkermans, B. Wielinga, and A.Th. Schreiber: Steps in Constructing Problem-Solving Methods. In N. Aussenac et al. (eds.), *Knowledge-Acquisition for Knowledge-Based Systems*, Lecture Notes in Artificial Intelligence (LNAI) 723, Springer-Verlag, Berlin, 1993.

[Akman & Surav, 1996]
V. Akman and M. Surav: Steps Toward Formalizing Context, *AI Magazine*, 17(3), 1996.

[Angele, 1993]
J. Angele: *Operationalisierung des Models der Expertise mit KARL*, Infix, St. Augustin, 1993.

[Angele et al., 1998]
J. Angele, D. Fensel, and R. Studer: Developing Knowledge-Based Systems with MIKE, *Journal of Automated Software Engineering*, 5(4):389-418, 1998.

[Angele & Studer, 1999]
J. Angele and R. Studer: A State Space Analysis of Propose-and-Revise, *International Journal of Intelligent Systems*,14(2), 1999.

[Arens et al., 1993]
Y. Arens, C.Y. Chee, C.-N. Hsu and C. Knoblock: Retrieving and Integrating Data From Multiple Information Sources, *International Journal of Intelligent Cooperative Information Systems*, 2(2):127—158, 1993.

[Baeten & Weijland, 1990]
J. C. M. Baeten and W. P. Weijland: *Process Algebra*, Cambridge Tracts in Theoretical Computer Science, no 18, Cambridge University Press, Cambridge, 1990.

Dieter Fensel: Problem-Solving Methods, LNAI 1791, pp. 133 - 154, 2000.
© Springer-Verlag Berlin Heidelberg 2000

[Bauer et al., 1987]
F. L. Bauer, H. Ehler, R. Horsch, B. Müller, H. Partsch, O. Paukner, and P. Pepper: The Munich Project CIP, vol II, *The Transformation System CIP-S*, Lecture Notes in Computer Science (LNCS) 292, Springer-Verlag, 1987.

[Benjamins, 1993]
R. Benjamins: *Problem-Solving Methods for Diagnosis*, Ph.D. Thesis, University of Amsterdam, Amsterdam, the Netherlands, 1993.

[Benjamins, 1995]
V.R. Benjamins: Problem Solving Methods for Diagnosis And Their Role in Knowledge Acquisition, *International Journal of Expert Systems: Research and Application*, 8(2):93—120, 1995.

[Benjamins, 1997]
R. Benjamins: Problem-Solving Methods in Cyberspace. In *Proceedings of the Workshop on Problem-Solving Methods for Knowledge-based Systems (W26) during the Fifteenth International Joint Conference on Artificial Intelligence (IJCAI-97)*, NAGOYA, Japan, August 23-29, 1997.

[Benjamins et al., 1996]
R. Benjamins, D. Fensel, and R. Straatman: Assumptions of Problem-Solving Methods and Their Role in Knowledge Engineering. In *Proceedings of the 12th European Conference on Artificial Intelligence (ECAI-96)*, Budapest, August 12-16, 1996.

[Benjamins et al., 1998]
V.R. Benjamins, E. Plaza, E. Motta, D. Fensel, R. Studer, B. Wielinga, G. Schreiber, Z. Zdrahal: An Intelligent Brokering Service for Knowledge-Component Reuse on the World-WideWeb. In Proceedings of the 11th Banff Knowledge Acquisition for Knowledge-Based System Workshop (KAW'98), Banff, Canada, April 18-23, 1998.

[Benjamins et al., 1999 (a)]
R. Benjamins, D. Fensel, S. Decker, and A. Gomez Perez: (KA)^2: Building ontologies for the internet: A mid-term report, *International Journal of Human-Computer Studies (IJHCS)*, 51, 1999.

[Benjamins et al., 1999 (b)]
V.R. Benjamins, B. Wielinga, J. Wielemaker, and D. Fensel : Brokering Problem-Solving Knowledge at the Internet. In Knowledge Acquisition, Modeling, and Management, Proceedings of the European Knowledge Acquisition Workshop (EKAW-99), D. Fensel et al. (eds.), Lecture Notes in Artificial Intelligence, LNAI 1621, Springer-Verlag, May 1999.

[Benjamins & Pierret-Golbreich, 1996]
R. Benjamins and C. Pierret-Golbreich: Assumptions of Problem-Solving Method. In N. Shadbolt et al. (eds.), *Advances in Knowledge Acquisition*, Lecture Notes in Artificial Intelligence (LNAI) 1076, Springer-Verlag, Berlin, 1996.

[Beys et al., 1996]
P. Beys, R. Benjamins, and G. van Heijst: Remedying the Reusability-Usability Trade-off for Problem-solving Methods. In *Proceedings of the 10th Banff Knowledge Acquisition for Knowledge-Based System Workshop (KAW'96)*, Banff, Canada, November 9-14, 1996.

[Bidoit et al., 1991]
M. Bidoit, H.-J. Kreowski, P. Lescane, F. Orejas and D. Sannella (eds.):
Algebraic System Specification and Development, Lecture Notes in Computer
Science (LNCS) 501, Springer-Verlag, 1991.

[Bonner & Kifer, 1993]
A. J. Bonner and M. Kifer: Transaction Logic Programming. In *Proceedings of
the 10th International Conference on Logic Programming (ICLP)*, Budapest,
Hungary, June 21-24, 1993.

[Bonner & Kifer, 1995]
A.J. Bonner and M. Kifer: *Transaction Logic Programming*, Technical Report
CSRI-323, 1995.

[Börger, 1995]
E. Börger: Why Use Evolving Algebras for Hardware and Software Engineering.
In M. Bartosek et al. (eds.), *SOFSEM'95: Theory and Practice of Informatics*,
Lecture Notes in Computer Science (LNCS) 1012, Springer-Verlag, 1995.

[Böttcher, 1995]
C. Böttcher: No Faults in Structure? - How to Diagnose Hidden Interactions. In
*Proceedings of the 14th International Joint Conference on Artificial Intelligence
(IJCAI-95)*, Montreal, Canada, August 20-25, 1995.

[Böttcher & Dressler, 1994]
C. Böttcher and O. Dressler: A Framework For Controlling Model-Based
Diagnosis Systems with Multiple Actions, *Annals of Mathematics and Artificial
Intelligence*, 11:241-261, 1994.

[Brazier et al., 1995]
F. Brazier, B. Dunin Keplicz, N.R. Jennings, and J. Treur: Formal Specification
of Multi-Agent Systems: a Real-World Case. In *Proceedings of the 1st
International Conference on Multi-Agent Systems (ICMAS-95)*, San Francisco,
CA, June 12-14, 1995.

[Bredeweg, 1994]
B. Bredeweg: Model-based Diagnosis and Prediction of Behavior. In [Breuker &
Van de Velde, 1994], pp. 121—153.

[Breuker, 1994]
J. Breuker: Components of Problem Solving. In L. Steels et al. (eds.), *A Future of
Knowledge Acquisition*, Springer-Verlag, Lecture Notes in Artificial Intelligence
(LNAI) 867, 1994.

[Breuker, 1997]
J. Breuker: Problems in Indexing Problem Solving Methods. In *Proceedings of
the Workshop on Problem-Solving Methods for Knowledge-based Systems (W26)
during the Fifteenth International Joint Conference on Artificial Intelligence
(IJCAI-97)*, NAGOYA, Japan, August 23-29, 1997.

[Breuker et al., 1987]
J. Breuker, B. Wielinga, M. van Someren, R. de Hoog, G. Schreiber, P. de Greef,
B. Bredeweg, J. Wielemaker, and j.-P. Billault: *Model-Driven Knowledge
Acquisition: Interpretation Models*, Esprit Project 1098, 1987.

[Breuker & Van de Velde, 1994]
    J. Breuker and W. Van de Velde (eds.): *The CommonKADS Library for Expertise Modeling*, IOS Press, Amsterdam, The Netherlands, 1994.

[Brodie, 1984]
    M.L. Brodie: On the Development of Data Models. In M.L. Brodie et al. (eds.), *On Conceptual Modeling*, Springer-Verlag, Berlin, 1984.

[Bundy, 1990]
    A. Bundy (ed.): *Catalogue of Artificial Intelligence Techniques*, 3rd ed., Springer-Verlag, Berlin, 1990.

[Buvac & Iwanska, 1997]
    T. Buvac and L. Iwanska (eds.): Context in Knowledge Representation and Natural Language. In *Working Notes AAAI-97 Fall Symposium Series*, MIT Cambridge, Massachusetts, November 8-10, 1997.

[Bylander, 1991]
    T. Bylander: Complexity Results for Planning. In *Proceedings of the 12th International Joint Conference on Artificial Intelligence (IJCAI-91)*, Sydney, Australia, August 1991.

[Bylander & Chandrasekaran, 1988]
    T. Bylander and B. Chandrasekaran: Generic Tasks in Knowledge-Based Reasoning. The Right Level of Abstraction for Knowledge Acquisition. In B. Gaines et al. (eds.): *Knowledge Acquisition for Knowledge-Based Systems*, vol I, pp. 65—77, Academic Press, London, 1988.

[Bylander et al., 1991]
    T. Bylander, D. Allemang, M.C. Tanner, and J.R. Josephson: The Computational Complexity of Abduction, *Artificial Intelligence*, 49:25—60, 1991.

[Chandrasekaran, 1986]
    B. Chandrasekaran: Generic Tasks in Knowledge-based Reasoning: High-level Building Blocks for Expert System Design. *IEEE Expert*, 1(3): 23—30, 1986.

[Chandrasekaran, 1990]
    B. Chandrasekaran: Design Problem Solving: A Task Analysis, *AI Magazine*, 1990, 59—71.

[Chandrasekaran, 1991]
    B. Chandrasekaran: Models Versus Rules, Deep Versus Compiled, Content Versus Form, *IEEE-Expert*, 6(2):75—79, 1991.

[Chandrasekaran et al., 1992]
    B. Chandrasekaran, T.R. Johnson, and J. W. Smith: Task Structure Analysis for Knowledge Modeling, *Communications of the ACM*, 35(9):124—137, 1992.

[Chandy & Sanders, 1995]
    K. M. Chandy and B. A. Sanders: Predicate Transformers for Reasoning about Concurrent Programs, *Science of Computer Programming*, 24, 1995.

[Chi et al., 1981]
    M.T.H. Chi, P.J. Feltovich, and R. Glaser: Categorization and Representation of Physics Problems by Experts and Novices, Cognitive Science, 5:121—152, 1981.

[Clancey, 1983]
W.J. Clancey, The Epistemology of a Rule-Based Expert System—a Framework for Explanation, *Artificial Intelligence* 20:215—251, 1983.

[Clancey, 1985]
W.J. Clancey: Heuristic Classification, *Artificial Intelligence*, 27:289—350, 1985.

[Clancey, 1993]
W. J. Clancey: The Knowledge Level Reinterpreted: Modeling Socio-Technical Systems, *The International Journal of Intelligent Systems*, 8(2), 1993.

[Console & Torasso, 1992]
L. Console and P. Torasso: A Spectrum of Logical Definitions of Model-Based Diagnosis. In W. Hamscher et al. (eds.), *Readings in Model-based Diagnosis*, Morgan Kaufman Publ., San Mateo, CA, 1992.

[Cornelissen et al., 1997]
F. Cornelissen, C.M. Junker, and J. Treur: Compositional Verification of Knowledge-Based Systems: A Case Study for Diagnostic Reasoning. In E. Plaza et al. (eds.), *Knowledge Acquisition, Modeling and Management*, Lecture Notes in Artificial Intelligence (LNAI) 1319, Springer-Verlag, 1997.

[Crow et al., 1995]
J. Crow, S. Owre, J. Rushby, N. Shankar, and M. Srivas: A Tutorial Introduction to PVS. In *Proceedings of the Workshop on Industrial-Strength Formal Specification Techniques (WIFT'95)*, Boca Raton, Florida, April 1995.

[Cox & Pietrzykowski, 1986]
P.T. Cox and T. Pietrzykowski: Causes of Events: Their Computation and Application. In *Proceedings of the 8th International Conference on Automated Deduction*, Oxford, England, July 27 - August 1, Lecture Notes in Computer Science (LNCS) 230, Springer-Verlag, 1986.

[Davis, 1984]
R. Davis: Diagnostic Reasoning Based on Structure and Behavior, *Artificial Intelligence*, 24:347—410, 1984.

[Davis & Hamscher, 1988]
R. Davis and W. Hamscher: Model-based Reasoning: Troubleshooting. In H. E. Shrobe (ed.), *Exploring AI: Survey Talks from the National Conference on AI*, Morgan Kaufman, San Mateo, CA, 1988.

[de Geus & Rotterdam, 1992]
F. de Geus and E. Rotterdam: *Decision Support in Anesthesia*, Ph.D. thesis, University of Groningen, 1992.

[de Kleer, 1986]
J. de Kleer: An Assumption-based TMS, *Artificial Intelligence,* 28, 1986.

[de Kleer & Brown, 1984]
J. de Kleer and J.S. Brown: A Qualitative Physics Based on Confluences, *Artificial Intelligence*, 24:7—83, 1984.

[de Kleer et al., 1992]
J. de Kleer, A.K. Mackworth, and R. Reiter: Characterizing Diagnoses and Systems, *Artificial Intelligence*, 56, 1992.

[de Kleer & Williams, 1987]
   J. de Kleer and B.C. Williams: Diagnosing Multiple Faults, *Artificial Intelligence*, 32:97—130, 1987.

[de Kleer & Williams, 1989]
   J. de Kleer and B.C. Williams: Diagnosis with Behavioral Modes. In *Proceedings of the 11th International Joint Conference on AI (IJCAI-89)*, Detroit, MI, 1989.

[Dijkstra, 1975]
   E.W. Dijkstra: Guarded Commands, Nondeterminancy, and Formal Derivation of Programs, *Communication of the ACM*, 18:453—457, 1975.

[Eriksson et al., 1994]
   H. Eriksson, Y. Shahar, S. W. Tu, A. R. Puerta, and M. A. Musen: *Task Modeling with Reusable Problem-Solving Methods*, research report, Knowledge Systems Lab., Stanford University, 1994.

[Eriksson et al., 1995]
   H. Eriksson, Y. Shahar, S. W. Tu, A. R. Puerta, and M. A. Musen: Task Modeling with Reusable Problem-Solving Methods, *Artificial Intelligence*, 79(2):293—326, 1995.

[Faltings & Freuder, 1996]
   B. Faltings and E. Freuder: *Configuration. Papers from the 1996 AAAI Fall Symposium*, Cambridge, Massachusetts, Technical Report FS-96-03, AAAI Press, November 9-11, 1996.

[Feijs & Jonkers, 1992]
   L.M.G. Feijs and H.B.M. Jonkers: *Formal Specification and Design*, Cambridge Tracts in Theoretical Computer Science 35, 1992.

[Fensel, 1995a]
   D. Fensel: Assumptions and Limitations of a Problem-Solving Method: A Case Study. In *Proceedings of the 9th Banff Knowledge Acquisition for Knowledge-Based System Workshop (KAW'95)*, Banff, Canada, January 26 - February 3, 1995.

[Fensel, 1995b]
   D. Fensel: *The Knowledge Acquisition and Representation Language KARL*, Kluwer Academic Publ., Boston, 1995.

[Fensel, 1995c]
   D. Fensel: Formal Specification Languages in Knowledge and Software Engineering, *The Knowledge Engineering Review*, 10(4), 1995.

[Fensel, 1997a]
   D. Fensel: An Ontology-based Broker: Making Problem-Solving Method Reuse Work. In *Proceedings of the Workshop on Problem-Solving Methods for Knowledge-based Systems (W26) during the Fifteenth International Joint Conference on Artificial Intelligence (IJCAI-97)*, NAGOYA, Japan, August 23-29, 1997.

[Fensel, 1997b]
D. Fensel: The Tower-of-Adapter Method for Developing and Reusing Problem-Solving Methods. In E. Plaza et al. (eds.), *Knowledge Acquisition, Modeling and Management*, Lecture Notes in Artificial Intelligence (LNAI) 1319, Springer-Verlag, 1997.

[Fensel & Benjamins, 1998 (a)]
D. Fensel and V.R. Benjamins: The Role of Assumptions in Knowledge Engineering, *International Journal of Intelligent Systems (IJIS)*, 13(8):715-748, 1998.

[Fensel & Benjamins, 1998 (b)]
D. Fensel and V.R. Benjamins: Key Issues for Problem-Solving Methods Reuse. In *Proceedings of the 13th European Conference on Artificial Intelligence (ECAI-98)*, Brighton, UK, August 1998, 63-67.

[Fensel et al., 1993]
D. Fensel, J. Angele, D. Landes, and R. Studer: Giving Structured Analysis Techniques a Formal and Operational Semantics with KARL. In *Proceedings of Requirements Engineering '93 - Prototyping -*, Bonn, April 25 - 27, 1993, Teubner Verlag, Stuttgart, 1993.

[Fensel et al., 1996b]
D. Fensel, H. Eriksson, M.A. Musen, and R. Studer: Conceptual and Formal Specification of Problem-Solving Methods, *International Journal of Expert Systems*, 9(4), 1996.

[Fensel et al., 1996c]
D. Fensel, A. Schönegge, R. Groenboom, and B. Wielinga: Specification and Verification of Knowledge-Based Systems. In *Proceedings of the 10th Banff Knowledge Acquisition for Knowledge-Based System Workshop (KAW'96)*, Banff, Canada, November 9-14, 1996.

[Fensel et al., 1997]
D. Fensel, E. Motta, S. Decker, and Z. Zdrahal: Using Ontologies For Defining Tasks, Problem-Solving Methods and Their Mappings. In E. Plaza et al. (eds.), *Knowledge Acquisition, Modeling and Management*, Lecture Notes in Artificial Intelligence (LNAI) 1319, Springer-Verlag, 1997.

[Fensel et al., 1998 (a)]
D. Fensel, S. Decker, M. Erdmann, and R. Studer: Ontobroker: The Very High Idea. In *Proceedings of the 11th International Flairs Conference (FLAIRS-98)*, Sanibal Island, Florida, USA, 131-135, May 1998.

[Fensel et al., 1998(b)]
D. Fensel, J. Angele, R. Studer: The Knowledge Acquisition and Representation Language KARL, *IEEE Transactions on Knowledge and Data Engineering*, 10(4):527-550, 1998.

[Fensel et al., 1998 (c)]
D. Fensel, R. Groenboom, and G.R. Renardel de Lavalette: Modal Change Logic (MCL): Specifying the Reasoning of Knowledge-based Systems, *Data and Knowledge Engineering (DKE)*, 26(3):243-269, 1998.

[Fensel et al., 1998 (d)]
D. Fensel, F. van Harmelen, W. Reif, and A. ten Teije: Formal Support for Development of Knowledge-Based Systems, *Information Technology Management: An International Journal*, 2(4):173-182, 1998.

[Fensel et al., 1999 (a)]
D. Fensel, J. Angele, S. Decker, M. Erdmann, H.-P. Schnurr, S. Staab, R. Studer, and A. Witt: On2broker: Semantic-Based Access to Information Sources at the WWW. In *Proceedings of the World Conference on the WWW and Internet (WebNet 99)*, Honolulu, Hawai, USA, October 25-30, 1999.

[Fensel et al., 1999 (b)]
Dieter Fensel, V. Richard Benjamins, Enrico Motta, and Bob Wielinga: UPML: A Framework for knowledge system reuse. In *Proceedings of the International Joint Conference on AI (IJCAI-99)*, Stockholm, Sweden, July 31 - August 5, 1999.

[Fensel et al., to appear]
D. Fensel, J. Angele, S. Decker, M. Erdmann, H.-P. Schnurr, R. Studer and A. Witt: Lessons Learned from Applying AI to the Web. To appear in *Journal of Cooperative Information Systems*.

[Fensel & Groenboom, 1996]
D. Fensel and R. Groenboom: MLPM: Defining a Semantics and Axiomatization for Specifying the Reasoning Process of Knowledge-based Systems. In *Proceedings of the 12th European Conference on Artificial Intelligence (ECAI-96)*, Budapest, August 12-16, 1996.

[Fensel & Groenboom, 1997]
D. Fensel and R. Groenboom: Specifying Knowledge-Based Systems with Reusable Components. In *Proceedings of the 9th International Conference on Software Engineering & Knowledge Engineering (SEKE-97)*, Madrid, Spain, June 18-20, 1997.

[Fensel & Schönegge, 1997]
D. Fensel and A. Schönegge: Using KIV to Specify and Verify Architectures of Knowledge-Based Systems. In *Proceedings of the 12th IEEE International Conference on Automated Software Engineering (ASEC-97)*, Incline Village, Nevada, November 3-5, 1997.

[Fensel & Schönegge, 1998]
D. Fensel and A. Schönegge: Inverse Verification of Problem-Solving Methods, *International Journal of Human-Computer Studies (IJHCS)*, 49(4):339-362, 1998.

[Fensel & Straatman, 1998]
D. Fensel und R. Straatman: The Essence of Problem-Solving Methods: Making Assumptions to Gain Efficiency, to appear in The *International Journal of Human Computer Studies (IJHCS)*, 48(2):181-215, 1998.

[Fensel & van Harmelen, 1994]
D. Fensel and F. van Harmelen: A Comparison of Languages which Operationalize and Formalize KADS Models of Expertise, *The Knowledge Engineering Review*, 9(2), 1994.

[Fridman Noy & Hafner, 1997]
    N. Fridman Noy and C.D. Hafner: The State of the Art in Ontology Design, *AI Magazine*, 18(3):53—74, 1997.

[Fuchß et al., 1995]
    Th. Fuchß, W. Reif, G. Schellhorn and K. Stenzel: Three Selected Case Studies in Verification. In M. Broy and S. Jähnichen (eds.): *Methods, Languages, and Tools for the Construction of Correct Software*, Lecture Notes in Computer Science (LNCS) 1009, Springer-Verlag, 1995.

[Gamma et al., 1995]
    E. Gamma, R. Helm, R. Johnson, and J. Vlissides: *Design Patterns,* Addison-Wesley Pub., 1995.

[Garlan & Perry, 1995]
    D. Garlan and D. Perry (eds.), *Special Issue on Software Architecture*, IEEE Transactions on Software Engineering, 21(4), 1995.

[Gennari et al., 1994]
    J. H. Gennari, S.W. Tu, T.E. Rothenfluh, and M. Musen: Mapping Domains to Methods in Support of Reuse. In *Proceedings of the 8th Banff Knowledge Acquisition Workshop (KAW-94)*, Banff, Canada, January 30 - February 4, 1994.

[Genesereth, 1984]
    M.R. Genesereth: The Use of Design Descriptions in Automated Diagnosis, *Artificial Intelligence*, 24:411-436, 1984.

[Genesereth et al., 1997]
    M.R. Genesereth, A.M. Keller, and O.M. Duschka: Infomaster: An Information Integration System. In *Proceedings of the ACM SIGMOD International Conference on Management of Data*, Tucson, AZ, May 1997.

[Gil & Melz, 1996]
    Y. Gil and E. Melz: Explicit Representations of Problem-Solving Strategies to Support Knowledge Acquisition. In *Proceedings of the 13th National Conference on AI (AAAI-96)*, Portland, Oregon, August 4-8, 1996.

[Goel et al., 1987]
    A. Goel, N. Soundararajan, and B. Chandrasekaran: Complexity in Classificatory Reasoning. In *Proceedings of the 6th National Conference on Artificial Intelligence (AAAI-87)*, Seattle, Washington, July 13-17, 1987.

[Goldblatt, 1982]
    R. Goldblatt: *Axiomatising the Logic of Computer Science*, Lecture Notes in Computer Science (LNCS) 130, Springer-Verlag, Berlin, 1982.

[Graham & Bailor, 1996]
    R.P. Graham, Jr. and P.D. Bailor: Synthesis of Local Search Algorithms by Algebraic Means. In *Proceedings of the 11th Knowledge-Based Software Engineering Conference (KBSE-96)*, 1996.

[Groenboom, 1997]
    R. Groenboom: *Formalizing Knowledge Domains - Static and Dynamic Aspects*, Ph.D. thesis, University of Groningen, Shaker Publ., 1997.

[Groenboom & Renardel de Lavalette, 1994]
R. Groenboom and G.R. Renardel de Lavalette: Reasoning about Dynamic Features in Specification Languages. In D.J. Andrews et al. (eds.), *Proceedings of Workshop in Semantics of Specification Languages*, October 1993, Utrecht, Springer Verlag, Berlin, 1994.

[Groenboom & Renardel de Lavalette, 1995]
R. Groenboom and G.R. Renardel de Lavalette: A Formalization of Evolving Algebras. In *Proceedings of Accolade 95*, Dutch Graduate School in Logic, Amsterdam, 1995.

[Gruber, 1993]
T.R. Gruber: A Translation Approach to Portable Ontology Specifications, *Knowledge Acquisition*, 5:199—220, 1993.

[Gruber, 1995]
T.R. Gruber: Toward Principles for the Design of Ontologies Used for Knowledge Sharing, *International Journal of Human-Computer Studies (IJHCS)*, 43(5/6):907—928, 1995.

[Guha, 1993]
R.V. Guha: *Context Dependence of Representations in Cyc*, MCC Technical Report, CYC 066-93, 1993.

[Guha & Lenat, 1990]
R.V. Guha and D.B. Lenat: Cyc: A Midterm Report, *AI Magazine*, 11:32—59, 1990.

[Gurevich, 1994]
Y. Gurevich: Evolving Algebras 1993: Lipari Guide. In E.B. Börger (ed.), *Specification and Validation Methods*, Oxford University Press, 1994.

[Harel, 1984]
D. Harel: Dynamic Logic. In D. Gabby et al. (eds.), *Handbook of Philosophical Logic, vol. II, Extensions of Classical Logic*, D. Reidel Publishing Company, Dordrecht (NL), 1984.

[Jones, 1990]
C.B. Jones: *Systematic Software Development Using VDM*, 2nd ed., Prentice Hall., 1990.

[Juellig et al., 1996a]
R. Juellig, Y. Srinivas, and J. Liu: SPECWARE: An Advanced Environment for the Formal Development of Complex Software Systems. In M. Wirsing et al. (eds.), *Algebraic Methodology and Software Technology*, Lecture Notes in Computer Science (LNCS) 1101, Springer-Verlag, Berlin, 1996.

[Jungclaus, 1993]
R. Jungclaus: *Modeling of Dynamic Object Systems - A Logic-based Approach*, Vieweg Verlag, 1993.

[Katz et al., 1989]
S. Katz, C.A. Richter, and K.-S. The: PARIS: A System for Reusing Partially Interpreted Schemas. In T. J. Biggerstaff et al. (eds.), *Software Reusability, vol I*, Addison-Wesley Publ., Menlo Park, 1989.

[Kifer et al., 1995]
M. Kifer, G. Lausen, and J. Wu: Logical Foundations of Object-Oriented and Frame-Based Languages, *Journal of the ACM*, 42:741—843, 1995.

[Klinker et al., 1991]
G. Klinker, C. Bhola, G. Dallemagne, D. Marques, and J. McDermott: Usable and Reusable Programming Constructs, *Knowledge Acquisition*, 3:117—136, 1991.

[Kozen, 1990]
D. Kozen: Logics of Programs. In J. v. Leeuwen (ed.), *Handbook of Theoretical Computer Science*, Elsevier Science Publ., B. V., Amsterdam, 1990.

[Kripke, 1959]
S.A. Kripke: A Completeness Theorem in Modal Logic, *Journal of Symbolic Logic*, 24:1—14, 1959.

[Kroeger, 1987]
F. Kroeger: *Temporal Logic of Programs*, Springer-Verlag, Berlin, 1987.

[Larkin et al., 1980]
J. H. Larkin, J. McDermott, D. P. Simon, and A. H. Simon: Expert and Novice Performance in Solving Physics Problems, *Science*, 208:1335— 1342, 1980.

[Ledru, 1996]
Y. Ledru: Using KIDS as a Tool Support for VDM. In *Proceedings of the 18th International Conference on Software Engineering (ICSE-96)*, Berlin, March 1996.

[Levesque, 1984]
H.J. Levesque: Foundations of a functional approach to knowledge representation, *Artificial Intelligence*, 23(2):155—212, 1984.

[Levy et al., 1996]
A.Y. Levy, A. Rajaraman, and J.J. Ordille: Query-Answering Algorithms for Information Agents. In *Proceedings of the National Conference on AI (AAAI-96)*, Portland, Oregon, August 4-8, 1996.

[Levy & Rousset, 1996]
A.Y. Levy and M.-C. Rousset: CARIN: A Representation Language Combining Horn Rules and Description Logics. In *Proceedings of the 12th European Conference on Artificial Intelligence (ECAI-96)*, Budapest, August 12-16, 1996.

[Linster, 1994]
M. Linster (ed.): Sisyphus '91/92: Models of Problem Solving, *International Journal of Human-Computer Studies (IJHCS)*, 40(3), 1994.

[Lloyd, 1987]
J. W. Lloyd: Declarative Error Diagnosis, *New Generation Computing*, 5:133— 154, 1987.

[Lowry, 1991]
M. Lowry: Automating the Design of Local Search Algorithms. In M. R. Lowry and R. D. McCartney (eds.), *Automating Software Design*, AAAI Press / The MIT Press, 1991.

[Lowry et al., 1994]
M. Lowry, A. Philpot, T. Pressburger, and I. Underwood: A Formal Approach to Domain-Oriented Software Design Environments. In *Proceedings of the 9th Knowledge-Based Software Engineering Conference (KBSE-94)*, Monterey, CA, September 20-23, 1994.

[Lydiard, 1992]
T.J. Lydiard: Overview of Current Practice and Research Initiatives for the Verification and Validation of KBS, *The Knowledge Engineering Review*, 7(2):101—113, 1992.

[Maes & Nardi, 1988]
P. Maes and D. Nardi: *Meta-Level Architectures and Reflection*, North-Holland, Amsterdam, 1988.

[Marcus, 1988]
S. Marcus (ed.): *Automating Knowledge Acquisition for Experts Systems*, Kluwer Academic Publisher, Boston, 1988.

[Marcus et al., 1988]
S. Marcus, J. Stout, and J. McDermott VT: An Expert Elevator Designer That Uses Knowledge-based Backtracking, *AI Magazine*, 9(1):95—111, 1988.

[Mark, 1996]
B. Mark: Special Issue on Data-Mining, IEEE-Expert, 11(5), 1996.

[McCarthy, 1993]
J. McCarthy: Notes on Formalizing Context. In *Proceedings of the 13th International Conference on Artificial Intelligence (IJCAI-93)*, Chamberry, France, 1993.

[McCarthy & Buvac, 1997]
J. McCarthy and S. Buvac: Formalizing Context (Expanded Notes). [Buvac & Iwanska, 1997].

[McCarthy & Hayes, 1969]
J.M. McCarthy and P.J. Hayes: Some Philosophical Problems from the Standpoint of Artificial Intelligence. In B. Meltzer et al. (eds.), *Machine Intelligence*, 4, 1969.

[McCluskey, 1956]
E.J. McCluskey: Minimizing of Boolean Functions, *Bell Systems Technology Journal*, 35(5):1417-1444, 1956.

[McIlraith, 1994]
S. McIlraith: Further Contribution to Characterizing Diagnosis, *Annals of Mathematics and AI*, 11(1-4), 1994.

[Meisels & Saaltink, 1996]
I. Meisels and M. Saaltink: The Z/EVES Reference Manual, ORA Canada, 1996. Available via http://www.ora.on.ca/z-eves/.

[Menzies, 1999] T. Menzies: Knowledge Maintenance: The State of the Art, to appear in *The Knowledge Engineering Review*, 14(1), 1999.

[Menzies & Clancey, 1999]
    T. Menzies and W.J. Clancey (eds.): Special Issue on Situated Cognition, *International Journal of Human-Computer Studies (IJHCS)*, 49, 1999.

[Mili, 1997]
    F. Mili: Transformational Based Problem Solving Reuse. In *Proceedings of the 9th International Conference on Software Engineering & Knowledge Engineering (SEKE-97)*, Madrid, Spain, June 18-20, 1997.

[Mili et al., 1995]
    H. Mili, F. Mili, and A. Mili: Reusing Software: Issues and Research Directions, *IEEE Transactions on Software Engineering*, 21(6):528—562, 1995.

[Minton, 1995]
    S. Minton: Quantitative Results Concerning the Utility of Explanation-Based Learning. In [Ram & Leake, 1995b].

[Minton et al., 1989]
    S. Minton, S. Carbonell, C. Knoblock, D.R. Kuokka, O. Etzioni, and Y. Gil: Explanation-based Learning: A Problem Solving Perspective, *Artificial Intelligence*, 40:63—118, 1989.

[Mittal & Frayman, 1989]
    S. Mittal and F. Frayman: Towards a Generic Model of Configuration Tasks. In *Proceedings of the 11th International Joint Conference on Artificial Intelligence - (IJCAI'89)*, San Mateo, CA, 1989.

[Motta, 1999]
    E. Motta: *Reusable Components for Knowledge Modeling*, IOS Press, Amsterdam, 1999.

[Motta & Zdrahal, 1996]
    E. Motta and Z. Zdrahal: Parametric Design Problem Solving. In *Proceedings of the 10h Banff Knowledge Acquisition for Knowledge-Based System Workshop (KAW'96)*, Banff, Canada, November 9-15, 1996.

[Muggleton & Buntine, 1988]
    S. Muggleton and W. Buntine: Machine Invention of First-Order Predicates by Inverting Resolution. In *Proceedings of the 5th International Conference on Machine Learning (ICML-88)*, Michigan, US, 1988.

[Muggleton & De Raedt, 1994]
    S. Muggleton and L. De Raedt: Inductive Logic Programming: Theory and Methods, *Journal of Logic Programming*, 19/20:629—679, 1994.

[Musen, 1989]
    M. A. Musen: An Editor for the Conceptual Models of Interactive Knowledge-Acquisition Tools, *International Journal of Man-Machine Studies (IJMMS)*, 31, 1989.

[Nebel, 1996]
    B. Nebel: Artificial Intelligence: A Computational Perspective. In G. Brewka (ed.), *Principles of Knowledge Representation*, CSLI publications, Studies in Logic, Language and Information, Stanford, 1996.

[Neches et al., 1991]
R. Neches, R.E. Fikes, T. Finin, T.R. Gruber, T. Senator, and W.R. Swartout: Enabling Technology for Knowledge Sharing, *AI Magazine*, 12(3):36—56, 1991.

[Nejdl et al., 1995]
W. Nejdl, P. Froehlich and M. Schroeder: A Formal Framework For Representing Diagnosis Strategies in Model-Based Diagnosis Systems. In *Proceedings of the 14th International Joint Conference on AI (IJCAI-95)*, Montreal, Canada, August 20-25, 1995.

[Newell, 1982]
A. Newell: The Knowledge Level, *Artificial Intelligence*, 18:87—127, 1982.

[Newell, 1991]
A. Newell: Formulating the Problem-Space Computational Model. In R. F. Rashid (ed.), *Carnegie-Mellon Computer Science: A 25-Year Commemorative Reading,* Addinson-Wesley, Reading, Mass., 1991.

[O'Hara & Shadbolt, 1996]
K. O'Hara and N. Shadbolt: The Thin End of the Wedge: Efficiency and the Generalized Directive Model Methodology. In N. Shadbolt (eds.), *Advances in Knowledge Acquisition*, Lecture Notes in Artificial Intelligence (LNAI) 1076, Springer-Verlag, Berlin, 1996.

[Papakonstantinou et al., 1995]
Y. Papakonstantinou, H. Garcia Molina, and J. Widom: Object Exchange Across Heterogeneous Information Sources. In *Proceedings of the IEEE International Conference on Data Engineering (ICDE)*, Taipei, Taiwan, March 1995.

[Park & Shaw, 1991]
C.Y. Park and A.C. Shaw: Experiments with a Program Timing Tool Based on Source-Level Timing Schema, *IEEE Computer*, 24(5):48—57, 1991.

[Parnas & Clements, 1986]
D.L. Parnas and P.C. Clements: A Rational Design Process: How and Why to Fake it, *IEEE Transactions of Software Engineering*, 12(2):251—257, 1986.

[Paulson & Nipkow, 1990]
L.C. Paulson and T. Nipkow: Isabelle: *Tutorial and Users Manual*, technical report, University of Cambridge, no 189, 1990.

[Penix & Alexander, 1997]
J. Penix and P. Alexander: Toward Automated Component Adaption. In *Proceedings of the 9th International Conference on Software Engineering & Knowledge Engineering (SEKE-97)*, Madrid, Spain, June 18-20, 1997.

[Penix et al., 1997]
J. Penix, P. Alexander, and K. Havelund: Declarative Specifications of Software Architectures. In *Proceedings of the 12th IEEE International Conference on Automated Software Engineering (ASEC-97)*, Incline Village, Nevada, November 1997.

[Perkuhn, 1997]
R. Perkuhn: Reuse of Problem-Solving Methods and Family Resemblances. In E. Plaza et al. (eds.), *Knowledge Acquisition, Modeling and Management*, Lecture Notes in Artificial Intelligence (LNAI) 1319, Springer-Verlag, 1997.

[Pierret-Golbreich & Talon, 1996]
C. Pierret-Golbreich and X. Talon: An Algebraic Specification of the Dynamic Behavior of Knowledge-Based Systems, *The Knowledge Engineering Review*, 11(2), 1996.

[Plant & Preece, 1996]
R. Plant and A.D. Preece (eds.): *Special Issue on Verification and Validation, International Journal on Human-Computer Studies (IJHCS)*, 44, 1996.

[Poeck, 1994]
K. Poeck: *Konfigurierbare Problemlösungsmethoden am Beispiel der Problemklassen Zuordnung und Diagnostik*, Ph.D. thesis, University of Würzburg, Germany, 1994.

[Poeck et al., 1996]
K. Poeck, D. Fensel, D. Landes, and J. Angele: Combining KARL And CRLM For Designing Vertical Transportation Systems. In [Schreiber & Birmingham, 1996].

[Poeck & Gappa, 1993]
K. Poeck and U. Gappa: Making Role-Limiting Shells More Flexible. In N. Aussenac et al. (eds.), *Knowledge Acquisition for Knowledge-Based Systems*, Lecture Notes in Artificial Intelligence (LNAI) 723, Springer-Verlag, 1993.

[Popper, 1959]
K.R. Popper: *The Logic of Scientific Discovery*, London, 1992 (reprint of 1959).

[Pos, 1997]
A. Pos: *Automated Redesign of Engineering Models*, Ph.D. thesis, University of Twente, the Netherlands, 1997.

[Preist & Welhalm, 1990]
C. Preist and B. Welham: Modeling Bridge Faults for Diagnosis in Electronic Circuits. In *Proceedings of the 1st International Workshop on Principles of Diagnosis*, Stanford, 1990.

[Przymusinski, 1988]
T.C. Przymusinski: On the Declarative Semantics of Deductive Databases and Logic Programs. In J. Minker (ed.), *Foundations of Deductive Databases and Logic Programming*, Morgan Kaufmann Publisher, Los Altos, CA, 1988.

[Puppe, 1993]
F. Puppe: *Systematic Introduction to Expert Systems: Knowledge Representation and Problem-Solving Methods*, Springer-Verlag, Berlin, 1993.

[Raiman, 1989]
O. Raiman: Diagnosis as a Trial. In *Proceedings of the Model Based Diagnosis International Workshop*, Paris, 1989.

148   References

[Raiman, 1992]
O. Raiman: The Alibi Principle. In W. Hamscher et al. (eds.), *Readings in Model-Based Diagnosis*, Morgan Kaufmann Publ., San Mateo, CA, 1992.

[Raiman et al., 1991]
O. Raiman, J. de Kleer, V. Saraswat, M. Shirley: Characterizing Non-Intermittent Faults. In *Proceedings of the 9th National Conference on AI (AAAI-91)*, Anaheim, CA, July 14-19, 1991.

[Ram & Leake, 1995b]
A. Ram and D.B. Leake (eds.): *Goal-Driven Learning*, The MIT Press, 1995.

[Reif, 1992]
W. Reif: Correctness of Generic Modules. In Nerode & Taitslin (eds.), *Symposium on Logical Foundations of Computer Science*, Lecture Notes in Computer Science (LNCS) 620, Springer-Verlag, 1992.

[Reif, 1995]
W. Reif: The KIV Approach to Software Engineering. In M. Broy and S. Jähnichen (eds.): *Methods, Languages, and Tools for the Construction of Correct Software*, Lecture Notes in Computer Science (LNCS) 1009, Springer-Verlag, Berlin, 1995.

[Reif & Stenzel, 1993]
W. Reif and K. Stenzel: Reuse of Proofs in Software Verification. In Shyamasundar (ed.), *Foundation of Software Technology and Theoretical Computer Science*, Lecture Notes in Computer Science (LNCS) 761, Springer-Verlag, 1993.

[Reiter, 1987]
R. Reiter: A Theory of Diagnosis from First Principles, *Artificial Intelligence*, 32:57—95, 1987.

[Renardel de Lavalette, 1997]
G.R. Renardel de Lavalette: *How to Change Your World—a Variant of Quantified Dynamic Logic*, Technical Report, CS-R9709, Dep. of Computer Science, University of Groningen, 1997.

[Renardel de Lavalette et al., 1998]
G.R. Renardel de Lavalette, R. Groenboom, E.P. Rotterdam, F. van Harmelen, and A. ten Teije: Formalization for Decision Support in Anesthesiology, *Artificial Intelligence in Medicine*, 11:189-214, 1998.

[Rich & Knight, 1991]
E. Rich and K. Knight: *Artificial Intelligence*, McGraw-Hill, New York, 2nd edition, 1991.

[Rouveirol & Albert, 1994]
C. Rouveirol and P. Albert: Knowledge Level Model of a Configurable Learning System. In L. Steels et al. (eds.), *A Future for Knowledge Acquisition*, Lecture Notes in Artificial Intelligence (LNAI) 867, Springer-Verlag, Berlin, 1994.

[Russell & Subramanian, 1995]
S. J. Russell and D. Subramanian: Provably Bounded-Optimal Agents, *Journal of Artificial Intelligence Research*, 2, 1995.

[Schönegge, 1995]
A. Schönegge: *Extending Dynamic Logic for Reasoning about Evolving Algebras*, research report 49/95, Institut für Logik, Komplexität und Deduktionssysteme, University of Karlsruhe, 1995.

[Schreiber, 1999]
A.Th Schreiber (ed.): *Knowledge Engineering and Management: The Commonkads Methodology*, MIT Press, 1999.

[Schreiber & Birmingham, 1996]
A.Th. Schreiber and B. Birmingham (eds.): *Special Issue on Sisyphus, International Journal of Human-Computer Studies (IJHCS)*, 44(3-4), 1996.

[Schreiber et al., 1991]
A.Th. Schreiber, J. M. Akkermans, and B. J. Wielinga: On Problems With the Knowledge Level Perspective. In L. Steels and B. Smith (eds.), *Proceedings AISB'91*: Artificial Intelligence and Simulation of Behavior, London, Springer-Verlag, 1991.

[Schreiber et al., 1993]
A.Th. Schreiber, B. J. Wielinga, and J. A. Breuker (eds.): *KADS: A Principled Approach to Knowledge-Based System Development*, vol 11 of Knowledge-Based Systems Book Series, Academic Press, London, 1993.

[Schreiber et al., 1994]
A.Th. Schreiber, B. Wielinga, J.M. Akkermans, W. Van De Velde, and R. de Hoog: CommonKADS. A Comprehensive Methodology for KBS Development, *IEEE Expert*, 9(6):28—37, 1994.

[Shapiro, 1982]
E.Y. Shapiro: *Algorithmic Program Debugging*, The MIT Press, 1982.

[Shaw, 1989]
A. Shaw: Reasoning About Time in Higher Level Language Software, *IEEE Transactions on Software Engineering*, 15(7):875—889, 1989.

[Shaw & Garlan, 1996]
M. Shaw and D. Garlan: *Software Architectures. Perspectives on an Emerging Discipline*, Prentice-Hall, 1996.

[Sitaraman et al., 1993]
M. Sitaraman, L.R. Welch, and D. E. Harms: On Specification of Reusable Software Components, *International Journal of Software Engineering and Knowledge Engineering*, 3(2):207—229, 1993.

[Smith, 1990]
D.R. Smith: KIDS: A Semiautomatic Program Development System, *IEEE Transactions on Software Engineering*, 16(9), 1990.

[Smith, 1996]
D.R. Smith: Towards a Classification Approach to Design. In M. Wirsing et al. (eds.), *Algebraic Methodology and Software Technology*, Lecture Notes in Computer Science (LNCS) 1101, Springer-Verlag, Berlin, 1996.

[Smith & Lowry, 1990]
   D.R. Smith and M.R. Lowry: Algorithm Theories and Design Tactics, *Science of Computer Programming,* 14:305—321, 1990.

[Spee & in 't Veld, 1994]
   J.W. Spee and L. in 't Veld: The Semantics of $K_{BS}SF$: A Language For KBS Design, *Knowledge Acquisition,* vol 6, 1994.

[Spivey, 1992]
   J.M. Spivey: *The Z Notation. A Reference Manual,* 2nd ed., Prentice Hall, New York, 1992.

[Spruit et al., 1992]
   P.A. Spruit, R. Wieringa, and J.-J. Meyer: Dynamic Database Logic: The First Order Case. In V.W. Lipeck and B. Thalheim (eds.), *Fourth International Workshop on Foundations of Models and Languages for Data and Objects,* Workshop in Computing, Springer-Verlag, Berlin, 1993.

[Spruit et al., 1995]
   P.A. Spruit, R. Wieringa, and J.-J. Meyer: Axiomatization, Declarative Semantics and Operational Semantics of Passive and Active Updates in Logic Databases, *Journal of Logic Computation,* 5(1), 1995.

[Steels, 1990]
   L. Steels: Components of Expertise, *AI Magazine,* 11(2), 1990.

[Steels, 1993]
   L. Steels: The Componential Framework and its Role in Reusability. In M. David et al. (eds.): Second Generation Expert Systems, Springer-Verlag, 1993.

[Stefik et al., 1983]
   M. Stefik, J. Aikins, R. Balzer, J. Benoit, L. Birnbaum, F. Hayes-Roth, and E. Sacerdoti: Basic Concepts for Building Expert Systems. In F. Hayes-Roth et al. (eds.), *Building Expert Systems,* Addison-Wesley Publ., 1983.

[Stefik, 1995]
   M. Stefik: *Introduction to Knowledge Systems,* Morgan Kaufman Publ., San Francisco, 1995.

[Sticklen et al., 1989]
   J. Sticklen, B. Chandrasekaran, and W.E. Bond: Applying a Functional Approach for Model Based Reasoning. In *Proceedings of the IJCAI Workshop on Model Based Reasoning,* Detroit, MI, 1989.

[Straatman & Beys, 1995]
   R. Straatman and P. Beys: A Performance Model for Knowledge-based Systems. In M. Ayel et al. (eds.): *EUROVAV-95 European Symposium on the Validation and Verification of Knowledge Based Systems,* University of Savoie, Chambery, June 26-28, 1995.

[Struss, 1992]
   P. Struss: Diagnosis as a Process. In W. Hamscher et al. (eds.), *Readings in Model-based Diagnosis,* Morgan Kaufman Publ., San Mateo, CA, 1992.

[Struss & Dressler, 1989]
P. Struss and O. Dressler: "Physical Negation" - Integrating Fault Models into the General Diagnostic Engine. In *Proceedings of the 11th International Joint Conference on AI (IJCAI-89)*, Detroit, MI, 1989.

[Studer et al., 1998]
R. Studer, V. R. Benjamins, D. Fensel: Knowledge Engineering: Methods and Principles, to appear in *Data and Knowledge Engineering*, 1998.

[Sutcliff & Maiden, 1994]
A.G. Sutcliff and N.A.M. Maiden (1994): Domain Modeling for Reuse. In *Proceedings of the 3rd International Conference on Software Reuse*, Rio de Janeiro, 1994.

[Tank, 1992]
W. Tank: Modellierung von *Expertise über Konfigurationsaufgaben*, Infix, Sankt Augustin, Germany, 1992.

[ten Teije, 1997]
A. ten Teije: *Automated Configuration of Problem Solving Methods in Diagnosis*, Ph.D. thesis, University of Amsterdam, the Netherlands, 1997.

[ten Teije & van Harmelen, 1994]
A. ten Teije and F. van Harmelen: An Extended Spectrum of Logical Definitions for Diagnostic Systems. In *Proceedings of the 5th International Workshop on Principles of Diagnosis (DX-94)*, New Paltz, New York, October 1994. Submitted for International Journal of Expert Systems.

[ten Teije & van Harmelen, 1996]
A. ten Teije and F. Van Harmelen: Using Reflection Techniques for Flexible Problem Solving (with Examples from Diagnosis), *Future Generation Computer Systems*, 12:217—234, 1996.

[Terpstra et al., 1993]
P. Terpstra, G. van Heijst, B. Wielinga, and N. Shadbolt: Knowledge Acquisition Support Through Generalized Directive Models. In M. David et al. (eds.): *Second Generation Expert Systems*, Springer-Verlag, 1993.

[Top & Akkermans, 1994]
J. Top and H. Akkermans: Tasks and Ontologies in Engineering Modeling, *International Journal of Human-Computer Studies (IJHCS)*, 41:585—617, 1994.

[Treur, 1994]
J. Treur: Temporal Semantics of Meta-Level Architectures for Dynamic Control of Reasoning. In L. Fribourg et al. (eds.), *Logic Program Synthesis and Transformation - Meta Programming in Logic, Proceedings of the 4th International Workshops, LOPSTER-94 and META-94*, Pisa, Italy, June 20-21, 1994, Lecture Notes in Artificial Intelligence (LNAI) 883, Springer Verlag, 1994.

[Treur & Wetter, 1993]
J. Treur and T. Wetter: *Formal Specification of Complex Reasoning Systems*, Ellis Horwood, New York, 1993.

[Van de Velde, 1988]
  W. van de Velde: Inference Structure as a Basis for Problem Solving. In *Proceedings of the 8th European Conference on Artificial Intelligence (ECAI-88)*, Munich, August 1-5, 1988.

[Van de Velde, 1991]
  W. Van de Velde: Tractable Rationality at the Knowledge-Level. In L. Steels and B. Smith (ed.), *Proceedings AISB'91: Artificial Intelligence and Simulation of Behavior*, London, Springer-Verlag, 1991.

[Van de Velde, 1994]
  W. Van de Velde: A Constructivist View on Knowledge Engineering. In *Proceedings of the 11th European Conference on Artificial Intelligence (ECAI'94)*, Amsterdam, August 1994.

[van Eck et al., 1997]
  P. van Eck, J. Engelfriet, D. Fensel, F. van Harmelen, Y. Venema, and M. Willems: Specification of Dynamics for Knowledge-based Systems. In *Proceedings of the Workshop on (Trans)Actions and Change in Logic Programming and Deductive Databases (DYNAMICS'97)*. Post-Conference of the International Logic Programming Symposium (ILPS-97), Port Jefferson, Long Island N.Y., USA, October 1997.

[van Harmelen & Aben, 1996]
  F. van Harmelen and M. Aben: Structure-preserving Specification Languages for Knowledge-based Systems, *International Journal of Human Computer Studies (IJHCS)*, 44:187—212, 1996.

[van Harmelen & Balder, 1992]
  F. van Harmelen and J. Balder: $(ML)^2$: A Formal Language for KADS Conceptual Models, *Knowledge Acquisition*, 4(1), 1992.

[van Harmelen & ten Teije, 1995]
  F. van Harmelen and A. ten Teije: Approximations in Diagnosis: Motivations and Techniques. In *Proceedings of the Symposium on Abstraction, Reformulation, and Approximation (SARA-95)*, Quebec, Canada, August 1995.

[van Harmelen & ten Teije, 1998]
  F. van Harmelen and A. ten Teije: Characterizing Problem Solving Methods by Gradual Requirements: Overcoming the Yes/No Distinction. In *Proceedings of the 11th Banff Knowledge Acquisition for Knowledge-Based System Workshop (KAW'98)*, Banff, Canada, April 18-23, 1998.

[van Heijst & Anjewerden:, 1996]
  G. van Heijst and A. Anjewerden: Four Propositions Concerning the Specification of Problem-Solving Methods. In *Supplementary Proceedings of the 9th European Knowledge Acquisition Workshop (EKAW-96)*, Nottingham, England, May 14-17, 1996.

[van Heijst et al., 1992]
  G. van Heijst, P. Terpstra, B. J. Wielinga and N. Shadbolt: Using Generalized Directive Models in Knowledge Acquisition. In T. Wetter et al. (eds.), *Current Developments in Knowledge Acquisition,* Lecture Notes in Artificial Intelligence (LNAI), Springer-Verlag, 1992.

[van Heijst et al., 1997]
G. van Heijst, A. T. Schreiber, and B. J. Wielinga: Using Explicit Ontologies in Knowledge-Based System Development, *International Journal of Human-Computer Studies (IJHCS)*, 46(6), 1997.

[van Langevelde et al., 1993]
I. van Langevelde, A. Philipsen, and J. Treur: A Compositional Architecture for Simple Design Formally Specified in DESIRE. In J. Treur and T. Wetter: *Formal Specification of Complex Reasoning Systems*, Ellis Horwood, New York, 1993.

[VanLehn, 1989]
K. VanLehn: Problem-Solving and Cognitive Skill Acquisition. In M. I. Posner (ed.), *Foundations of Cognitive Science*, The MIT Press, Cambridge, 1989.

[Vissers et al., 1991]
C.A. Vissers, G. Scollo, M. van Sinderen, and E. Brinksma: Specification Styles in Distributed System Design and Verification, *Theoretical Computer Science*, 98:179—206, 1991.

[Voss & Voss, 1993]
H. Voss and A. Voss: Reuse-Oriented Knowledge Engineering with MoMo. In *Proceedings of the 5th International Conference on Software Engineering and Knowledge Engineering (SEKE93)*, San Francisco Bay, June 14-18, 1993.

[Weiß, 1995]
G. Weiß: Adaption and Learning in Multi-Agent Systems: Some Remarks on a Bibliography. In G. Weiß et al. (eds.), *Adaption and Learning in Multi-Agent Systems*, Lecture Notes in Artificial Intelligence (LNAI) 1042, Springer-Verlag, 1995.

[Wiederhold, 1992]
G Wiederhold: Mediators in the Architecture of Future Information Systems, *IEEE Computer*, 25(3):38—49, 1992.

[Wielinga et al., 1993]
B. J. Wielinga, W. Van De Velde, A. Th. Schreiber, and J. M. Akkermans: Towards a Unification of Knowledge Modeling Approaches. In J.-M. David et al. (eds.), *Second Generation Expert Systems*, Springer-Verlag, Berlin, 1993.

[Wielinga et al., 1995]
B. Wielinga, J. M. Akkermans, and A. TH. Schreiber: A Formal Analysis of Parametric Design Problem Solving. In *Proceedings of the 9th Banff Knowledge Acquisition for Knowledge-Based System Workshop (KAW'95)*, Banff, Canada, January 26 - February 3, 1995.

[Wirsing, 1990]
M. Wirsing: Algebraic Specification. In J. van Leeuwen (ed.), *Handbook of Theoretical Computer Science*, Elsevier Science Publ., 1990.

[Wirsing, 1995]
M. Wirsing: Algebraic Specification Languages: an Overview. In *Proceedings of the 10th Workshop on Specification of Abstract Data Types*, Springer-Verlag, Lecture Notes in Computer Science (LNCS) 906, 1995.

[Wirth, 1983]
N. Wirth: Program Development by Stepwise Refinement, *Communications of the ACM*, 26(1), 1983.

[Wordsworth, 1996]
J.B. Wordsworth: *Software Engineering with B*, Addison-Wesley, 1996.

[Yost & Rothenfluh, 1996]
G.R. Yost and T.R. Rothenfluh: Configuring Elevator Systems, *International Journal of Human-Computer Studies (IJHCS)*, 44(3/4):521—568, 1996.

[Zdrahal & Motta, 1995]
Z. Zdrahal and E. Motta: An In-Depth Analysis of Propose & Revise Problem Solving Methods. In *Proceedings of the 9th Banff Knowledge Acquisition for Knowledge-Based System Workshop (KAW'95)*, Banff, Canada, January 26 - February 3, 1995.

[Zilberstein, 1996]
S. Zilberstein: Using Anytime Algorithms in Intelligent Systems, *AI Magazine*, 17(3), 1996.

Lecture Notes in Artificial Intelligence (LNAI)

Lecture Notes in Computer Science

Vol. 1899: H.-H. Nagel, F.J. Perales López (Eds.), Articulated Motion and Deformable Objects. Proceedings, 2000. X, 183 pages. 2000.

Vol. 1900: A. Bode, T. Ludwig, W. Karl, R. Wismüller (Eds.), Euro-Par 2000 Parallel Processing. Proceedings, 2000. XXXV, 1368 pages. 2000.

Vol. 1901: O. Etzion, P. Scheuermann (Eds.), Cooperative Information Systems. Proceedings, 2000. XI, 336 pages. 2000.

Vol. 1902: P. Sojka, I. Kopeček, K. Pala (Eds.), Text, Speech and Dialogue. Proceedings, 2000. XIII, 463 pages. 2000. (Subseries LNAI).

Vol. 1903: S. Reich, K.M. Anderson (Eds.), Open Hypermedia Systems and Structural Computing. Proceedings, 2000. VIII, 187 pages. 2000.

Vol. 1904: S.A. Cerri, D. Dochev (Eds.), Artificial Intelligence: Methodology, Systems, and Applications. Proceedings, 2000. XII, 366 pages. 2000. (Subseries LNAI).

Vol. 1905: H. Scholten, M.J. van Sinderen (Eds.), Interactive Distributed Multimedia Systems and Telecommunication Services. Proceedings, 2000. XI, 306 pages. 2000.

Vol. 1906: A. Porto, G.-C. Roman (Eds.), Coordination Languages and Models. Proceedings, 2000. IX, 353 pages. 2000.

Vol. 1907: H. Debar, L. Mé, S.F. Wu (Eds.), Recent Advances in Intrusion Detection. Proceedings, 2000. X, 227 pages. 2000.

Vol. 1908: J. Dongarra, P. Kacsuk, N. Podhorszki (Eds.), Recent Advances in Parallel Virtual Machine and Message Passing Interface. Proceedings, 2000. XV, 364 pages. 2000.

Vol. 1910: D.A. Zighed, J. Komorowski, J. Żytkow (Eds.), Principles of Data Mining and Knowledge Discovery. Proceedings, 2000. XV, 701 pages. 2000. (Subseries LNAI).

Vol. 1912: Y. Gurevich, P.W. Kutter, M. Odersky, L. Thiele (Eds.), Abstract State Machines. Proceedings, 2000. X, 381 pages. 2000.

Vol. 1913: K. Jansen, S. Khuller (Eds.), Approximation Algorithms for Combinatorial Optimization. Proceedings, 2000. IX, 275 pages. 2000.

Vol. 1914: M. Herlihy (Ed.), Distributed Computing. Proceedings, 2000. VIII, 389 pages. 2000.

Vol. 1917: M. Schoenauer, K. Deb, G. Rudolph, X. Yao, E. Lutton, J.J. Merelo, H.-P. Schwefel (Eds.), Parallel Problem Solving from Nature – PPSN VI. Proceedings, 2000. XXI, 914 pages. 2000.

Vol. 1918: D. Soudris, P. Pirsch, E. Barke (Eds.), Integrated Circuit Design. Proceedings, 2000. XII, 338 pages. 2000.

Vol. 1919: M. Ojeda-Aciego, I.P. de Guzman, G. Brewka, L. Moniz Pereira (Eds.), Logics in Artificial Intelligence. Proceedings, 2000. XI, 407 pages. 2000. (Subseries LNAI).

Vol. 1920: A.H.F. Laender, S.W. Liddle, V.C. Storey (Eds.), Conceptual Modeling – ER 2000. Proceedings, 2000. XV, 588 pages. 2000.

Vol. 1921: S.W. Liddle, H.C. Mayr, B. Thalheim (Eds.), Conceptual Modeling for E-Business and the Web. Proceedings, 2000. X, 179 pages. 2000.

Vol. 1922: J. Crowcroft, J. Roberts, M.I. Smirnov (Eds.), Quality of Future Internet Services. Proceedings, 2000. XI, 368 pages. 2000.

Vol. 1923: J. Borbinha, T. Baker (Eds.), Research and Advanced Technology for Digital Libraries. Proceedings, 2000. XVII, 513 pages. 2000.

Vol. 1924: W. Taha (Ed.), Semantics, Applications, and Implementation of Program Generation. Proceedings, 2000. VIII, 231 pages. 2000.

Vol. 1925: J. Cussens, S. Dżeroski (Eds.), Learning Language in Logic. X, 301 pages 2000. (Subseries LNAI).

Vol. 1926: M. Joseph (Ed.), Formal Techniques in Real-Time and Fault-Tolerant Systems. Proceedings, 2000. X, 305 pages. 2000.

Vol. 1927: P. Thomas, H.W. Gellersen, (Eds.), Handheld and Ubiquitous Computing. Proceedings, 2000. X, 249 pages. 2000.

Vol. 1931: E. Horlait (Ed.), Mobile Agents for Telecommunication Applications. Proceedings, 2000. IX, 271 pages. 2000.

Vol. 1766: M. Jazayeri, R.G.K. Loos, D.R. Musser (Eds.), Generic Programming. Proceedings, 1998. X, 269 pages. 2000.

Vol. 1791: D. Fensel, Problem-Solving Methods. XII, 153 pages. 2000. (Subseries LNAI).

Vol. 1932: Z.W. Raś, S. Ohsuga (Eds.), Foundations of Intelligent Systems. Proceedings, 2000. XII, 646 pages. (Subseries LNAI).

Vol. 1933: R.W. Brause, E. Hanisch (Eds.), Medical Data Analysis. Proceedings, 2000. XI, 316 pages. 2000.

Vol. 1934: J.S. White (Ed.), Envisioning Machine Translation in the Information Future. Proceedings, 2000. XV, 254 pages. 2000. (Subseries LNAI).

Vol. 1937: R. Dieng, O. Corby (Eds.), Knowledge Engineering and Knowledge Management. Proceedings, 2000. XIII, 457 pages. 2000. (Subseries LNAI).

Vol. 1938: S. Rao, K.I. Sletta (Eds.), Next Generation Networks. Proceedings, 2000. XI, 392 pages. 2000.

Vol. 1939: A. Evans, S. Kent, B. Selic (Eds.), «UML» – The Unified Modeling Language. Proceedings, 2000. XIV, 572 pages. 2000.